the genius and the impostor

the genius and the impostor

The Neuroscience of Unlocking Human Potential

Josh Turknett

TARCHER
an imprint of Penguin Random House
New York

Tarcher
an imprint of Penguin Random House LLC
1745 Broadway, New York, NY 10019
penguinrandomhouse.com

Book design by Shannon Nicole Plunkett

Library of Congress Cataloging-in-Publication Data
has been applied for.

Hardcover ISBN: 9780593850992
eBook ISBN: 9780593851012

Printed in the United States of America
1st Printing

The authorized representative in the EU for product safety and compliance is Penguin Random House Ireland, Morrison Chambers, 32 Nassau Street, Dublin D02 YH68, Ireland, https://eu-contact.penguin.ie.

For all who march to the beat of their own drummer.

Please don't stop.

contents

the genius and the impostor

why the genius and the impostor?

You know how sometimes you procrastinate on the things that matter most to you? You get an email from an old friend that's too important for a quick reply, so you put it off? Then the days turn to weeks as you wait for the perfect moment that never comes.

This book is like that email.

For years I've carried around what feels like a secret. Not the kind of secret you should keep to yourself, but the kind that needs to be shared. One that I think can do a whole lot of good.

Which is also why I put off writing this book for so long. Not because it wasn't important. But because it was more important than anything, and nothing felt good enough for the message I hoped to deliver. Like I said, it's easy to put off doing the things that matter most, precisely because they matter most.

The secret I've been carrying comes from a lifetime studying the brain. From classroom to research lab to the neurology wards and beyond, decades of work in a variety of areas led me to the inescapable conclusion that we'd gotten the story of our brain terribly wrong. That much of what we believe about intelligence, ability, and potential is a fiction. A story based on speculation rather than science.

That fiction has had huge consequences. Ones that keep me awake at night. I've agonized over how much of our collective potential has been devoured by that narrative. I've cringed every time I hear people equate intelligence with IQ. I've wondered how many lives have been quietly rerouted because of a myth. How many ambitions abandoned, skills left unexplored, and identities prematurely narrowed.

Our brain is astonishing beyond comprehension. Every single one. But all this time, we've been obsessing over limitations when we should have been marveling at the possibilities.

And it wasn't just individuals affected. From the classroom to the boardroom, entire systems have been built on flawed assumptions about how brains work.

But challenging and overturning deeply held beliefs is no small feat, especially when they've shaped our identity and worldview since childhood. To have any chance of success, I'd need to share my secret in the clearest and most effective way possible.

Years went by as I wrestled with how to do that.

Then one summer afternoon while preparing for a talk on these ideas, the Genius and the Impostor arrived in my mind. Not the book, but the characters. When they did, I knew they were the right vehicle for delivering the science and for sharing the secret.

I used those characters in the talk, and the response was immediate and overwhelming. It didn't just help the audience relate to the science better; it seemed to change how they saw themselves.

But what surprised me most was the effect it had on *me*.

I've given many talks before. I know the anxiety and self-doubt that creep in before stepping onstage. And I'd learned techniques for succeeding in spite of them.

This time felt different. I felt at ease in a way I hadn't known in a very long time. It was a surreal moment. The very framework I was using to explain my audience's potential was helping me unlock my own.

You've probably had moments like that, too. Times when you surprised yourself. When you performed better than you thought you could, spoke more eloquently than usual, solved a problem that had seemed impossible. Almost as if another version of you took over. A part of you that was calm, capable, and unencumbered by doubt.

And then it vanished as quickly as it came. You wondered if it was a fluke, a random accident you could never re-create.

But that part of you is still there. It's always been there. It's the truest version of you, but you don't see it nearly enough.

My aim in this book is to bring that part of you out of hiding. To make it not an unpredictable visitor but a permanent presence.

I've thought about the Genius and the Impostor every day since that talk. I've *used* it every day since. It shapes how I learn and make decisions, and how I show up when it matters. I consider it the most useful lens I've found for building a life that's authentically my own. Those I've shared it with feel the same.

That's my goal for you, too.

Yes, there's neuroscience in these pages. The fact that this framework is grounded in and emerges from neuroscience is what makes it so powerful. You're going to learn things about your brain that will shock you. You're going to *unlearn* the myths and misconceptions that pollute the popular conversation. I think you'll find the Genius and the Impostor framework to be a helpful conceptual anchor for the neuroscience, helping you unlock a new level of understanding about yourself.

But, more importantly, I hope you find this framework as useful and transformative as I have. That it transforms how you learn and live so that you can fully realize the gift of that wet, squishy miracle sitting between your ears.

You may not believe your brain is capable of what I'm claiming. I'd expect nothing less. The voice resisting that message is exactly the phenomenon this book explains.

I know that every brain is so much more extraordinary than we realize. Not some of them. All of them. Including yours.

It's about time you learned why.

1

the special brain ~~story~~ lie

I am, somehow, less interested in the weight and convolutions of Einstein's brain than in the near certainty that people of equal talent have lived and died in cotton fields and sweatshops.

—Stephen Jay Gould (evolutionary biologist)

Mrs. Patterson methodically walked through the rows of desks, placing the graded math quizzes face-down on each one as she went. Hearts pounded. The air smelled like Elmer's glue and terror. One by one, faces transformed into expressions of disappointment or relief as each glimpsed its fate.

Sarah took a deep breath as she slowly lifted the corner of the page, like a bomb might explode if she went too fast.

And then she saw it. Like a dagger into her soul, "64%" written in a hostile shade of red marker. Next to it: a large letter "F."

Her stomach dropped. Out of the corner of her eye she could see her best friend, Jen, vibrating with delight. "I can't believe I got an A," Jen whispered. "How'd you do?" she asked.

Choking down tears, Sarah just shook her head from side to

side as she flipped her paper back over. "Oh," said Jen, her voice dripping with soul-crushing pity.

That afternoon, Sarah's mom picked her up early for a dentist appointment. In the car, Sarah mentioned the quiz.

"A sixty-four?" Her mom's voice carried that careful tone Sarah had learned to dread. "Sweetie, you know what? Not everyone is good at math. Your father wasn't either." She glanced over with a reassuring smile. "You're more of a creative type. That's your gift."

Sarah was seven years old.

She's thirty-four now. She works in marketing, which she's "naturally good at" because she's "creative, not analytical." She hasn't attempted anything involving numbers more complex than splitting a dinner check in more than two decades.

When someone mentions statistics or data analysis, she laughs and says, "Oh, I'm terrible at math. Always have been." To her, it feels no different from saying she has brown eyes or a size 8 shoe. A part of who she is that she had no control over.

The memory of Mrs. Patterson's classroom, or the red "64%," or the car ride with her mom is long gone. The idea that she's not a math person has been a part of who she is for so long she can't imagine it any other way.

IIIIIIIIIIIIIIIIIIIIIIII

You've been lied to. So has Sarah. So have I.

I'm not talking about some vast right-wing conspiracy. Or left wing. There are no wings for us to blame here. That's because we're the ones responsible for spreading the lie. We were told it when we were very young, and we fell for it. We've been obediently parroting it to each other ever since.

Who's been telling us this lie?

You have. I have. We all have.

Because there's a voice in our heads that's been narrating our lives since early childhood. It explains who you are, what you're capable of, and how you compare to others. It feels like your own thoughts, your own beliefs, your own understanding of yourself.

But it's not.

I call it the Impostor. The Impostor is a compulsive liar, and his masterpiece is the Special Brain Story.

That story is a lie about human potential itself. The lie says that we're all born with very different brains with very different abilities. It says that the brain we're born with is what determines what we're good and not so good at, no matter how hard we try.

According to this story, your job in childhood is to figure out which brain you got, then stay in your lane. If you try to do something your brain wasn't designed to do, you will look foolish. For example, you shouldn't waste time pursuing engineering if you didn't get a math brain. Or don't embarrass yourself buying that guitar if you didn't get a music brain, for goodness' sake.

Figuring this out is very important because it allows you to set the right expectations for yourself.

Childhood is also when you find out how smart you are, especially in relation to other brains. School is very helpful for sorting this out for you. That's because, in addition to its innate abilities and limitations, your brain also contains a very specific amount of a thing called *intelligence*.

Your innate abilities and intelligence are determined by your genes, since these contain the instructions for building your brain. This is why you can trace the source of these things to a particular relative, if you look hard enough. Like how you can thank Grandpa Joe for your artistic talent, your mom for your quick wit, and Aunt Mildred for your unique fashion sense.

In school, you can even take a test to find out how much intelligence is in your brain, in the form of a very precise number! The earlier you find out this number, the better. That way, if you find yourself in possession of one of those gifted brains, you can go to classes only for gifted brains and minimize the time you spend consorting with the ordinary ones, bless their little hearts.

At the tippy top of the intelligence hierarchy are the geniuses. These freaks of nature were born with brains that can solve problems and imagine things no ordinary brain can match. These are the only brains capable of generating the ideas and inventions that change the world. The rest of us ordinary-brained folk should limit ourselves to ordinary-brained pursuits while awaiting the fruits of their intellectual labor.

This entire narrative, from sorting children by innate ability to worshipping rare geniuses, is the Special Brain Story. It reflects the popular conception of how our brains work, and it has shaped virtually every aspect of how we think about human potential. It seems so obviously true that questioning it feels almost absurd. For many years, I didn't.

Yet, having spent my adult life in neuroscience, I have concluded that this popular view of the brain is—to use the scientific terminology—"total bullshit."

One of the first holes in the Special Brain Story was exposed a few decades ago after a very famous and special brain was placed under the microscope.

The Genius Brain

When you hear the word "genius," I bet I know what pops into your head.

Wild, gravity-defying tendrils of white frizz. Eyes deep-set and weary from countless hours of contemplation. Rumpled, ill-fitting clothing and a total indifference to fashion trends. Perhaps an equation-filled chalkboard in the background.

Albert Einstein's name is so synonymous with the word "genius" that we can't help but conjure his image when we hear the word. If you have an untamed mop of hair atop your scalp, people will just assume you're too busy writing theorems to bother with a hairbrush. His name has become a universal symbol for intelligence, whether wielded genuinely or ironically, as in "Great thinking, Einstein!"

Of course, Einstein's position as the proverbial genius is well deserved. After all, he discovered secrets of the universe including the existence of gravitational waves, black holes, and time dilation, just by conducting experiments *in his mind*. Many of those secrets are at odds with some of our deepest intuitions, which is one reason why they'd eluded all the brilliant minds that came before him. Super-impressive stuff, to say the least.

So, Einstein is a fitting place to begin our story. Though we're going to start at the end. The end of his life, that is.

You see, when Einstein died, the scientists were all quite excited. Not because he died, because that'd be rude. Plus, his death was a loss to humanity. He'd advanced the science of theoretical physics more than anyone else in history, after all, and it wasn't clear who was gonna pick up the mantle of uncovering the nature of reality while pedaling around aimlessly on a bicycle.

No, what they were excited about was the prospect of getting to see his brain. Because clearly something wondrous was happening there. Prior to his death, people could only imagine what his brain might look like. Einstein lived years before we had imaging technologies like CT and MRI scans that could give us detailed pictures of a living brain.

The reason the scientists wanted to see his brain so badly was because many believed in the Special Brain Story when it came to geniuses. That story says that in order to be a genius, you had to be born with a brain that was very unusual. A brain equipped with special bits that were unlike the bits found in other brains. Problem was, nobody knew what those bits were. Though many were certain it was true, the Special Brain Theory lacked any proof.

And it wasn't like genius brains were dropping into pathology labs every day. First off, genius brains are rare. Geniuses willing to donate their brains to science are also rare. I'm no Einstein, but I know that the odds of one rare thing and another rare thing happening together is even more of a rare thing.

So, this was a big moment. We were going to learn so much about human intelligence. About the neurobiology of being a smarty-pants. About the special brain bits that power genius. Maybe we'd even find a special molecule in Einstein's brain that we could manufacture and shove inside a pill to make us all equally brilliant. Or at least help us remember where we put our car keys.

Needless to say, many scientists wanted to get their hands on his brain. Literally. In academia, you see, science is a competitive sport. All the glory would go to the first one to identify and publish about what gave a brain its genius powers. So there wasn't a shortage of scientists clamoring for a morsel of his neural tissue.

The analysis of Einstein's brain began, as all postmortem brain analyses do, by taking its weight. At the time, the thing scientists were probably most certain of was that Einstein's brain was going to be *big*! More brain equals more smarts was a leading formula at the time. I told you these were top scientists.

The average adult male brain weighs between 1,300 and 1,400 grams. Surely, Einstein's would be somewhere north of 2,000.

So what did the scale read when Einstein's brain was set upon it?

A measly 1,230 grams.

Talk about awkward! The poster child for smartness had a brain that was *smaller* than average. The Special Brain Story was not off to a great start.

After this momentary setback, the scientists brushed off their egos and pressed on. Sure, the big brain theory of genius was wrong. But that probably just meant the answer would reveal itself under the microscope. That was where they'd find all of Einstein's special brain bits!

In the spirit of fairness, the pathologist who conducted Einstein's autopsy, Dr. Thomas Stoltz Harvey, shipped twenty equal slices of Einstein's brain to twelve leading pathologists (incidentally, it remains unclear if Einstein had consented to this analysis prior to his death). And the race was on.

The top pathologists polished off their finest microscopes and examined Einstein's neurons every which way. They stained them with dyes. They looked at them from every angle. They squinted harder than they'd ever squinted before. Some made faces that would've frightened small children.

And do you know what they found?

Zilch.

Einstein's brain was subjected to one of the most thorough pathological analyses of any brain in history, and yet nobody found anything special about it. Yes, there were a few features that were somewhat unique. But nothing out of the ordinary.

There was no smoking gun with genius bullets. No golden neurons. No diamond-tipped synapses. If you saw it in a lineup of brains, you wouldn't pick it out as the one that figured out time dilation. Because Einstein's brain was profoundly, boringly normal.

When all was said and done, the consensus was clear: the most extraordinary thing about Einstein's brain was that it was entirely ordinary.

Again, this was all quite unexpected, not to mention disappointing. What were we to make of this failure to find anything remarkable?

Perhaps we just needed better and more powerful tools and technology. Maybe the secrets of genius would only reveal themselves at the level of individual atoms. Or maybe even quantum forces. If so, we'd need way more powerful microscopes.

Or maybe, just maybe, it meant that the Special Brain Story was wrong.

Maybe they didn't find anything special about his brain because genius doesn't come from being born with special brain bits. Maybe genius has more to do with how somebody uses the bits that we all have. Maybe Einstein just used his regular brain in an irregular way. Maybe his genius was not about the brain he was born with, but about what his brain *became*?

And so, after this disappointing and unexpected little episode, everyone took a long, hard look at all the evidence and decided to pretend like nothing had ever happened. We continued right on telling the Special Brain Story like we always had. The ordinariness of Einstein's brain was no match for its seductive appeal.

Neither the scientists of the time nor the general public was prepared to let it go just yet. After all, what was the alternative? That any old brain was capable of Einstein's brilliance? Preposterous! If that were true, why was it such a rare thing?

Einstein Was Right . . . Again

Einstein died in 1955. Even at that time, there was already enough evidence to call into question the belief that genius was innate. In fact, guess what scientist of that era didn't subscribe to the Special Brain Story?

Einstein.

Many times in his writings and public comments, Einstein downplayed or dismissed the idea that he possessed any special abilities. In one representative example, he said, "It is an irony of fate that I myself have been the recipient of excessive admiration and reverence from my fellow-beings, through no fault, and no merit, of my own. The cause of this may well be the desire, unattainable for many, to understand the few ideas to which I have with my feeble powers attained through ceaseless struggle."

Einstein believed that he wasn't born with a unique brain,

but that he molded a unique mind by relentlessly following his curiosity, and not the herd, wherever it led. He believed that intelligence wasn't born but built through curiosity-driven learning.

And I agree with him.

The Genius and the Impostor

What I've learned from decades of studying brains is that the Special Brain Story isn't just wrong. It's *backward.*

I've spent my career as a neurologist examining how brains work and what happens when they break. And I've also helped thousands tap into and realize their cognitive potential. Through that work I've learned that every brain, including yours, contains two very different forces.

The first force is what I call the Genius. It's been with you since birth. It's the extraordinary learning machinery that enabled you to master language without instruction, recognize thousands of faces effortlessly, and navigate a three-dimensional world with precision. The Genius is the source of all that you value in yourself: every skill you've ever acquired, every problem you've ever solved, every capability you possess. And it's still within you now, ready to be summoned.

The second force is the Impostor. The Genius is his sworn enemy. The Impostor's job is to construct and narrate a story about who you are, what you're capable of, and how you stack up against your peers. Critically, that story isn't based on reality. That's because the Impostor doesn't care whether that story is true. Later on you'll learn the surprising reason why we all have a compulsive liar in our brains, and why we're predisposed to believing every word he says. Including the Special Brain Story.

The Genius built your capabilities. The Impostor narrates them, and those stories have consequences. One of those consequences is that most people spend their lives operating far below their actual potential. Not because they lack ability, but because they've internalized the Impostor's most powerful lie.

This book is about understanding these two forces—where they come from, how they operate, and most importantly, how to shift the balance back in favor of the Genius.

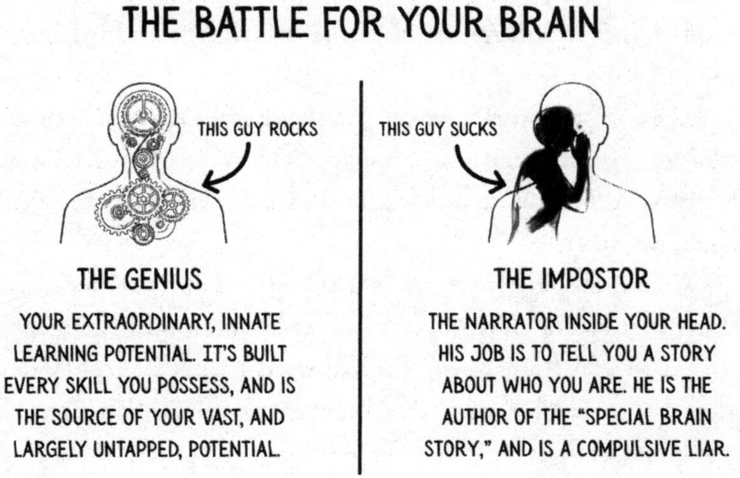

Why Stories Matter

Another thing that cognitive neuroscience research has taught us time and time again is that the stories we tell ourselves matter.

Not just in how we feel, but in how our bodies and brains actually function.

The placebo effect is a textbook and rigorously studied example. The placebo effect shows us that expecting something to help you makes it more likely that it will help you. Give someone a sugar pill and tell them it will make them sleepy, and chances are it will. Why? Because their brain started using its influence to make that story a reality. Ultimately, it was nothing but a story that made them sleepy.

On the flip side, expecting something bad to happen makes that thing more likely to happen, which is known as the "nocebo effect." If you expect a pill will make you nauseous, there's a very good chance it will make you nauseous. Again, nothing but a story making you feel ill.

Likewise, the stories we tell about what we're capable of, or what we expect of ourselves, impact us in exactly the same way. If we expect we can do more, chances are we will do more. If we don't, we won't.

What is absolutely certain is that you will never achieve anything that you don't think is possible. The reason Einstein continued to contemplate the fundamental nature of reality day after day, week after week, year after year was that he thought he had a shot of figuring it out. Otherwise, why bother?

The reason the Wright brothers built a flying machine was that they thought it was possible. Otherwise, why bother?

If you don't believe, because of the simple fact that you have a brain, that you are capable of the same extraordinary feats as other ordinary brains, then there's no chance that you'll achieve those feats. Getting more out of your brain than you previously thought possible starts with believing that there's more to get!

The Stakes

It may seem audacious to claim that much of what you think you know about the brain is wrong. But the thing is, we've been telling the Special Brain Story for a very long time. Centuries, at a minimum.

As a species, admitting our ignorance isn't our forte. Confidently making up stories about things we know nothing about? That's where we excel! Before the advent of science and its methodologies, these stories were all we had for explaining how the world worked.

Once science arrived, however, those stories quickly fell apart. The earth wasn't really the center of the universe. Lightning wasn't the anger of the gods. Demons didn't cause disease. Over time, most of us stopped telling the stories we conjured and started telling the ones based on facts, evidence, and reason.

But neuroscience is a young science. While fields like physics, chemistry, and astronomy have been subjected to rigorous inquiry for centuries, neuroscience is, by comparison, still in its infancy. The brain is considered science's last great mystery. That's not because understanding it hasn't been a priority, but because we only recently developed the tools and technology needed to do so.

Our brain also happens to be the most complex object in the known universe. In short, it's the most complex thing we've ever studied, and we've been studying it for the least amount of time. This is why our popular narrative around the brain is one of the last remaining fabrications that still enjoys widespread acceptance.

Although we still have a very long way to go in understanding the brain, we've made significant progress. We now have more than enough evidence to know that the story we invented in the absence of facts was, unsurprisingly, wrong.

The stakes aren't just personal. Because how we think about human potential shapes how we educate children, structure workplaces, and organize society.

If the Impostor is right and abilities are fixed, intelligence is predetermined, and your potential has a ceiling, then it's reasonable to make peace with your limitations, play to your strengths, and avoid your weaknesses.

If the Impostor is wrong and capabilities are determined by experience, intelligence is malleable, and your potential is limitless, then we've only been realizing a fraction of what's possible both individually and collectively.

So, this story matters. And an update is long overdue.

Your potential is not a myth. But the story you've been told about it is.

The Plan

So here's where we're headed:

First, we'll rebuild your understanding of what a brain is actually for and how it accomplishes its mission. You'll discover that the principles underlying all learning are more universal and powerful than you think.

Then you'll meet the Genius, to understand the source of your vast potential, and exactly why you've underestimated it for so long. You'll learn that your brain isn't a fixed hard drive but a wet, squishy, constantly changing ball of magic and wonder that can rewire itself until the day you die. You'll learn why the gifts you already possess rival the most celebrated feats of the human mind.

Next, it's time to peel back the curtain on the Impostor. You'll learn his fascinating origin story, along with his favorite tricks for undermining your potential.

Finally, I'll show you how to reclaim what's yours and unlock the potential that's been there all along.

So that's the plan. Rebuild your foundation, meet your genius, unmask the Impostor, and reclaim what's yours. By the end, you'll understand why Einstein credited "ceaseless struggle" over innate gifts. Why breakthrough discoveries often come during walks rather than at desks. Why children learn so effortlessly while adults struggle. And why you're capable of far more than you currently believe.

chapter summary

- **The Special Brain Story is a lie:** We've been told that we're born with brains of varying abilities and intelligence, and that our job is to figure out what kind of brain we got and stay in our lane. This story is bogus.

- **Einstein's brain was ordinary:** The most celebrated genius in history had a brain that was built just like yours, without any special bits.

- **Every brain contains two forces:** The Genius is the extraordinary learning machinery that built all your capabilities. The Impostor constructs and narrates a fictional story about who you are and what you're capable of.

- **Stories shape reality:** What we believe shapes what we become.
- **The stakes are enormous:** The Special Brain Story has shaped how we educate children, structure workplaces, and organize society. If it's wrong, we've only been realizing a fraction of what's possible.

2

the survival machine

We have a brain for one reason and one reason only, and that is to produce adaptable and complex movements.

—Daniel Wolpert (neuroscientist)

The year is 87,555 BC. You and your best pal, Thog the Skull Smasher, are shooting the breeze inside your favorite cave when suddenly a portal from the future opens up and spits a can opener onto the floor. Thog picks it up and holds it out in front of him.

"Careful, Thog," you say.

"Why? What is it?" Thog asks.

"I don't know. But that's my point."

Thog pulls the handles back and forth, twists the crank a few times.

"Why? What do you think it's for, Thog?"

"Probably skull smashing!" he replies excitedly as he raises the can opener over his head.

"Well, that was predictable. Seems overengineered, though."

"Mmm . . . yes." Thog reconsiders. "Maybe . . . finger smashing?!"

You sigh, resigned to the fact that Thog will be of little help in solving this mystery. Though, to be honest, you don't have much of a clue, either. It's by far the most advanced tool you've ever seen, and it's clear it was designed to do something useful. But you haven't the foggiest idea what that might be.

After a few more rounds of guessing, you and Thog give up, throw the can opener into the junk pit, and get back to your game of dodge rock.

The Survival Project

It's all but impossible to figure out how something works if we don't know what it's for, or the problem it was designed to solve. Even the brightest prehistoric human would have no hope of figuring out the workings of a can opener without first knowing about canned goods and their lack of convenient openings. Show him an unopened can, however, and even Thog the Skull Smasher could solve the riddle.

In many ways, our brain is like a mysterious object from another realm. We didn't make it. We just found it, sitting there on the floor of our skulls, all wrinkled and spongy. In fact, it does kind of look like it's from another planet. And let's be honest, visually it's less impressive than a can opener. You certainly can't tell much about what it's for or how it works just by looking at it.

Unlike organs with obvious jobs—your heart with its chambers for pumping blood, your lungs with their air sacs for gas exchange, your stomach as the place where your pizza ends up—

the brain's purpose isn't self-evident upon initial inspection. As with any found object, if we hope to make any progress in understanding how it works, we must first figure out what it's for. Or, more specifically, we need to know the problem it solves.

Finding the Brain's Purpose

The first clue comes from where we find our brain: inside a body. And we know that the primary mission of a human body is to stay alive long enough so it can reproduce and package its genetic material into another human body. The only reason you're currently alive and reading this sentence is because every strand of your DNA, which contains your assembly instructions, managed to survive for every generation before you came along.

Ultimately, then, the job of every organ is to help us fulfill that mission of living to see another day. Of course, keeping a human body alive is seriously complicated. To simplify things a bit, animals like us take a divide-and-conquer approach to the task, splitting up duties among a team of specialist organs.

Hearts pump oxygen-rich blood to the tissues. Lungs grab oxygen out of the air and expel carbon dioxide back into it. Stomachs and intestines absorb nutrients from food and eliminate waste. Spleens do whatever it is that a spleen does. And so on.

Each of these tasks helps us stay alive.

So what about the brain? What is the brain's specialty, and how does it contribute to the survival project?

The Spaghetti Factory

To get a handle on those questions, we'll use humanity's most time-honored investigative technique, formally known as "smash it open and see what's inside." Or, if we want to act like professionals, we'll call it a "dissection." Now, I realize you don't have a human brain in front of you that you can slice open (fingers crossed!), so I'll tell you what you'd see if you did.

You'd see nerves. Everywhere.

You'd see roughly eighty billion neurons crisscrossing the brain like the world's most elaborate mess of spaghetti. Zooming in farther, you'd find that each neuron consists of a bloblike cell body with scores of tiny little arms sticking out, known as "dendrites." Extending from the cell body is also a thin, wirelike projection known as an "axon," which can traverse very long distances.

THE NEURON

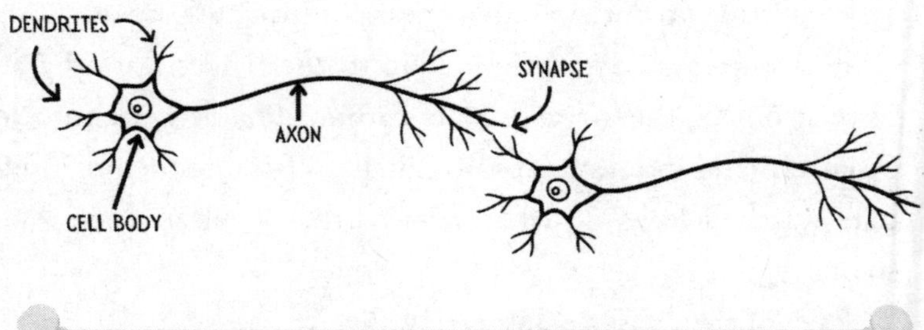

NEURONS ARE THE BASIC UNITS OF THE BRAIN.

THE PRIMARY COMPONENTS ARE THE CELL BODY, WHICH CONTAINS THE NUCLEUS, THE DENDRITES, WHICH RECEIVE SIGNALS FROM OTHER NEURONS, AND THE AXON, WHICH CARRIES THE SIGNAL TO THE SYNAPSE.

At first glance, it all looks hopelessly complicated. But if we trace where the neurons begin and end, we find an order in the apparent chaos. Specifically, if we organize them according to where they start (the location of the cell body) and end (where the axon terminates), we can group them into three main categories.

First are the nerves whose cell bodies reside near a sensory organ, like the skin, eyes, ears, nose, and so on. The axons from these cell bodies project *into* the brain.

Next are the nerves whose cell bodies sit inside the brain or spinal cord. Their axons project *out of* the brain and into the muscles.

Last are the nerves whose cell bodies and axonal projections exist entirely *within* the brain. They project from one neuron to another.

What are these three different kinds of nerves doing? Let's briefly review each of them in turn.

The Inbox (Sensory Nerves)

The nerves whose axons project from sensory organs *into* the brain are formally known as "sensory nerves." These nerves carry information from those sensory organs into the brain for processing and analysis. Nerves from the eyes connect to the visual cortex in the back of the brain. Nerves from the inner ear connect to areas that process sound. Nerves from the nasal cavity and taste buds connect to areas for smell and taste. Nerves from the skin connect to areas that process touch, pressure, and temperature.

Why do we have sensory nerves? To understand what's

happening in the world outside the brain. Our brain spends its entire life in total darkness. A lonely blob floating in a dark tank of fluid. These sensory nerves are its only access to the mysterious land beyond the skull. These sensory nerves are *your* only access to the mysterious land beyond the skull! Everything you've ever known and will know about the world comes by way of these nerves, including all that you're perceiving this very instant!

It's fairly obvious that knowing what's happening outside of us is pertinent to our central mission of staying alive. We need to know if there are apples to pick, rivers to cross, or tiny spiders to overreact to. And so our brain integrates all the information it receives through our sense organs to create an internal model of the world.

But our brain doesn't just need to know about what's happening in the world outside us. It also needs to know about what's happening inside us. Fortunately, we've got nerves for that, too!

There are nerves in our muscles, joints, and tendons that help us monitor the position of our bodies and limbs. There are nerves inside every major organ that transmit critical information about their moment-to-moment function.

In sum, we have nerves for collecting detailed information about the world outside us (exteroception) and inside us (interoception). Which brings us to the crux of what our brain does, which is to acquire, process, and analyze information. The formal term for this is "cognition."

The sensory nerves that we've just described are the foundation of our *perceptual* system, carrying critical information into our brain so that it can make sense of it. But knowing what's happening doesn't do us much good unless we can do something about it, right? For it to be able to help us survive, we must be able to act on that information. Which brings us to our next category of nerves.

The Outbox (Motor Nerves)

The formal name for the nerves whose axons project out of the brain is motor nerves. These nerves are about taking action! They make things happen in the world inside and outside our bodies. They're the reason you can walk, talk, and give constructive hand gestures toward your fellow drivers.

3 KINDS OF NERVES

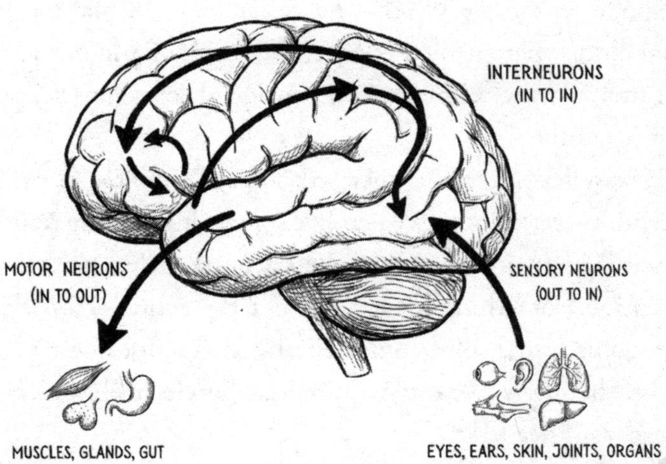

NERVES FALL INTO 3 CATEGORIES BASED ON WHERE THEY TRANSMIT INFORMATION TO AND FROM:

#1 - OUTSIDE TO INSIDE (SENSORY)
#2 - INSIDE TO OUTSIDE (MOTOR)
#3 - INSIDE TO INSIDE (INTER)

Nerves that originate in our brainstem and spinal cord send signals to our organs and glands. Nerves that originate in the motor cortex send signals down through the spinal cord and into the muscles. These nerves are the foundation of our motor system, enabling us to take actions inside and outside our bodies.

The Perception-Action Loop

If all we had were single neurons carrying signals in and out, our perceptual and motor abilities would be quite primitive. In fact, we are born with just these sorts of primitive abilities, in the form of our innate reflexes.

When a doctor taps on your patellar tendon, it triggers the firing of a sensory nerve. That nerve carries the signal into the spinal cord, where it then triggers the firing of a motor nerve. That motor nerve terminates on your quadriceps muscle, causing it to contract.

Basic reflexes like the knee jerk are the simplest form of a perception-action loop. We perceive something, and we respond with an action. In the case of the knee jerk reflex, neither the perception (something hit my leg) nor the action (kick leg) is very sophisticated. Not coincidentally, this reflex doesn't even involve the brain. We often appropriately refer to brainless responses as "knee-jerk."

But if we want to perceive anything more advanced than "something tapped me on the knee" or execute a movement more complex than aimlessly kicking out our leg, we need more processing power. We need a way to bridge the gap between the incoming sensory signals and the outgoing motor signals with more sophistication.

THE PERCEPTION-ACTION LOOP
(SIMPLE REFLEX)

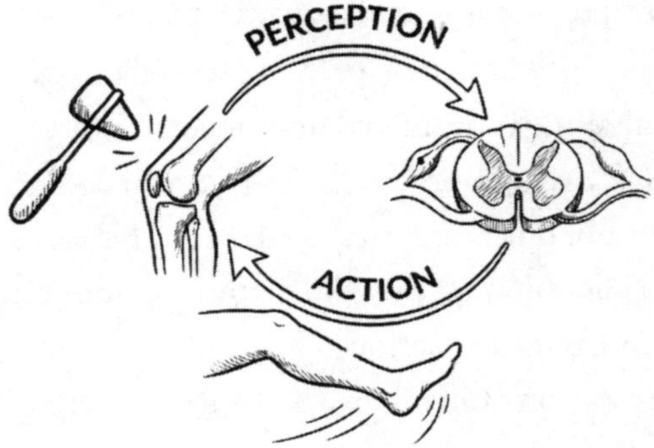

EVERYTHING THE BRAIN DOES RESTS ON THE PERCEPTION-ACTION LOOP, THE CYCLE OF SENSING AND ACTING THAT KEEPS US ALIVE AND ADAPTING.

THE SIMPLEST LOOPS ARE OUR INNATE REFLEXES. A SENSORY SIGNAL TRIGGERS A DIRECT MOTOR RESPONSE, OFTEN WITHOUT INVOLVING THE BRAIN.

Which brings us to our third and final category of nerves: the interneurons.

These are the neurons whose cell bodies and projections exist entirely within the brain. They don't touch the outside world; they talk only to each other.

It takes the processing, analysis, and integration of loads of neuronal activity to recognize your mother's face, tie your shoes, or decide whether to have the steak or the chicken. This processing is "cognition" and it is powered by the 100 trillion connections among these interneurons that transmit signals entirely within the brain.

Altogether, then, we have a vast network of nerves dedicated to perceiving what's happening, and a vast network of nerves dedicated to making things happen. To ensure those nerves do useful things, we have cognitive networks in our cerebral cortex for making sense of our perceptions ("perceptual skills"), and cognitive networks for making coordinated movements ("motor skills").

We perceive, decide, and we act. In fact, you could argue that the whole point of our perceptual system is to help us decide and guide our next action, and the whole point of our brain is to decide and execute our next action.

The brain's job crystallizes into a simple, perpetual cycle that began the moment you entered this world: perceive threats and opportunities, decide what to do, act on that decision.

And the goal of those decisions is to maintain homeostasis, or the stable internal conditions necessary for survival. Threats are forces that move us out of balance and endanger our survival—and are to be avoided. Opportunities are chances to bring us into balance and promote our survival—and are to be pursued.

An example will help us bring this all together: Imagine you've skipped breakfast before a session on your stationary bike. As you pump your legs on your miserable journey to nowhere, the metabolic activity in your heart, lungs, and muscles increases. That activity churns through glucose in your blood, causing levels to drop. Glucose-sensing neurons in the hypothalamus detect the dip. As a short-term response to the impending energy crisis, the hypothalamus sends signals to the adrenal glands to release epinephrine, prompting the liver to break down glycogen and liberate glucose into the bloodstream. Meanwhile, in hopes of achieving a longer-term solution, neurons in the insula respond by producing the sensation of hunger, so that you'll literally get off your butt and find some food. Networks in the basal ganglia and cerebellum initiate a series of motor programs for dismounting the bike and walking up the stairs to the kitchen. Networks in the visual system readily identify the sight of a glorious, ripe banana sitting in the fruit basket. Motor programs for reaching, grabbing, peeling, biting, chewing, and swallowing commence. The banana is digested and absorbed into the bloodstream and glucose levels rise. The brain has used all its sensing and moving apparatus to restore energy balance.

THE PERCEPTION-ACTION LOOP

(COMPLEX "REFLEX")

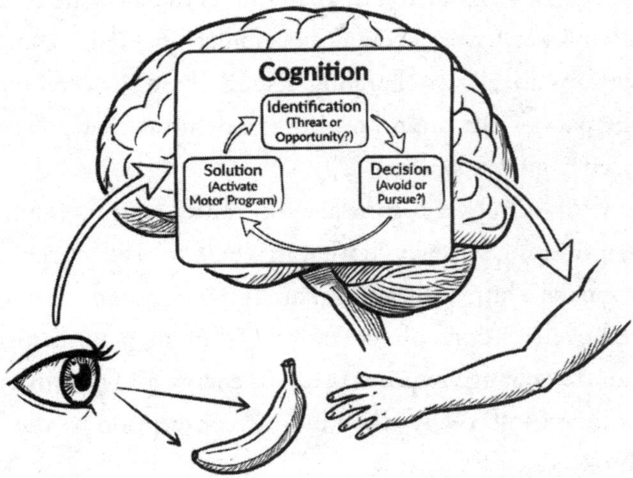

A COMPLEX BRAIN ENABLES ADDITIONAL PROCESSING ("COGNITION") IN BETWEEN PERCEPTION AND ACTION TO ENABLE MORE ADVANCED ANALYSIS, DECISION MAKING, AND MOVEMENT PATTERNS.

IN THE BRAIN, THE ONLY DIFFERENCE BETWEEN THE SIMPLEST AND MOST SOPHISTICATED LOOPS IS HOW MANY NEURONS PARTICIPATE IN THAT CHAIN.

To answer the question posed at the beginning of this chapter, our brain is for maintaining homeostasis throughout the body. It is the master coordinator of our life-sustaining functions, and perception-action loops are how it gets that done.

But how exactly does our brain know how to do all this? How does it know that a banana will provide the rush of energy it needs? How does it know to distinguish an edible banana from a rotten one?

Change Is a Constant

Picture yourself shrunk down to the size of a synapse, exploring the intricate wiring of the human brain. As you navigate through this complex network, you notice something remarkable: its connections are always changing. Especially in the cerebral cortex, the part of our brain housing the neurons that power our advanced cognitive skills.

None of our other organs are constantly rearranging themselves, mind you. Nor would we want them to. The blueprint for how to make a human heart and lungs has been refined and optimized over millions of generations. Why mess with success? Plus, all that change requires precious energy and resources. So, what's the payoff? Why is the brain the exception to the "if it ain't broke, don't fix it" rule?

The Turtle and the Toddler

As we've discussed, our perceptual skills enable us to identify threats and opportunities in our environment, while our motor skills enable us to respond to those threats and opportunities in a way that enhances our odds of survival.

Now, imagine you're charged with designing a brain and you're given a choice. The first is to hardwire all those skills into the brain from birth. Once the wiring is complete, it's fixed and final. All your behavior is nothing but pure instinct.

The second option is to "softwire" the brain. In this approach, you're born with no cognitive skills and instead create them and the necessary wiring as you go.

Each approach has its merits.

On the one hand, hardwiring all our skills means we can be independent, fully autonomous creatures right out of the starting gate. It also means we can have simpler brains, since we don't need all that fancy learning equipment. A simpler brain requires less energy and fewer resources to maintain. That's also a win.

But there are disadvantages, too. What happens if our conditions change? Hardwiring all our perceptual and motor skills for perceiving and responding appropriately to threats and opportunities in our environment makes good sense if we know in advance the full spectrum of threats and opportunities that we'll encounter over the course of our lives. If our environment is completely stable and predictable, then baking it all in and running on instinct is the way to go. But if our environment is unstable, we're in trouble. Hardwiring makes us rigid. Softwiring makes us adaptable.

The plight of the sea turtle underscores the disadvantages of hardwiring. When sea turtles hatch, which usually occurs at night, they instinctively move toward the brightest horizon. Why? Because the sea turtle brain comes hardwired with the skill of finding the ocean. Which seems like a very reasonable thing to have done. For millions of years, the brightest horizon at night marked the location of the ocean as the sea reflected the light of the moon and the stars. It seemed a safe bet that things would stay that way, so might as well hardwire that bit of knowledge in their turtle brains.

Then Thomas Edison and his bright idea ruined everything. In a post-lightbulb world, the "brightest horizon always marks the ocean" heuristic is no longer true. Now that brightest horizon might be coming from the horizon or from the lights of a city, luring an instinct-bound turtle straight into harm's way. Hardwiring in navigational skills conferred a survival advantage for the sea turtle when the heavens were the only source of light. Now that decision is an existential threat. With hardwired navigational skills tailored for a different world, sea turtles must now rely on conscientious humans to ensure a safe journey to the sea.

So, if you're going to choose the "hardwire all cognitive skills" approach to designing a brain, then you'd better be sure that the environment that brain will navigate is entirely stable and predictable. If you want a brain that's optimized for adaptability, on the other hand, then softwiring is the way to go. And this is the decision *our* brain has made. We wire up our skills as needed. We're not born with them, so we must *learn* them instead.

Not having any cognitive skills at birth does have its downsides. You are likely aware of these downsides if you've ever had to parent an unskilled baby human. Caring for these helpless creatures is a full-time job. For much of our childhood, we depend on the cognitive skills of the adults in our lives to keep us alive. Having the longest period of helplessness in the animal kingdom is the price we pay for a softwired and highly adaptable brain.

So far, this trade-off has worked out pretty well for us. Despite having evolved mostly in East Africa, we humans have since spread to every region of the world. We can learn to live in the jungle, or the desert, or New Jersey. Trading childhood self-sufficiency for cognitive adaptability is one of the reasons we've been able to thrive in more habitats than any other species on the planet.

From Vibrations to Meaning

We now know what the brain is for and why it's designed the way it is. But we haven't yet answered the question of *how* it accomplishes its mission. How does this modest mass turn air vibrations into your mother's voice, or photons of light into the face of a friend?

To help us develop some sense of how we get from electrical impulses to the execution of a backflip or the taste of a cheeseburger, let's take a tour of what happens when we hear a sound, using the timeless example of a tree falling in the woods.

When the tree strikes the ground, the impact disrupts air molecules, creating a wave of vibrating air that spreads outward like ripples in a lake. If your ear is within range, those vibrations funnel into your ear canal and crash against your eardrum, and your eardrum begins vibrating. Those vibrations rattle the bones of your middle ear, slosh the fluid in your cochlea, and jostle the hair cells that line its walls. And finally, the moment of truth: the movement of the hair cells triggers the firing of a neuron.

The firing of a neuron in response to the falling tree is the pivotal moment, because it's the moment when information from the outside world (vibrations of air molecules) is turned into brain activity. Or, to use the common jargon, it's been translated into a neuronal "spike"—a reference to the visual appearance of a firing neuron on an oscilloscope.

The conversion of physical stimuli into spikes is the first step in every sensory organ. Photons of light are converted into spikes in the retina. Mechanical pressure and temperature change are converted into spikes in our skin's mechanoreceptors and thermoreceptors. Dissolved chemicals in fluids are converted into spikes in our taste buds. Volatile organic compounds in the air are transmitted into spikes in the olfactory epithelium.

Why is this? Because the brain's cognitive machinery only speaks the language of spikes. Like a computer that only understands binary code, or an American who only speaks English, all information must first be translated into that language in order for the brain to interpret it.

But what makes this information useful? Remember, our goal here is to use these spikes to figure out what's going on out there. In this example, it's to identify the sound of a tree falling in the woods. We've painstakingly turned vibrations of air into neural impulses, but how exactly does that help us identify that sound?

It helps us because each source has its own unique, signature *pattern*.

The pattern of air vibrations created by a falling tree differs from those of a barking dog. The pattern created when your mother says "hello" differs from when your sister says it. The pattern of photons bouncing off a car differs from those bouncing off a motorcycle. And patterns of various kinds are converted into patterns of neuronal activity by your sensory organs, so that your brain can decode them.

The ability to decode and generate patterns in neural firings is your brain's core competency. Every cognitive skill you possess depends on it.

Think about what's happening here. A tree falls in the forest, creating a specific pattern of air vibrations. That pattern gets preserved as a pattern of eardrum vibrations. That becomes a pattern of fluid waves in your cochlea. That becomes a pattern of hair cell movements. That becomes a pattern of neuronal spikes traveling into your brain.

At each step, the pattern is transformed but preserved. And if the pattern of spikes triggered by a fallen tree is preserved in the spiking patterns of neurons in your auditory cortex, then identifying the source becomes a matter of detecting and recognizing patterns of spikes. If you've learned to recognize the spiking pattern for "falling tree," then the tree does indeed make a sound. In your mind, at least.

This same mechanism applies across all your senses. With vision, patterns of light become patterns of neural activity that let you recognize faces, read words, navigate spaces. With touch, patterns of pressure and temperature become patterns that distinguish a cat's fur from sandpaper. With taste, patterns of chemical signals become patterns that distinguish chocolate from coffee. With smell, patterns of airborne molecules become patterns that distinguish roses from gasoline.

And it's not just perception. Skilled movements like throwing a ball, playing piano, and writing your name are all precisely timed *patterns* of neural firing that trigger coordinated muscle

FROM THE AIR TO YOUR BRAIN

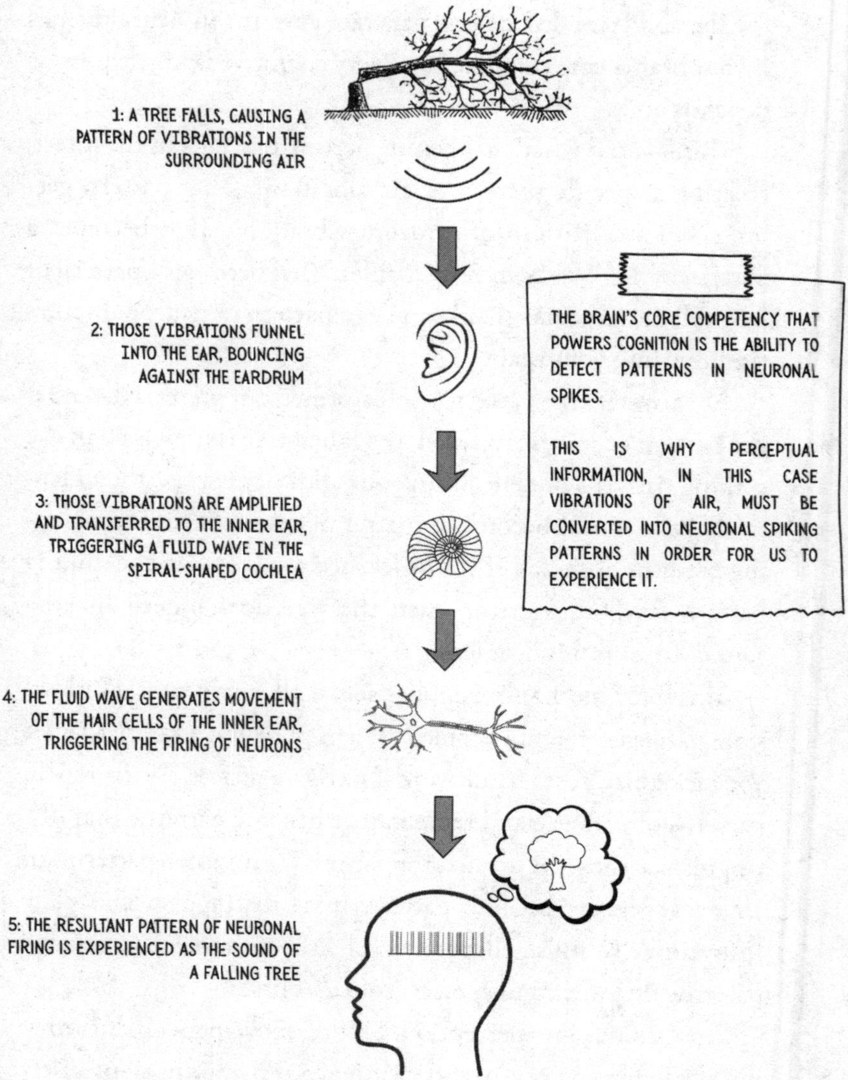

contractions. The core competency covers both pattern detection and pattern generation.

But your brain's pattern proclivities extend beyond processing the world around you. As we'll see next, the most revolutionary application of this mechanism happens when your brain turns it inward.

The Revolution Within

We now understand how your brain transforms air vibrations into your mother's voice and photons into a friend's face. In each case, it achieves those feats by detecting patterns in neural spikes. It must do it this way, because spikes are the language of all animal brains. And up to this point, what we've covered is true of all brains.

But your brain has one more trick up its sleeve. A trick that equipped the human brain with a superpower that would change the world forever.

The First Revolution: Self-Generated Patterns

Imagine you're lost in the woods. You haven't eaten in days, and you're getting desperate. You've noticed some rabbits hopping around, but they're too quick to catch on foot. Then you remember something important: you have a brain!

You start to *think*. A plan takes shape in your mind. You recall that rabbits tend to follow the same paths through the grass. You've also observed that they love to eat clover. You imagine digging a pit along one of their trails, covering it with sticks and leaves to create a fake forest floor, and then placing some clover on top as bait. In your mind's eye, you see a rabbit hopping onto your trap and falling through, securing your dinner and your survival.

Now, here's a question for you: Where did the information for that mental plan come from?

Images of rabbits and clovers and twig-covered pits danced around in your mind, but they didn't come through your sense organs. The pit didn't exist yet. You weren't looking at clover or watching bunnies bounce. While you were hatching your plans, the information your brain was processing wasn't coming from outside your skull at all. It was coming from the *inside*.

This ability to generate information internally represents one of the most consequential innovations in the history of life on Earth. For hundreds of millions of years, the pattern-recognition machinery in animal brains served a single purpose: to make sense of sensory input. Eyes detected patterns of light; ears detected patterns of sound. The brain identified those patterns to understand the world as it is right now.

Then, sometime in our evolutionary history, the brain figured out a way to reverse-engineer the process. It learned to *generate* the patterns itself.

Consider what happens when you imagine a sound, like the barking of a dog. When an actual dog barks, specific neurons in your auditory cortex fire in a specific pattern. But when you merely *imagine* that sound, many of those same neurons fire in nearly the same pattern. Your brain re-creates the pattern internally—no sound waves required. It generates the pattern, then recognizes what it just generated.

This cycle of pattern generation and analysis is the essence of thinking. It's the brain talking to itself. And it gave us a transformative new capability: the ability to *simulate* the world.

When our mental life was tethered to the outside world, our behavior was driven entirely by the present moment. We reacted to the world as it was. With this new capability, we could imagine worlds that didn't exist yet. We could simulate possible futures, run mental experiments—like building a rabbit trap—and choose the best course of action before committing to it. The ability to imagine meant we could prepare today for the challenges of tomorrow.

A BRAIN THAT TALKS TO ITSELF

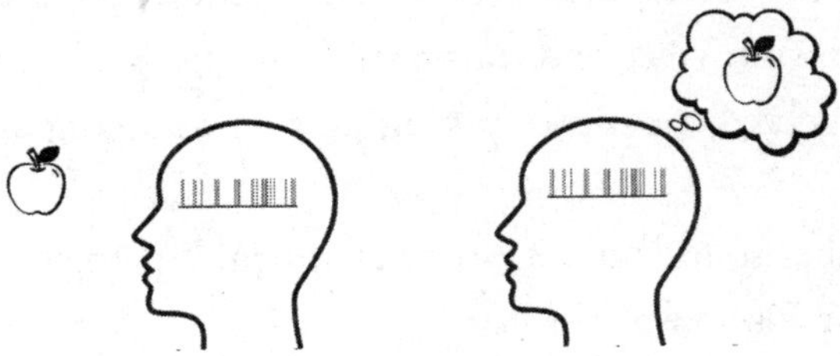

WHEN WE PERCEIVE AN OBJECT THROUGH OUR SENSES, IT ELICITS A PATTERN OF NEURONAL SPIKES. THE ANALYSIS OF THAT PATTERN RESULTS IN OUR PERCEPTUAL EXPERIENCE.

WHEN WE IMAGINE AN OBJECT, OUR BRAIN IS GENERATING A PATTERN OF NEURONAL SPIKES. THE ANALYSIS OF THAT PATTERN RESULTS IN OUR PERCEPTUAL EXPERIENCE. IN THIS CASE, THE BRAIN IS GENERATING THE PATTERN THAT IT THEN ANALYZES.

However, this first revolution had its limits. We could only simulate what we'd already *experienced*. We could recombine memories to create scenarios we'd never directly perceived, like rabbits falling into pits, but we were still bound by the raw materials of our direct perceptions. To break those chains and think about things we had never seen or touched, we would need a second revolution.

One that would create the greatest mental technology the world has ever known.

The Second Revolution: Symbolic Patterns

Our brain's ability to generate patterns opened an unexpected possibility. If you could reliably re-create the pattern for "rabbit" in your mind, then you could also use *something else* to trigger that pattern. For example, you could invent a sound that you made with your voice and train your brain so that hearing that sound triggered the same spiking pattern as seeing an actual "rabbit".

Now that sound, and its associated neural pattern, *stood for* rabbit. The sound was a *symbol.*

This move to using symbols might not seem noteworthy, but it was a revolutionary step. If you and I both agree that the same sound meant "rabbit," I could activate the rabbit pattern in *your* brain just by making that sound. I could make you think about rabbits without a rabbit anywhere in sight. Now humans could transfer their mental simulations to other human minds through symbols.

This sharing of symbolic sounds is what we call language, and it became humanity's most transformative adaptation. The ability to share thoughts, coordinate actions, and pass along knowledge through sounds provided such a profound survival advantage that it drove our capability for symbolic thinking.

Humans who used language could warn others about distant dangers, coordinate complex hunts, share discoveries about food and shelter, and pass accumulated wisdom across generations. The massive survival advantage conferred by language created an intense selection pressure, reshaping our brain in ways that made it really good at manipulating symbols. Language was both a product of symbolic thinking and the force that created it.

For our purposes, the crucial point about this new capability of symbolic thinking is that it is still all about patterns. It was a case of repurposing our core competency for a new use. With symbolic sounds, we were creating patterns of neural activity that represented *other patterns* of neural activity. And there is no limit to how far you can take this, as the evolution of language illustrates.

Language began simply with sounds that represented things in the world. The sound "banana" came to represent that crescent-shaped object with the tasty insides. The sound "donk" represented the sound a rock made when it struck Thog's skull. One sound stood for one thing.

But why stop there? Why not create symbolic patterns that refer to *other* symbolic patterns? And so we created sounds not just for specific objects, but for categories. The sound "food" didn't refer to any specific edible item, like a banana, but to *all* edible items. With a word such as "food," we had a neural pattern that wasn't referencing anything specific in the real world, but rather another symbolic pattern in our own brain!

Then we needed our symbols to do things. Trees fall. Rivers flow. Animals run. So we developed sounds for actions, and rules for how the order of sounds changed their meaning.

In this way, we began creating an entire system of symbols.

To expand what we could do with that system, our system needed rules. So we created sounds that only made sense within the symbolic system itself. The only job of words like "the" and "whereas" and "therefore" is to specify relationships between other symbols. Which is to say they're patterns that specify relationships between other patterns.

The fancy term for embedding structures within structures—like sentences within sentences or patterns within patterns—is "recursion." And recursion can just keep going and going. Recursion is what makes human language infinitely expressive with a finite set of sounds, exponentially expanding not only our ability to communicate but our ability to *think*.

A Tool for the Mind

Language didn't just enhance communication. It fundamentally transformed what we could think.

For millions of years, humans had been making tools for their hands: Spears for hunting. Scrapers for hides. Hammers for breaking. Each tool extended our physical capabilities, letting us do things our bare hands couldn't.

Language was the first tool for your mind, one that multiplied your thinking abilities. By collapsing complex concepts into single sounds, you could manipulate ideas that would otherwise be too big to hold in your head all at once.

Furthermore, once the neural circuits for language had been built, they could be repurposed for other forms of symbolic thinking. The same circuits that enabled language are what enabled other forms of symbolic thinking, such as mathematics, logic, written language, and musical notation—each a new tool for the mind, each enabled by the machinery language created.

Same Machinery, Different Input

Crucially, once we get down to the level of neural firing, there's little difference between perceptual skills and thinking skills. The neural machinery that learned to recognize your mother's face also learned to imagine a dog's bark, and that same machinery learned to understand grammar and manipulate abstract symbols.

What differs is just the source and nature of the patterns. When you learn to recognize faces, you're training pattern-detection networks on visual input from your eyes. When you imagine or mentally simulate, you're generating those same types of patterns internally. When you learn language and symbolic thinking, you're training pattern-detection networks to work with patterns that represent other patterns.

As biologist François Jacob put it, "Evolution is a tinkerer, not an engineer." In the case of the brain, it has continued to tinker with pattern recognition to take our cognitive powers to new heights. First, it learned to recognize patterns from the world generated by our sense organs (perception). Then, it learned to generate and recognize its own patterns (imagination/simulation). Finally, it learned to create patterns that represent other patterns (symbolic thinking).

A UNIVERSAL PROCESS

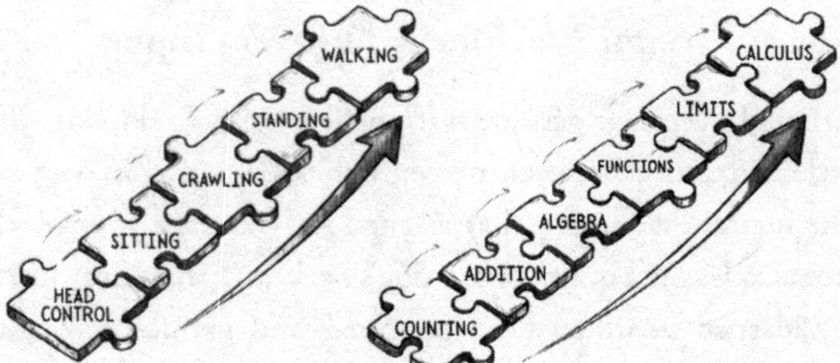

WE MISTAKENLY TREAT "THINKING SKILLS" LIKE MATH AND LOGIC AS IF THEY BELONG TO A SPECIAL CATEGORY.

IN REALITY, THE MECHANISMS THAT TAUGHT YOU TO WALK ARE THE EXACT SAME ONES THAT CAN TEACH YOU TO WRITE CODE. THE PROCESS THAT BUILT YOUR ABILITY TO RECOGNIZE FACES IS THE SAME ONE THAT BUILDS YOUR ABILITY TO UNDERSTAND PHYSICS. THE PATH THAT TRANSFORMED YOU FROM A HELPLESS INFANT INTO A CAPABLE ADULT IS THE SAME PATH THAT CAN TAKE YOU ANYWHERE ELSE YOU WANT TO GO.

A Universal Process

If perceptual, motor, and thinking skills all rely on the same pattern-recognition machinery, then they all develop through the same process.

The mechanisms that taught you to walk are the exact same ones that taught you to talk. The process that built your ability to recognize faces is the exact same process that built your ability to understand grammar. While motor, perceptual, and thinking skills may look different on the outside, they are powered by the identical engine on the inside.

This matters because it means we have been looking at human potential all wrong. We have treated "thinking skills"—like math, logic, and chess—as if they belong to a separate category of magic, reserved for those lucky few born with special "smart" brains.

But the neuroscience tells a different story. It tells us that thinking skills aren't special. They are just another application of the same pattern-recognition machinery that powers everything else you do.

This implies that the insights we have about how a baby learns to walk or how a toddler learns to speak apply directly to how an adult learns calculus or how to write code. The path that transformed you from a helpless infant into a capable adult is the same path that can take you anywhere else you want to go.

That machinery—the force that weaves these patterns into skills, the force that turned you into a virtuoso of walking and talking without you even realizing it—is what I call the Genius.

And as you will discover next, the Genius has a very specific way of working.

chapter summary

- **The brain's mission is survival:** The brain maintains homeostasis through perpetual perception-action loops, perceiving threats and opportunities, deciding what to do, and executing actions to keep the body in balance.

- **We are built for adaptability, not instinct:** Unlike animals with hardwired behaviors, the human brain is "softwired." We trade instinct for adaptability.

- **Pattern recognition is the brain's core competency:** Every cognitive skill, from recognizing faces to understanding grammar, depends on detecting and generating patterns of neural spikes. It's the brain's universal language.

- **Thinking emerged from perception:** The brain's most revolutionary trick was learning to generate patterns internally rather than only receiving them from the senses. This enabled imagination, simulation, and planning for the future.

- **Symbolic cognition repurposed ancient machinery:** Language, math, and abstract reasoning emerged from repurposing the same pattern-recognition machinery that powers perception and movement. The process that taught you to walk is the same process that can teach you calculus.

3

genius in training

We are faced with a paradox: the fantastic palace that is our brain contains a hundred thousand times more detail than the architect's blueprints that are used to build it!

—Stanislas Dehaene (cognitive neuroscientist)

Imagine you've just bought a computer. A really, really expensive one. It has the most advanced hardware in the known universe, consisting of nearly 100 billion processing units and trillions of connections.

You turn it on. You wait for the operating system to load. And . . . nothing. Just a blank screen.

This is the human infant. In the language of computing, when we first plop out on the scene, we're all hardware and no software. Unlike a foal, which hits the ground running (literally), or a sea turtle, which knows exactly which way the ocean is, the human baby is the definition of incompetence.

This is because, unlike a computer, our brain must write its own software. And rather than storing algorithms in patterns of ones and zeros, it encodes them in intricate networks of neuronal connections. To develop any cognitive abilities, we must first build those connections.

The challenge our brain faces here is monumental. It must learn to make sense of the torrent of sensory information flooding in from the eyes, ears, skin, and other sense organs. It must learn to control a body with dozens of joints and hundreds of muscles. It must learn to decode and produce the complex sounds of human language. It must learn to distinguish safe from dangerous, edible from inedible, mother from stranger.

And it must do so without an instruction manual.

The Genius is the unconscious learning engine that took you from a flailing, milk-obsessed blob to a creature capable of decoding the patterns of squiggles on this page. And if we look closely at how the Genius operates, we find that it follows a strict, mathematical logic.

The brain begins chipping away at this challenge from day one. It processes patterns in its sensory data. It attempts movements and observes the results. In the laboratory of the real world, it steadily builds the neural scaffolding that will support advanced perceptions, movements, and thinking.

At first, progress seems agonizingly slow. For months, a baby can't do anything useful with its limbs. Months of aimless flailing about before it can intentionally hit a target within reach. Underneath the hood, though, massive changes are afoot. Each near-miss, each accidental success is valuable feedback for constructing the neural networks that will eventually enable precise, purposeful movement.

The same process unfolds in parallel across every domain. In vision, the brain begins detecting basic features such as edges, contrasts, movement. In hearing, it starts deciphering different frequencies and patterns of sound. In touch, it maps the relationship between sensations and body parts.

By around six months, the first indicators of that network building start to emerge. The baby can sit up, reach for objects with some accuracy, and distinguish familiar faces from strangers. By twelve months, most can pull themselves up to stand, say a few words, and understand simple instructions. By eighteen months, they're walking, their vocabulary is exploding, and they're beginning to engage in pretend play.

By age three, they might as well be a new kind of life-form. That flailing, unskilled blob of a newborn has become a capable, curious, communicative little human. Walking, talking, thinking, playing, imagining. A budding virtuoso in the core skills of human cognition.

This magical cognitive transformation doesn't just happen in a few gifted brains. It is nearly universal. Every intact brain that's placed in the right conditions acquires these exceptional skills.

But what's even more remarkable is that, when we look closer at how these skills develop, we find the same pattern every time. Whether it's motor skills like walking, perceptual skills like parsing a sentence, or thinking skills like solving problems, the process of skill building is the same. The domains may be different, but the underlying structure is the same. A structure that betrays their shared underlying mechanism.

And the architect behind this construction project is the Genius. It is the unconscious learning engine that built your cognitive abilities. And it built them from scratch.

The Genius Blueprint

So now let's dig into the Genius's methods. Doing so not only reinforces the universality of a learning process that has been shaped by millions of years of evolution but it also provides the template for how to learn anything. By understanding these patterns, we can unlock the Genius blueprint.

Feature #1: It's Always the Same Sequence

If you're a parent, then chances are, you're familiar with the developmental milestones. These are the predictable stages of physical, cognitive, and social development that mark a child's progress, such as sitting up, learning first words, and walking. Besides being an excellent source of crippling parental anxiety for the first few years of a child's life, they also function as an indicator of the health of the nervous system.

This is because, barring injury or disease, every child passes through these milestones. In Western culture, parents often pay extra attention to when specific milestones occur. Hitting language milestones early is often taken as a sign of intellectual giftedness. Early motor milestones are often construed as indicators of future athletic prowess. Being late to achieve a milestone is often cause for consternation.

But, by and large, parents attach far too much significance to the timing of these events than they merit, especially when it comes to predicting future capabilities. That's because, in the end, what really matters in determining whether a child develops these skills is not when they hit these milestones, but whether they hit them at all. What matters is that they pass through the sequence, because it's the sequence that matters.

For those of us interested in understanding the learning process, this is the feature that is most telling. Milestones always occur in the same order, and over similar time frames. Which is precisely why they can be printed on a chart in the pediatrician's office.

Just as no child has ever come out of the womb walking and talking, no child has started speaking words before babbling, learned to skip before learning to walk, or learned to read before recognizing letters. The order never varies.

With language development, for example, babies spend an extensive period of time learning how to produce the sonic building blocks of their native tongue. And this process doesn't begin until several months, because it depends on the perceptual machinery that can identify what those building blocks are in the sounds we hear, and that must be built first.

And there's an order to babbling itself, even across languages. It begins with the soothing "oohs" and "ahs" of cooing, representing the first attempt at vowel sounds. That's followed by plosives, nasals, glides, fricatives, and affricatives. Bringing up the rear, sometimes by a wide margin, are the "l" and "r" sounds, often a bittersweet parental moment where a child loses their last vestiges of "baby talk."

Skills always emerge in a particular order, and each one takes a minimum amount of time to develop. There is no skipping steps. And there are no shortcuts.

But all those who move through the sequence end up at the same destination. It's not how fast you move along the path that determines whether mastery is achieved, it's whether you complete the sequence.

Feature #2: The Sequence Is Cumulative and Hierarchical

Why is the sequence so critical? Why is it always the same?

Because the Genius is a structural engineer. Learning requires building physical structures in the brain, and the sequence matters when building anything. You can't build the penthouse of a skyscraper before you've poured the concrete for the lobby. There's a necessary sequence to the construction process, as each new floor depends on the stability of what's below. At any point in time, what you can build depends on the existing *scaffolding*.

The brain is constrained by the same rules of construction. What we can learn at any point in time also depends on the cognitive scaffolding we've built, implemented in our neural connections. Our tangible neurological scaffolding produces our abstract cognitive scaffolding, and both determine what can and can't be built next in the neural and cognitive realms. And all of it is a product of what we've learned up until that moment.

Once again, take the case of a baby learning to articulate the sounds of language. She must begin with the movement patterns that are available to her, based on her existing neurological scaffolding. She can't start with fricatives because the neurological scaffolding required to generate those movements doesn't exist yet. Just as you can't build the fifth floor after the first, she must first learn her plosives, nasals, and glides in order to build the necessary structural supports.

This may not seem too surprising when it comes to motor skills. Though we may try to shortcut the process, on some level we realize that we can't run before we can walk or juggle three balls before we can catch one.

But, crucially, the same rules apply to the development of our thinking skills, as demonstrated by the sequence in which words are learned. Once again, there is a stereotyped progression in the order they appear. Only in this case the order is determined by the *class* of words. Children learn nouns first, then verbs, adjectives before adverbs, and so on. Why would this be?

It's not because we lack the required motor scaffolding. Verbs aren't inherently harder to pronounce than nouns. Rather, it's because thinking skills require *conceptual* scaffolding. We only learn to pronounce the words we understand. And we only understand what our conceptual scaffolding allows. Nouns refer to concrete objects in the world. Conceptually, they are the simplest class of words.

Verbs refer to actions we take in the world but are an abstraction. Adverbs, conjunctions, and prepositions only exist within our symbolic system, representing the most conceptually advanced classes of words. This stereotyped progression in our use of words occurs because thinking skills, which rely on the same learning mechanisms, require neurological and cognitive scaffolding.

In this way, what we can learn next is always constrained by what we have learned. Across all domains, our existing neural scaffolding determines our "Goldilocks Zone," or the limits of current capabilities, and the kind of scaffolding we can build next. It's the zone where things are hard but not impossible. Anything beyond that zone is biologically impossible for us to attain, no matter how hard we try.

In sum, the learning sequence matters because our cognitive skills are built from the ground up, layer by layer, in a process that is cumulative and hierarchical. It's a process I'll refer to as "progressive composition" to highlight the fact that it is both building upward from previous achievements and combining simpler elements into more complex wholes.

SKILLS REQUIRE SCAFFOLDING

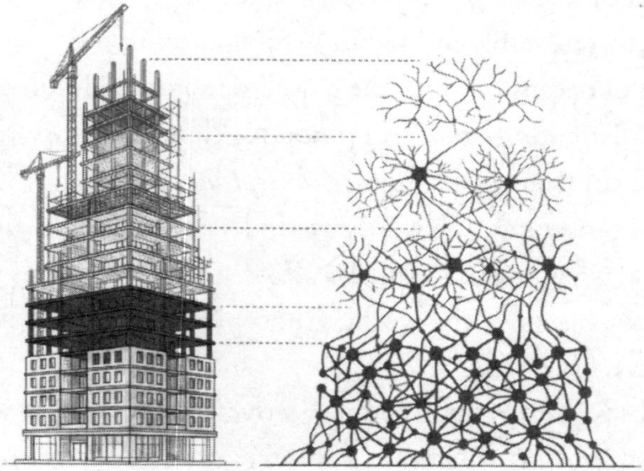

THE SEQUENCE OF MILESTONES IS STEREOTYPICAL BECAUSE LEARNING REQUIRES BUILDING PHYSICAL STRUCTURES IN THE BRAIN. LIKE A SKYSCRAPER, EACH NEW FLOOR DEPENDS ON THE STABILITY OF WHAT'S BELOW.

WHAT WE CAN LEARN—WHETHER IT'S A MOTOR, PERCEPTUAL, OR THINKING SKILL—ALWAYS DEPENDS ON AND IS DETERMINED BY THE COGNITIVE SCAFFOLDING WE'VE ALREADY BUILT.

This explains why the sequence matters and why it's always the same. But there's something else about this process that we haven't addressed yet. Who's supervising it all? Who's planning out the sequence in the first place and making sure each step is completed properly?

Feature #3: There Is No Teacher

We tend to think of learning as something that happens in classrooms. It involves teachers and textbooks. It requires somebody overseeing the process, laying out exactly how we'll get from point A to point B. And it probably has to be a little unpleasant. It's something we do while wishing we were doing something else, like playing outside or talking to our friends.

But who taught you how to walk and talk? Who taught you how to distinguish the faces of joy and anger?

Nobody did, of course. When it comes to learning our core cognitive abilities, there are no teachers. We are self-taught. There are no classrooms. No syllabus, assignments, or pop quizzes.

Nor could there be. None of us has any earthly idea how we learned to walk or talk. We couldn't teach each other how to do it if we tried.

Yet, while we don't teach our children these skills, we aren't entirely superfluous, either. We actually play a critical role, which is to provide the conditions that allow their brain to learn them.

For example, I bet you've noticed how differently adult humans speak to infants. You've likely done it yourself. You may have even felt ridiculous about it. Though you'd have felt even more ridiculous if you were to talk to an adult like you talk to an infant. Just accept that there's no way to sound cool when talking to a baby.

Though we may not be consciously aware of it, what we're doing when engaging in "baby talk" is providing the infant brain a simpler form of language. A baby doesn't have the neural scaffolding needed to parse and comprehend all the sounds and concepts of mature, adult-level speech. So we provide them with a form of speech that they can potentially parse and comprehend. We're giving training data that's in the Genius's Goldilocks Zone.

There are no schools for learning our core cognitive skills. In most cases, however, our culture and environment provide the necessary conditions for the Genius to acquire them.

Feature #4: Deprivation Disrupts Development

How do we know that our culture and environment provide the necessary conditions for the acquisition of our core cognitive skills?

Because of what happens when a brain doesn't get them.

There are two scenarios in which children don't end up mastering the core human cognitive skills. The first is when there's dysfunction of the brain's hardware due to disease or injury, when there's dysfunction of the machinery that powers learning and cognition. In this case, development may not occur at all or may arrest at a particular stage.

The second scenario where a normally functioning young brain doesn't develop the core cognitive skills is when it's deprived of the necessary inputs. Unfortunately, we know this because of some historical episodes where children were subjected to settings of extreme deprivation.

From the day they're born, most children are surrounded by the sounds of their native language. In many cases, those sounds are being directed toward them. We talk to babies not because they understand, but so they can learn to do so. Our speech is their training data.

What happens when a brain isn't exposed to the sounds of any language, verbal or nonverbal? Language ability doesn't develop. Children who aren't exposed to a language don't end up learning to speak or understand speech normally.

The same happens if the motor system is deprived of its necessary inputs. From the day they're born, most children are free to explore an open world with their bodies. When allowed to do so, they develop a full repertoire of complex motor skills, again in stereotyped sequence. If they aren't free to explore the world around them, however, those motor skills, and the neural structures that enable them, don't develop properly.

It doesn't necessarily have to be designed this way. Another option would've been to program the development of our cognitive skill networks into our DNA, in the same way that our brain and other organ systems develop in utero according to a genetically encoded script. That'd still be a form of hardwiring, since it wouldn't be environmentally driven. But were that true, deprivation should not disrupt the development of those skills, which it does. Brains aren't born with abilities; they're born with potential.

What does this tell us? It tells us that, in normally functioning brains, variabilities in skill development are the result of variabilities in the environment. From variability in the learning path.

Feature #5: Motivation Comes from Within

If there's no teacher or grown-up planning and overseeing the learning process, no grades or gold stars to strive for, no threats of summer school, then why does a child try to learn at all?

As we've reviewed, learning occurs in a predictable sequence. The steps we've cleared determine the next step we need to make. And when it's time to work on the next skill in the progression, we do so with single-minded, relentless intensity.

When rolling over is in a child's Goldilocks Zone of motor skills, for example, rolling over becomes the most important thing in the world. They're obsessed with it. They work on it relentlessly. Until they learn it. And then it's on to the next step.

But where does that obsession come from? We don't decide to start learning to roll over or pronounce phonemes because there's a test tomorrow, or to pad our résumé. We do it because these skills are matters of life and death. For us humans, learning to walk, talk, socialize, and make sense of the world are essential survival skills.

From the moment we're born, our sensory cortices are bombarded with information from our sensory organs. But none of it makes any sense. The world is a chaotic blur and we need to identify the Milk-Giver! But we're born without the perceptual skills needed to do so. And so the Genius gets to work building hierarchies of feature-detection networks.

At birth, we're incapable of moving our body in any meaningful fashion and must depend on the generosity of others to move us anywhere. We do possess the neural hardware needed to move on our own; we just don't know how to control it yet. And so the Genius begins constructing the neural machinery required to make useful movements of our limbs and body.

We can't perceive, move, or communicate, which puts us at serious risk. And so our motivation comes from needing to solve very important problems. We learn what we care about. We learn it because, at that point in time, nothing matters more. What we care about determines what we pay close attention to, and what we pay attention to determines what we learn.

The Genius is driven by curiosity and necessity. No external rewards or punishments required. The drive to understand and master the world is built in.

Feature #6: Virtuosity by Default

Plop a normally functioning infant brain anywhere in the world, and it's virtually guaranteed that its brain will attain the highest levels of expertise in the core skills of human cognition. It will master the physics of bipedal motion and the complex grammar of a language. It will become an expert at facial recognition. When it comes to those core skills, we are all virtuosos.

There is virtually no meaningful variability across humans in these core cognitive abilities. Least of all in our skills of perception. We're all about equally adept at identifying the sight of a tree or a dog or a dandelion, or the sound of a bird or a laugh or a trumpet. In light of what we now know about how the Genius learns, this makes perfect sense. We're all born on the same planet, exposed to roughly the same natural elements. For all practical purposes, our perceptual training data is identical.

Similarly, when it comes to our common advanced motor skills, especially walking, we also all find ourselves exploring a similar world. And we all become highly skilled at moving through it.

Culture shapes the communication skills we learn, of course. Languages and social norms depend on where we're born. However, barring deliberate attempts at deprivation, every brain receives loads of high-quality training data in these domains. While the specifics may be culturally dependent—another indicator that environment is the driver—virtuosity is still reliably attained.

In sum, brains that are placed in the same conditions, with the same goals, will write the same neural code, evident in the stereotyped sequence of milestones that every brain passes through on the path to virtuosity.

The transformation from helpless newborn to capable three-year-old isn't a miracle reserved for special brains. It's what happens to every intact brain when given the right conditions. Virtuosity is the default outcome.

Progressive Composition: The Universal Pattern

We've just explored the six features that characterize how the Genius learns. Features that reveal a universal process for developing expertise in any domain.

I call this universal process progressive composition. "Progressive" means it happens in stages, step by step, building forward continuously. "Composition" means that complex skills are composed of simpler skills combined.

Progressive composition is how expertise always develops, because it is the *only* way expertise can develop. It is how the Genius builds our complex cognitive skills. Understand how it works, and you have the skeleton key for how to learn anything.

The pattern is remarkably consistent across all domains:

Step #1: Build simple skills first. Start with what's possible given your current scaffolding. A baby can't walk before learning to sit, sit before learning head control, or speak words before babbling phonemes. Each skill must be within reach, or in the Goldilocks Zone—challenging but attainable.

Step #2: Combine simple skills into complex skills. Once simpler skills are in place, the Genius combines them. Head control plus torso control becomes sitting. Sitting plus leg coordination becomes crawling. Phonemes combine into words.

Step #3: Repeat indefinitely. When skills are built in this way, there is no ceiling. The cycle of learning and growth can continue indefinitely.

This is progressive composition. Everything your brain is currently capable of was constructed layer by layer, each depending on what came before, each determining and enabling what comes next. You built yourself, brick by neural brick, layer by

PROGRESSIVE COMPOSITION: HOW SKILLS ARE BUILT

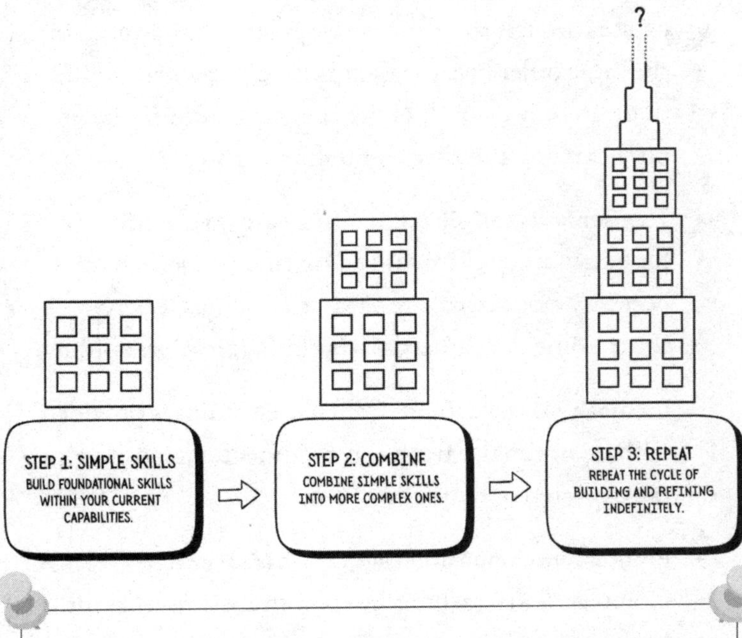

REGARDLESS OF THE DOMAIN (MOTOR, PERCEPTUAL, CONCEPTUAL), THE GENIUS CONSTRUCTS OUR COGNITIVE SKILLS THROUGH THE PROCESS OF PROGRESSIVE COMPOSITION.

ALL OUR COGNITIVE ABILITIES ARE ACQUIRED IN THIS WAY.

layer, driven by obsession and guided by a master architect who doesn't quit until the job is done.

It's the process that transformed you from a helpless infant to the capable person you are today. The best part, as you will soon discover? You can still do this.

chapter summary

- **Learning follows a universal sequence:** Every brain passes through the same developmental milestones in the same order because each skill requires scaffolding that can only be built on what came before. There are no shortcuts, and there is no skipping steps.
- **The Genius is self-directing:** There are no teachers for our core cognitive skills. Driven by curiosity and necessity, not external rewards, the Genius seeks out the training data it needs to build cognitive scaffolding.
- **Virtuosity is the default:** When the Genius is provided with an optimal learning environment, virtuosity is the expected outcome.
- **Progressive composition is the universal pattern:** Complex skills are built by combining simpler skills, layer by layer, in a cumulative and hierarchical process. This is how expertise develops in every domain—motor, perceptual, and conceptual—because it is the only way expertise *can* develop.

4

the problem solver

All life is problem solving.

—Karl Popper (philosopher of science)

The Genius builds skills through progressive composition. But what is the Genius actually building? What's the result of all this learning?

I'll tell you. The Genius is building *intelligence.*

Does that claim make you squirm a bit? Does that feel at odds at all with how you think about intelligence? If so, that's understandable. It's a term that's thrown around a lot, often by those with only a loose concept of what it means. And it's a term that comes with a lot of baggage, a product of being attached to some very flimsy ideas. All in all, the popular conversation around intelligence is clouded by confusion and contradiction.

So, before we go any further, I want you to pause and try to define intelligence for yourself. I'll be here when you're finished.

Did you struggle? If so, you're in good company. Lots of very intelligent people (whatever that means!) have—and continue to—struggle to define intelligence. Even among those who study the subject for a living.

For example, one of the grand goals in the field of artificial intelligence (AI) is the creation of an artificial "general intelligence," or AGI. But the people trying to build it aren't sure what that actually means. We're on a grand quest to build AGI, yet we're not sure we'll even know when we've completed it! Some say that, at the time of this writing, we've already done it. Others say we're decades away, at minimum. One reason for that discrepancy is the underlying biases and assumptions people bring to the topic.

Smart Like Us?

To some, an AGI would be able to do all things that a human brain can do. That's because we tend to think of ourselves as the standard-bearers of intelligence, thank you very much. And "general intelligence" is that special thing our brain does better than any other animal on the planet. It's why we're the only species that has invented rockets and sprayable ham. Intelligence is the quality that makes smart people smarter than less smart people. So, whatever intelligence is, by definition, we humans must have the most of it.

Yet, when we try to pin down exactly what it is that we humans have so much more of, we struggle. Do we struggle because intelligence is just such an advanced concept that it eludes comprehension? How ironic would that be?!

Or might there be something flawed in our assumptions? Perhaps our assumption that intelligence is a general quality that brains can have more or less of, and that human brains have the most of, is the very reason we struggle to define it!

So, let's attempt the audacious task of trying to build a definition of intelligence from the ground up. And we'll do so without preconceptions. That includes any preconception that intelligence must be a quantifiable property that humans have the most of. That may well turn out to be true (cross your fingers!), but we won't try to shoehorn our definition just to make it so.

Acting Intelligently

Even though we find it hard to define, we easily recognize intelligence when we see it. Which brings up an important feature of intelligence, which is that it is demonstrated by actions. Or, perhaps more accurately, intelligence is a judgment about behavior.

Is a rock intelligent? Or a chair? Or a lamp?

It doesn't seem like it. But the question doesn't even really make sense, does it? It's like asking if silence has an accent.

That's because the only way to assess the intelligence of something is by evaluating how it behaves. The only way to tell the difference between something that's intelligent from something that isn't is by what it does. As the saying goes, "Better to remain silent and be thought a fool than to speak and remove all doubt."

Rocks, chairs, and lamps don't *do* anything. They just sit there. Like a rock, appropriately enough. Intelligence requires agency.

Jack and Jill Fetch Some Punch

So, if intelligence is an assessment of the actions of entities with agency, then what is the signature feature of intelligent behavior? How does intelligent behavior differ from unintelligent behavior? Let's consider some examples.

Jack and Jill are at a party and they start to get thirsty. Jill looks around and spots a punch bowl. She walks over, ladles a healthy portion of punch into a cup, and drinks it. Jill's thirst is quenched.

Jack looks around and spots a bottle of dish soap. He picks it up and squirts some in his mouth. His thirst remains unquenched. And his stomach hurts.

Whose behavior would you consider to be more intelligent?

Here's another scenario: Jack and Jill, who both live in the same neighborhood and are equally fastidious about oral hygiene, are out of toothpaste. Jill recalls the location of the closest drugstore, drives there, and buys the toothpaste. She's back home and brushing her teeth in under 20 minutes.

Jack hops in his car and starts driving. His plan is to drive, making turns when the urge strikes him, until he encounters a convenience store. He arrives at one 90 minutes later and purchases his toothpaste. Now in an unfamiliar part of town, he gets lost and must ask for directions several times. He arrives home over five hours later. In addition to the $3 he spent on toothpaste, he's spent $28 on gas.

If you had to describe in a single word the difference between Jill's behavior as compared to Jack's, what would you say? Most likely, you'd say that her behavior was "smarter" than Jack's. Or you might say her behavior was more "intelligent." There's really no better word for it, is there? Based on these stories, if we could distill the difference between Jack and Jill into one word, it would be "intelligence."

We know intelligence when we see it, then. In these two examples, the distinction between intelligent and unintelligent behavior is obvious. So, what's the difference? What are we noticing in Jill's behavior that makes it more intelligent than Jack's?

In each example, Jack and Jill had a goal and had to solve a series of problems to achieve that goal. In the first example, their goal was hydration. Here, Jill achieved the goal but Jack did not. Jill's solution was clearly superior to Jack's.

In the second example, their goal was to acquire a tube of toothpaste (to achieve their larger goal of dental hygiene or cavity avoidance). In this case, both of them achieved that goal. However, I think we'd all agree that Jack's solution was inferior to Jill's. Why? Because he expended considerably more energy and resources to achieve the same goal.

What's the recurring theme? Intelligence is about solving problems.

Goals are our desired outcomes. Problems are the obstacles between you and those goals. Intelligence is how well you solve problems to reach your goals, or the quality of your solutions. More effective and efficient solutions demonstrate more intelligent behavior.

You might be used to thinking of intelligence mainly in the context of taking tests in school, and our definition works just fine there as well. When taking a test, our goal is a good grade. And the problems that stand between us and our goal are oftentimes referred to as literal problems. The better our solutions to those problems, the closer we get to achieving our goal.

Note here, though, that, even in this instance, intelligence can only be assessed by our actions, whether it's the movements of our wrist to control a pencil, our fingers to select options on a keypad, or our vocal cords to speak words.

But what we do in a school classroom, which usually involves thinking skills of some kind, comprises only a tiny fraction of our total intelligent behavior. Our brain is solving problems continuously. Walking to the kitchen requires solving a navigation problem. Making breakfast requires solving a coordination problem. All require intelligence.

We rely on intelligent behavior each and every day, long before and long after our formal education begins and ends. And solving problems that require thinking skills is no more "intelligent" than solving problems that require perceptual or motor skills (most real-world problems require a combination of them all).

While outwardly they may appear different, as we now know,

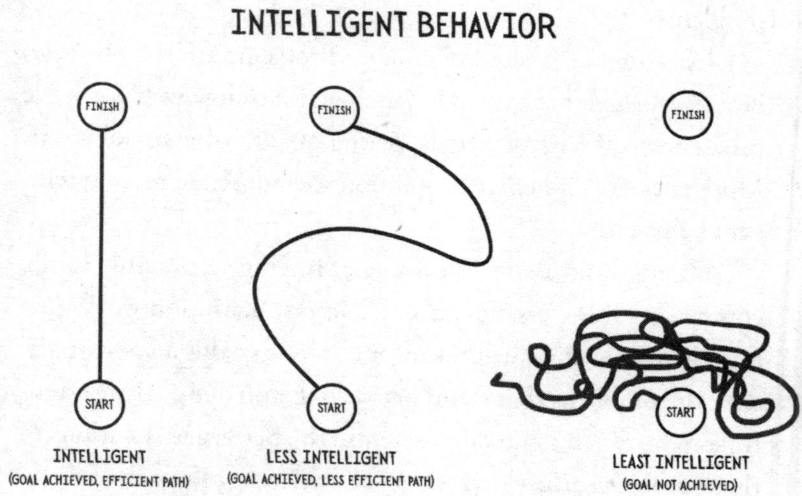

it's all implemented by the same neural mechanisms and machinery. The nature of the problem determines the cognitive skills required to solve it.

Intelligent Animals

Having reached a satisfying working definition of intelligence, let's revisit the question of our place in the hierarchy of intelligent beings. Are we humans the top animal at solving problems to achieve our goals?

Well, it depends. It depends on the goals, and the problems that must be solved to reach them.

Are humans better than bats at sharing our thoughts through spoken language? Undoubtedly. We possess the cognitive skill set required for language, and bats do not.

How about navigating a dark cave by echolocation? I'm afraid that one goes to the bats. Bats possess the perceptual skills required to navigate with sonar, while we'd end up concussed by a stalactite.

So, then, who is the more "intelligent" animal, humans or bats? The question doesn't even make sense. It certainly doesn't to me. It all depends on the context, or the problem being solved.

Intelligence isn't some general quality that we can have more or less of, as we have been inclined to think. It is contextual. It depends on the situation. It only makes sense in relation to specific kinds of problems and specific goals. There's a vast landscape of problems, and different brains are wired to solve different ones. Asking if one person or species is more or less intelligent than another is like asking whether a submarine is better at "transportation" than a helicopter.

I'm afraid we have no choice but to concede that humans are not at the tippy top of the intelligence heap. But that's only because there's no heap. There is no intelligence hierarchy.

The fact that we don't end up as the supreme planetary intelligence doesn't mean our definition is wrong; it just means that our assumptions were.

For over a century, the popular framework for conceptualizing intelligence has been the intelligence quotient, or IQ, a single number meant to capture your overall "smartness." A number that told you where you ranked in the intelligence hierarchy. Given our preceding discussion, it's a concept that should now sound—ironically enough—a bit unintelligent! It's grounded in a set of flawed assumptions and dubious logic. You can't reduce context-dependent problem-solving ability to a single score any more than you can rank a submarine and helicopter by asking which is better at "transportation." And the fact that we're the only animal that could be deemed intelligent on the IQ test is a clear giveaway that our pro-human bias has scrambled our thinking on the topic. We've only chosen to assess the kinds of problems we're better at solving.

So, we need a framework for conceptualizing intelligence that reflects our updated definition. One that captures the fact that intelligence is idiosyncratic and contextual.

The Solution Space

At any moment in our lives, we have a set of problem-solving abilities wired into our brains. These abilities are determined by the perceptual, motor, and thinking skills we've acquired up until that point. We can think of this complete set of problems we can solve as our "solution space." Imagine a piece of land surrounded by fencing. Everything inside the fencing is your solution space, or the problems you've already mastered.

Reading this sentence is safe inside those borders. If you couldn't read, these words would be meaningless squiggles. But you built the perceptual and conceptual skills required to decode written language, so reading is inside your fence. Walking across your bedroom without crashing into the furniture is inside the fence. Making toast is inside the fence. Distinguishing between a bus and a bicycle is inside the fence.

Problems you can't yet solve lie beyond the fence. Playing Rachmaninoff's third concerto is probably outside the fence. As is understanding whale song.

Critically, that solution space is a product of what you've learned. Want to expand the borders? Then develop more problem-solving skills.

The Impostor looks at that fence and sees a concrete wall. A boundary fixed at birth by your genetics. That's the Special Brain Story of intelligence. It's the story that fuels the concept of IQ, and a story the Impostor authored. The Impostor tells you that what's inside is "who you are," and what's outside is "who you aren't" and never will be.

The Genius knows that the fence is just a temporary perimeter. One that he built, and that he can expand at any time. It's just a reflection of where you are at this particular moment in time and nothing more.

This distinction is critical because any problem outside the fence is biologically impossible for your brain to solve. You simply don't have the necessary neural and cognitive scaffolding yet. It's not that you're "stupid" or "untalented," it's just that you haven't claimed that ground yet.

What's out there beyond the fence? Anything outside your current solution space. Speaking a language you've never heard. Playing an instrument you've never touched. Solving math problems in a field you've never studied. You simply don't have the wiring because the Genius hasn't built it.

What's in your solution space, and what's out of reach, is a direct result of your existing cognitive skills. How, then, does your solution space expand? Through learning. Period.

Learning is the act of digging up the fence posts and moving

SOLUTION SPACE: THE BOUNDARIES OF INTELLIGENCE

OUR SOLUTION SPACE REPRESENTS THE SET OF PROBLEMS WE CAN CURRENTLY SOLVE, BASED ON OUR EXISTING SCAFFOLDING.

IT ALSO DEFINES OUR GOLDILOCKS ZONE, WHICH ARE THE SKILLS THAT ARE WITHIN REACH BUT NOT YET MASTERED.

ANYTHING OUTSIDE THE GOLDILOCKS ZONE ARE PROBLEMS WE ARE PRESENTLY INCAPABLE OF SOLVING.

them outward to expand our solution space. Learning is what *creates* intelligence.

Your current solution space—your current "intelligence"—is simply the land you have fenced off so far. Expanding that space requires stepping past the boundary and staking a new claim.

Moravec's Paradox

It was in the mid-twentieth century that computer scientists began seriously exploring the possibility of creating thinking machines, or artificial intelligence. It was an audacious idea, and many were skeptical. So the AI-enthusiasts figured they should start with something easy. First show that the concept was viable, then get more ambitious. Which meant identifying some easy problems to tackle first.

Since many considered human intelligence to be the gold standard, the researchers naturally assumed that the problems that humans found hardest would be the hardest to program into computers, and the problems humans found easiest would be easiest to program. Seems obvious enough. We consider activities like chess, mathematics, and trivia to be the pinnacle of human intelligence. High levels of skill at these pursuits have long been considered hallmarks of smarts.

Why do we think this way? Partly because these are all thinking skills enabled by symbolic cognition, which is the most distinctive feature of the human brain. If we're the pinnacle of intelligent species and these are the sorts of problems only human brains can solve, then these must require the highest quantities of intelligence, right?

Furthermore, humans show enormous *variability* in these

skills. Talking is a thinking skill, but everyone can do it, so it mustn't be special. Only a small percentage excel at chess or advanced math, on the other hand. Most people find those things to be quite challenging, which must mean that those abilities are more advanced forms of intelligence.

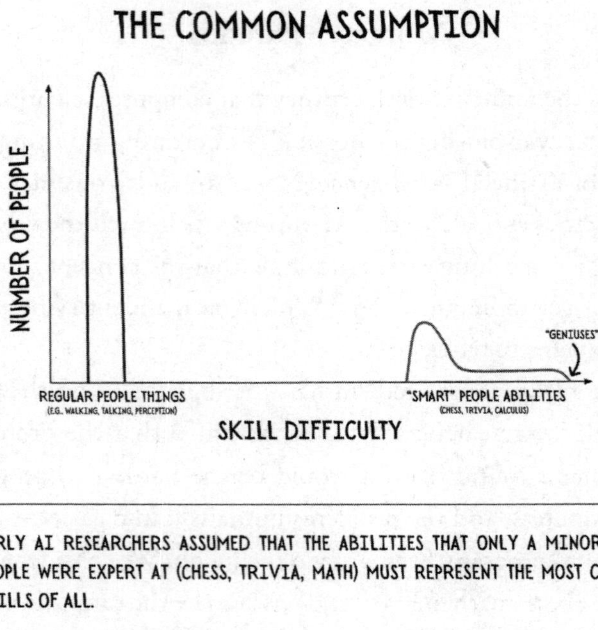

EARLY AI RESEARCHERS ASSUMED THAT THE ABILITIES THAT ONLY A MINORITY OF PEOPLE WERE EXPERT AT (CHESS, TRIVIA, MATH) MUST REPRESENT THE MOST COMPLEX SKILLS OF ALL.

ON THE OTHER HAND, THE ABILITIES THAT A MAJORITY OF PEOPLE WERE EXPERT AT (WALKING, TALKING, PERCEPTION) MUST REPRESENT SIMPLER SKILLS.

In short, the computer scientists assumed that the problems that most human brains found the hardest to solve would pose the greatest challenge for computers, too. Meanwhile, the problems that virtually all humans solve easily should prove relatively straightforward to program.

Turns out they had it totally backward.

Programming a computer to solve math problems, play chess, or answer trivia questions ended up being relatively easy. We've had pocket calculators since the 1970s. IBM's Deep Blue beat world chess champion Garry Kasparov back in 1997. Watson took down the best humans at trivia in 2011 to become a *Jeopardy!* champion.

But programming a computer to walk across a cluttered room without falling? To recognize a face from any angle in any lighting? To fold laundry while having a conversation about your holiday travel plans? These turned out to be much more challenging. We've only recently developed machines that can hold a conversation at the level of a young child, and we still don't have ones that can navigate unpredictable terrain as well as a toddler, recognize faces as reliably as you do, or tell a halfway-decent joke.

This unexpected discovery came to be known as Moravec's Paradox, named after computer scientist Hans Moravec, who first described it. In his words:

> *It is comparatively easy to make computers exhibit adult level performance on intelligence tests or playing checkers, and difficult or impossible to give them the skills of a one-year-old when it comes to perception and mobility.*

The paradox is that the thinking skills that humans find most challenging—the ones we built entire educational systems around—turned out to be relatively simple to program into computers. Meanwhile, the basic perceptual and motor skills that every healthy child acquires—the ones we barely think about—turned out to be massively more complex.

It's a paradox that revealed how little we understood about our own intelligence. The problems we all solve daily aren't simple at all. They represent a massive solution space and an incomprehensibly complex computational challenge. We'd assumed they were easy because they *feel* easy to us. It's a paradox that forces us to reexamine the most basic assumptions about our own intelligence and how it should be measured.

And if our concept of what intelligence is was inverted, what does that say about what we've long considered the most exceptional feats of the human mind? Are they as truly exceptional as we've thought?

Real Genius

When we use the word "genius" to describe a person, we're usually referring to someone who has accomplished an extraordinary intellectual feat. Most often, these are feats in the realm of thinking skills, like a breakthrough in science, a revolutionary mathematical proof, or a work of literature that transforms how we see the world.

Occasionally, we apply the label to achievements beyond pure thought. A musician who invents an entirely new technique. An athlete whose innovation transforms their sport forever.

In either case, for a feat to earn the genius label, it typically must fulfill two criteria. First, it must be considered sufficiently complex. It has to push the boundaries of what we thought was possible. It has to seem quite hard or downright impossible to most of us.

Second, and crucially, it must be rare. Genius, in our common usage, is by definition singular. If everyone could do it, we wouldn't call it genius. If every child wrote *Hamlet* or derived the theory of relativity, Shakespeare and Einstein would lose their genius cards. We celebrate them precisely because their accomplishments were *unique*.

In other words, feats we label as genius are unique solutions to challenging problems.

Why does this distinction matter? Because as Moravec's Paradox reveals, we've failed to appreciate humanity's most remarkable cognitive achievements precisely because they aren't rare. We've overlooked them because they're common, which led us to conclude that feats of "genius" must be enabled by fundamentally

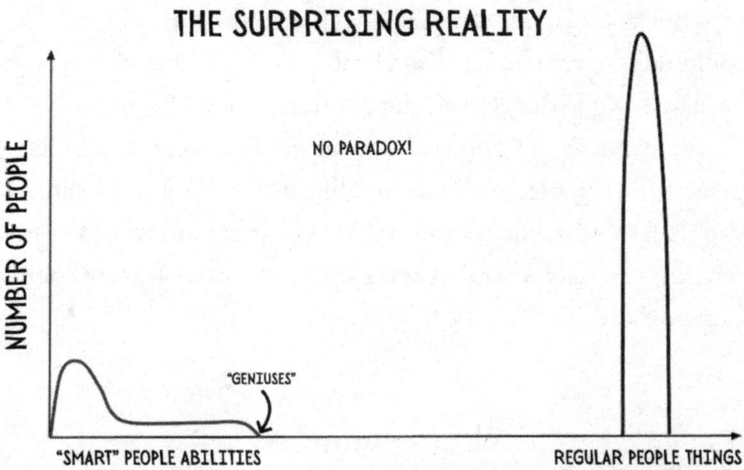

AS IT TURNED OUT, THE COMMON ABILITIES THAT MOST EVERYONE EXCELS AT ENDED UP BEING THE MOST CHALLENGING.

WE'D MISTAKENLY ASSUMED THAT THE FACT THAT THESE SKILLS WERE NEARLY UNIVERSAL AND FELT EASY MEANT THEY ARE LESS COMPLEX.

different brains and not by the neurobiological machinery we all share.

Our universal cognitive skills all represent elegant solutions to extraordinarily challenging problems. Based on their computational complexity, as revealed by Moravec's Paradox, these skills stand at the pinnacle of intellectual achievement. As feats of problem solving, they rival or exceed the celebrated breakthroughs of Einstein and Shakespeare. But they are not unique, nor do they feel hard.

You solve massively complex problems every single day, thanks to the gigantic solution space the Genius has built. The only reason you don't feel like a genius is because everyone else can do it, too. But you can be sure that if you were the only person who could talk, recognize faces, or climb a staircase, scientists would be clamoring to dissect your brain after you died.

Yet you have no appreciation of anything remarkable happening, of the extraordinary intelligence pulling it all off. As you'll learn next, the very fact that your extraordinary gifts *feel* trivial is precisely what makes these extraordinary feats of cognition possible.

chapter summary

- **Intelligence is about solving problems:** Intelligence is simply the ability to solve problems to achieve goals, not a mystical quality some brains possess more of than others.
- **Intelligence is contextual, not general:** Intelligence is

contextual rather than general. Comparing human and bat intelligence only makes sense relative to specific problems, which is why reducing it to IQ numbers is fundamentally flawed.

- **Your solution space is what you've learned:** At any moment, your brain's solution space is determined by what you've learned. The Impostor sees this as a fixed boundary; the Genius knows it can expand.
- **Moravec's Paradox reveals our blind spot:** The skills we find easiest proved hardest to program into computers, revealing how we underestimate what feels effortless. Yet effortlessness is the signature of mastery, not simplicity.
- **Common genius is still genius:** We don't call everyday cognitive feats "genius" only because everyone achieves them, yet by any objective measure, they rival the celebrated works of Einstein and Shakespeare.

5

the engine of intelligence

Civilization advances by extending the number of important operations which we can perform without thinking about them.

—Alfred North Whitehead (mathematician and philosopher)

When you were born, your solution space was teeny tiny. You possessed a few rudimentary reflexes, the most useful of which was the ability to suck on a milk-filled nipple if it kindly found its way into your mouth. And you could summon another human by screaming at the top of your lungs. This pretty much sums up the newborn repertoire of "intelligent" behavior.

By age three, however, your solution space had grown. Exponentially. You could walk, run, and climb. You could talk in sentences, understand thousands of words, and identify thousands of objects. Your social skills had skyrocketed. You'd become a master of manipulation, able to plead, negotiate, or deceive to get what you wanted.

And by now, your solution space is massive. You could do any number of things that, to your childhood self, would've looked like magic.

We've discussed the phenomenon of progressive composition that makes learning possible. On the surface, it is quite simple. Almost pedestrian. Plod along one step at a time, adding layer upon layer. How is it, then, that such a mundane and incremental procedure could produce such staggeringly complex behavior? Staggeringly complex behavior that feels simple.

To see how it's done, let's talk about another one of your brain's amazing tricks. One that you've probably been told it can't do.

The Multitasking Myth

Have you heard the sad news? We humans can't multitask. The productivity gurus tell us it's the reason why, in this age of distraction, we feel so unproductive.

As much as we may try, we simply can't simultaneously surf the internet, scramble eggs, and pay the electric bill. In our effort to try to consume and do more, we end up doing less. Our brains weren't made for these modern times. Our pitiful little one-track minds just can't handle it.

They tell us the solution is to single task. Focus on one thing at a time. Close those browser tabs, turn off notifications, and accept your biological limits. Stop asking your poor, overstimulated brain to be something it's not.

Is this really true? Are we really incapable of multitasking?

Let's consider the following scenario:

You're exiting the parking lot on your way home from work when your cell phone rings. You answer, and on the other end is

Billy Blankenship, a childhood friend you haven't spoken to in years! You'd love to talk to him, but you also know that your family is at home expecting you for dinner in 20 minutes.

Now you're in a quandary. Do you pull over, talk to Billy, and shirk your familial obligations? Or do you spurn your childhood friend to maintain the peace at home?

And then, you remember something very important. Which is that you can talk and drive at the same time!

So, over the course of the next 20 minutes you successfully navigate your way home, all the while reminiscing with Billy about that time Ryan Chesney shot chocolate milk out of his eyeball. You have no trouble whatsoever making it home safe and sound while engrossed in conversation with your old pal.

Now consider all you had to do to pull this off. First, just to safely operate your motor vehicle and make it to your desired destination, you had to monitor the location and movements of all the other cars on the road, identify and execute the appropriate turns, change into the necessary lanes, monitor traffic signals and obey all applicable laws, maintain proper speed by monitoring the speedometer and modifying force on the accelerator appropriately, make steering wheel micro-adjustments to maintain lane position, read and interpret road signs, calculate stopping distances based on weather and road conditions, maintain proper following distance, and so on.

But that's just the half of it! Because in order to maintain a coherent conversation with Billy, you had to instantly identify the words from the continuous stream of sounds coming into your ear, attach them to their associated meaning, apply the proper rules of grammar and syntax, filter out background noise to isolate Billy's voice, process his emotional tone and inflection patterns, access memories triggered by his stories, interpret cultural references, sarcasm, and inside jokes, and so much more. When it was your turn to talk, you essentially had to do all of that in reverse to choose what you wanted to say, in addition to selecting the appropriate motor program for vibrating your vocal cords so your selected sounds came out appropriately and were intelligible to Billy.

And you had to perform all those tasks at the same time.

What do you have to say for yourself now, Mr. Productivity Guru? What we have here isn't just a modest little bit of multitasking. This is multitasking of the highest order. This is elite, mind-blowing stuff. It's the sort of multitasking you have to see to believe. The sort of multitasking even our most powerful computers are not yet capable of pulling off, mind you.

Yet there was a time when you could do none of that.

You probably recall the first time you got behind the wheel of a car. Or, if you've parented a teenage child, you more recently remember the first time they got behind the wheel. Being a novice driver is nerve-racking. Being a passenger in a car with a novice driver requires backup undergarments.

Because, as a novice, you truly can only perform one task at a time. Every single one requires your full and undivided attention. And you're lousy at those tasks, too. The very fact that a novice driver can't multitask is precisely why novice drivers are so dangerous! They require a second set of eyes and ears just to safely navigate their way around an empty parking lot.

Now, before we concede that Mr. Productivity Guru was right all along with his multitasking admonishments, let's see if we can make sense of this apparent contradiction. Answering these kinds of complex questions is exactly why we invented scientists, so let's invite them to come to our rescue here.

The Science of Automaticity

In a 2005 study published in the *Journal of Neuroscience*, participants were trained on what's known as a "serial reaction time" (SRT) task. In the task, colored squares appeared on a screen in front of them in one of four locations. Their job was to press a corresponding button for each square as fast as possible. Unbeknownst to the participants, the squares were presented in a twelve-item repeating sequence.

Participants underwent four training sessions over two weeks, practicing this button-pressing task. Before training began, researchers tested their ability to multitask. While pressing buttons in response to the colored squares, participants also had to count auditory tones that played.

As you might expect, when having to press the right buttons and count tones at the same time, their performance suffered. They could not multitask. Because they had to constantly switch back and forth between the two tasks, they were slower to respond and less accurate.

After two weeks of training, however, their performance on the SRT skyrocketed. Their responses were much faster and more accurate. They'd memorized the twelve-square sequence, though they hadn't "tried" to memorize anything, and weren't aware of having done so.

But the most fascinating part was that now when they were

asked to perform the SRT while counting tones, their performance did not suffer. Their responses were just as fast and accurate as they were when not having to count tones!

After weeks of training, they were much better than they'd been at first, and the task no longer required any conscious attention.

In other words, they could multitask. Really, really well. Even when distracted by the tones, their performance on the SRT was far better than it was when they were novices doing it with no distractions. Importantly, their improvement in the SRT seemed to *coincide* with their ability to multitask, suggesting a link between those two phenomena.

In addition to the change in their performance over the course of their training, there was also a marked change in their brain activity. Initially when performing the SRT task, there was considerable activity in the dorsolateral prefrontal cortex (DLPFC), an area known to be involved in conscious control. After training, activity in the DLPFC diminished, and there was an increase in activity in the putamen, supplemental motor area, and cerebellum—areas involved with motor control that run without conscious control. Their performance improvement and ability to multitask was associated with a shift in the parts of the brain controlling their behavior.

So what's happening here? Through training, the brains of the study subjects built an algorithm, stored in their brains as a pattern of neuronal firing, for executing the SRT task. A pattern stored in nonconscious networks. A pattern that, once activated, could run automatically while their attention was diverted elsewhere.

How does a pattern of neural activity become permanent? Primarily through the strengthening of the connections between neurons. With each practice session, the synapses between the neurons firing in that pattern strengthen, or *consolidate*. The pattern that was once temporary neural activity becomes encoded in the physical structure of the brain itself. This is how neural scaffolding is built, as permanent infrastructure wired into your brain tissue.

Importantly, this consolidation of connections to form permanent networks happens primarily during sleep. While you're unconscious, your brain replays the patterns (aka "memories") you practiced during the day, strengthening the synaptic connections that support them and pruning those that don't. What began as fleeting electrical activity transforms into lasting physical change. And you wake up the next day a little bit better. This is the process by which practice leads to progress.

INTELLIGENCE BY AUTOMATION

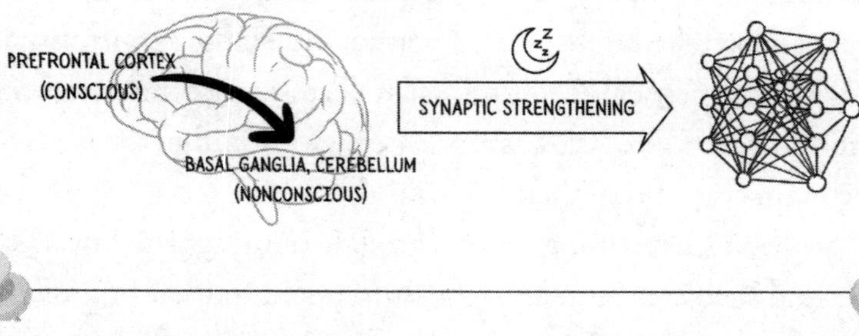

THROUGH LEARNING AND PRACTICE, BRAIN ACTIVITY SHIFTS FROM THE CONSCIOUS PREFRONTAL CORTEX TO AUTOMATED REGIONS LIKE THE BASAL GANGLIA AND CEREBELLUM.

THIS PROCESS, ENABLED BY SYNAPTIC STRENGTHENING AND SLEEP CONSOLIDATION, "WIRES" BEHAVIORS INTO ROBUST NEURAL NETWORKS THAT CAN RUN AUTOMATICALLY.

As we will see, this process of writing problem-solving algorithms into the connections of our nonconscious networks isn't just something our brain does to get good at button pushing, it's something our brain does—and must do—when it gets good at anything.

Easy ≠ Simple

What do we consider the hallmark of an expert? Making something look easy. The beginner struggles with the basics despite trying hard. The expert performs complex tasks while hardly trying.

The better we get at something, the easier and more effortless it becomes. For the novice, driving is challenging and effortful. For the expert, it is easy and effortless. Not because the task has changed, but because our brain has. Our brain has built a solution we no longer need to think about.

With algorithms etched into our brain tissue, we can accomplish the same task with far fewer cognitive resources, which we experience as less effort.

As Michelangelo famously admitted, "If people knew how hard I worked to get my mastery, it wouldn't seem so wonderful at all."

Resolving the Paradox

Now that we appreciate the relationship between automation and cognitive load, it's easy to see why the intuitions of early AI researchers were so far off. The skills that we find easy were harder to program because they are more complex skills! We don't find them easy because they're simple; we find them easy because we've automated their execution. There was no paradox, just a fundamental underappreciation of the sophistication of our own intelligence.

We've uncovered a core truth about ourselves that naturally inverts our intuitions about the complexity of our own behavior. The better we get, the easier it feels. The most remarkable feats of the human mind are the ones we're most prone to dismiss as trivially simple. It's not just the computer scientists who overlooked the common genius in every human brain. We all did.

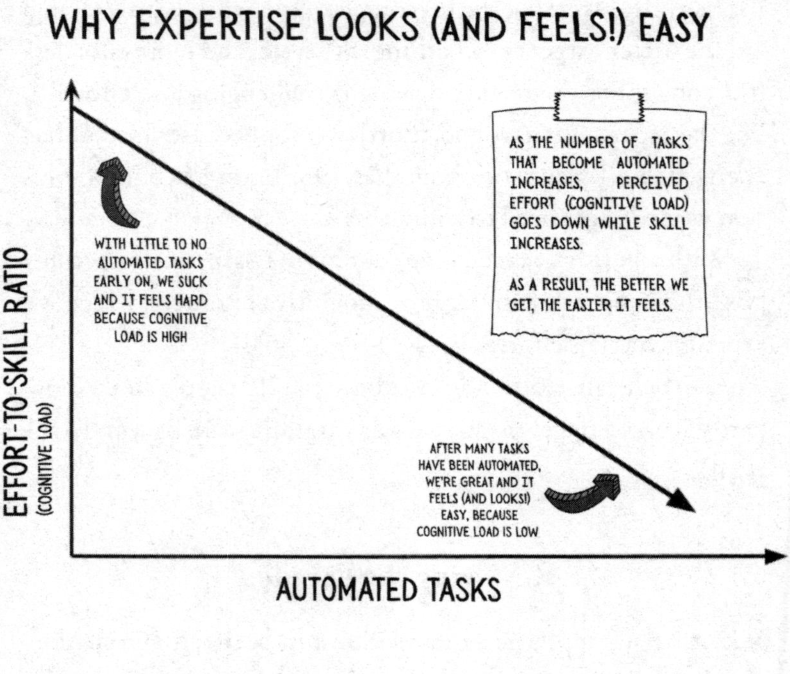

The Conscious Bottleneck

As your eyes scan across these words, your comprehension is immediate and effortless. There's no sense of having to "try" to do it. It just happens. It's no different from when you hear someone speaking in your native language. The transfer of information is immediate and effortless. You may have to exert some effort to tune out distractions, but the language decoding itself is effortless.

Of course, the ease with which you do this belies the extraordinary complexity of the task. Consider what's happening under the hood when you read. The first problem your brain must solve is perceptual. It must identify the letters and words from the string of shapes and squiggles (regardless of font size, color, or style). It must take the visual information it receives from this page (or screen) and identify the symbols.

This perceptual decoding operation is something you trained your brain to do when first learning to read. The very first step was to train it to recognize letters. And with practice, you automated recognition of the entire alphabet. Before you built your letter recognition networks, that consciously mediated process felt really, really hard.

Then you automated the recognition of words. Now, you likely have anywhere from thirty thousand to seventy thousand words you can identify on the spot (in any font, color, or size, mind you). All thanks to the development of automaticity for all those perceptual subtasks so that word decoding bypasses the bottleneck of conscious attention. Once that transition to unconscious competence is complete, the conversion from word symbol to its associated sound is instantaneous and effortless. To the brain, reading a word and catching a ball are variations of the same challenge of building the circuits to automate the process.

But deciphering the words is just half the problem. For these words to convey information, you must also comprehend them. And comprehension requires automation of understanding. It requires *conceptual* automaticity.

While complex motor skills are enabled by motor automaticity and complex perceptual skills are enabled by perceptual automaticity, complex thinking skills are enabled by conceptual automaticity. The effortless and instantaneous comprehension you experience right now as you read this sentence is possible not just because you can automatically decode the symbols, but because you can effortlessly and instantaneously decode their *meaning*. That task requires that you not only automatically grasp the meaning of each word, but also that you automatically apply the rules of grammar and syntax to understand entire sentences. All your unskilled conscious mind has to do is keep your attention on this page so that those nonconscious networks can work their magic, crunching all the data and delivering it into awareness as a tidy little package of comprehension.

It's much easier to appreciate the role of progressive composition through automation when it comes to complex motor skills. We can see it, literally. When we watch an expert athlete or musician, we witness the simultaneous execution of many motor tasks. That's part of what makes it extraordinary to watch. The scaffolding is on display. Scaffolding that was built, layer by layer, through years of training.

When it comes to advanced perceptual or thinking skills, however, the scaffolding is hidden. It's natural to think these skills are built and work differently. But—as the preceding discussion illustrates—they are constructed in the same way. They, too, require years of training to build countless automated subskills to create the necessary scaffolding.

No Automation, No Intelligence

There is no intelligence without automation. Without the ability to automate, our finite cognitive resources would preclude intelligent behavior. And there is no automation without learning. Intelligence is what emerges when the brain turns problem-solving into routine.

Without automation, you're stuck in the conscious bottleneck forever. You can only solve one problem at a time. You can't build complex skills because there's no scaffolding to support you. Your solution space stays tiny, so your intelligence cannot grow.

Now you understand the mechanism. Progressive composition through automation. Simple skills combine into complex skills. Automated skills free cognitive resources. Freed resources

ESCAPING THE BOTTLENECK

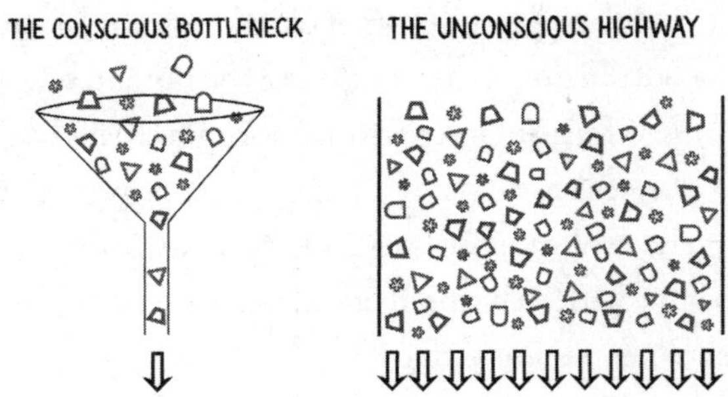

AUTOMATION ALLOWS US TO ESCAPE THE BOTTLENECK OF THE SINGLE-TASKING CONSCIOUS MIND.

ONCE TASKS ARE AUTOMATED AND CONTROLLED BY NONCONSCIOUS NETWORKS, THEY CAN RUN SIMULTANEOUSLY. THIS MECHANISM ENABLES PROGRESSIVE COMPOSITION, AND THUS IS WHAT MAKES THE ACQUISITION OF COMPLEX MOTOR, PERCEPTUAL, AND THINKING ABILITIES POSSIBLE.

enable even greater complexity. The cycle continues indefinitely, scaling intelligence exponentially.

This engine exists in every brain. This is how your brain built every capability you possess.

So where does the Special Brain Story come from? If everyone has the same engine, if the process works the same way for all of us, why do we see such dramatic differences in ability?

The Impostor has an answer ready: some brains are just born with better hardware, more horsepower under the hood. But as we'll see, that's not where the differences come from at all.

Exponential Growth

The ability to perform multiple tasks simultaneously, or to multitask, is deceptively powerful. Why? Because when we run multiple tasks at the same time, our performance doesn't scale linearly, it *multiplies*. Multitasking allows us to harness the power of compounding to produce exponential growth. As mentioned earlier, the breakthrough innovation in the human brain was the repurposing of learning mechanisms for movement and perception into the realm of symbolic cognition, a project that was driven by the evolution of language. Not surprisingly, it is language that provides the perfect example of why automaticity enables exponential growth.

So let's use language as an example to illustrate the exponential nature of multitasking. Since it's notoriously challenging for us to wrap our minds around the scale of exponential growth, we'll use real numbers to demonstrate how communication abilities grow as we automate word knowledge.

At eighteen months, the typical child has automated the use of about ten words. They can produce and understand those words without conscious effort. With ten words, they can produce roughly five to ten possible sentences, or coherent sentence fragments.

By age two, vocabulary increases to about fifty words. With that relatively small change in vocabulary size, the number of possible coherent sentences increases to around four thousand. In the span of six months, communication ability has already grown four hundred to eight hundred times larger.

By age three, vocabulary hits around three hundred words. Now the number of potential coherent sentences has grown to about ten million.

By age five, it's three thousand words and fifty billion possible sentences. And by age fifteen, it's twenty thousand words and a *quadrillion* possible coherent sentences. In the span of fifteen years, we've gone from zero to a number so large, we can't even comprehend it. Thanks to the combinatorial explosion enabled by automaticity.

Automation allows all components to be available simultaneously. They can combine in innumerable ways, allowing the solution space to grow exponentially.

The same principle applies across all domains, of course. With motor cognition, automated movements combine into complex behaviors. Walking plus reaching plus grasping plus balancing equals limitless possible actions. For perceptual skills, automated feature detection combines into object recognition.

Edges plus shapes plus colors plus textures equals the ability to recognize anything. For thinking skills, automated concepts combine into complex thoughts. Ideas plus logic plus language plus memory equals limitless reasoning possibilities.

This is why the solution space can grow from tiny to incomprehensibly massive in just a few years.

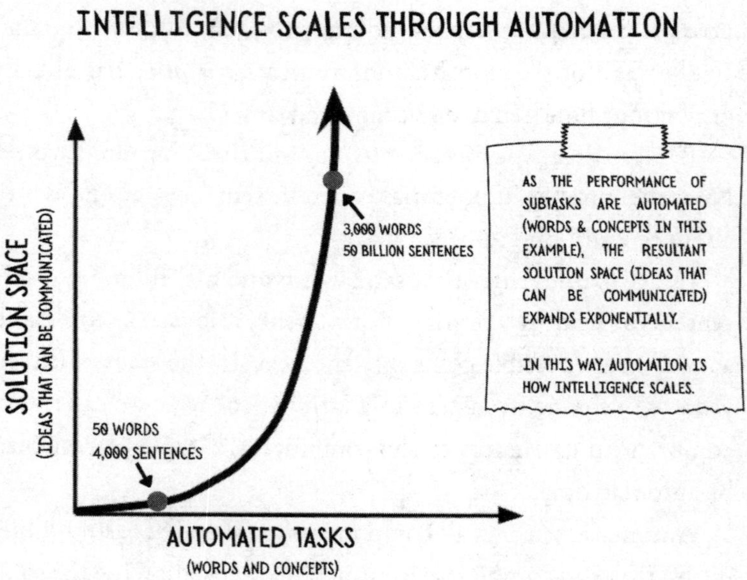

This kind of exponential growth is impossible with hardware improvements alone. You can't evolve "better neurons" that give you ten billion times more capacity. But you can learn unlimited skills that combine in unlimited ways.

Yet we still act like the hardware we inherit is destiny. Why?

The Hardware Myth

When we look at the world, we only ever see the end result. You've been practicing guitar for years, suffered through bleeding fingers and tedious scale exercises, and then you watch someone crush a solo that feels as out of reach as your high school waistline. And she's in the third grade.

Or you've spent months trying to write your first novel, then you read a few lines of Hemingway and chuck your draft—and your aspirations—in the trash.

You see twelve-year-olds doing advanced math, teenagers who speak five languages fluently, a coworker picking up new technologies with ease.

It's enough to make you wonder, *What's wrong with my brain?*

The Special Brain Story is ready with an answer. Some people are just born with certain gifts, thanks to their genes. Genes create your brain's hardware, and it's your brain's hardware that determines the sorts of things you can be good at, along with the sorts of things you shouldn't bother with.

This narrative is everywhere. It's in how we talk about children ("she's a natural"), how we excuse ourselves ("I'm just not a math person"), and how we interpret the achievements of others ("well, they were born with it").

The IQ test is the quintessential embodiment of that belief. It is the Special Brain Story distilled into a single number. A number that tells you, with numerical precision, how smart you are. A trait you've been told is as fixed as the color of your eyes. You can make the most of what you've got but should also accept your limits. Don't embarrass yourself by reaching beyond what your hardware can do.

The IQ test doesn't just reflect our ideas about intelligence and our cognitive potential; it has *created* them. To many, IQ is synonymous with intelligence, and the terms are often used interchangeably. The problem is, IQ and intelligence are not the same thing. Not even remotely.

Unfulfilled Promise

When the first widely used IQ test arrived in America in 1916, people were captivated. Finally, we had a scientific means of quantifying smarts. An exact number we could rank brains against from worst to first! For sorting the gifted from the ordinary and predicting future success.

The test caught on like wildfire. Schools adopted it eagerly. Businesses used it for hiring. Psychologists built entire theories around it. It was used to support all sorts of beliefs about human potential, about who could and couldn't achieve certain things. People not only bought into the idea that intelligence was a fixed, genetically encoded trait that could be measured, but they also bought into the idea that the IQ test was good at measuring it. After all, it says so right there in the name!

Intelligence, which we've defined as problem-solving ability, is quite a useful thing. That's not a controversial claim. The more problems in your life you can solve, the better. There isn't a downside to more intelligence. If you can solve more problems, you should be happier, more successful, more fulfilled. In short, a good test of intelligence should be a very good predictor of life satisfaction.

The IQ test is not. IQ scores are a poor predictor of life satisfaction or happiness. They're also not good at predicting who will make breakthrough discoveries in science or math. To be fair, an IQ test is exceedingly good at predicting your chances of getting into clubs that require high IQ scores for entry.

Now I can hear some of you thinking, *Hold on a minute. I know some "high IQ" people who struggle socially. IQ doesn't always predict life satisfaction because smart people sometimes have poor social skills.*

If you thought that, then you've just made my point—because you're equating intelligence with getting a high score on an IQ test. Being able to navigate social situations, which is to say being able to solve social problems, is, by definition, intelligence. Social problems are as complex and challenging as they come, which is why brains must devote boatloads of neural resources to solving them!

So one reason the IQ test has had such poor predictive power is that it only assesses a tiny slice of the pie of possible intelligent behaviors. Getting a good score on it means you are good at the particular kinds of problems it poses. And it's only a snapshot in time. Meaning that it only tells you how good you are at those skills at that point in time.

The Flynn Effect

If the Special Brain Story were true and each brain contained a genetically encoded amount of intelligence as measured by the IQ test, then the average scores of the human species should remain stable over time. Evolution is a slow, plodding process. It takes many thousands of generations to make significant upgrades to our biological hardware through genetic change.

But that's not what the data shows.

In the 1980s, researcher James Flynn uncovered a trend that blew a planet-sized hole in IQ's credibility. Flynn found that IQ scores had been steadily *rising* throughout the twentieth century at a rate of about three points per decade.

Perhaps three points doesn't sound like much at first, but the cumulative shift over time is so massive that an "average" teenager today would be considered a near-genius by the scoring standards of 1910. Conversely, an average adult from 1900 would score low enough on a test today to be classified as intellectually disabled!

Did the human brain spontaneously evolve superneurons in just three generations? Did our hardware get a massive upgrade in the blink of an evolutionary eye? Of course not. The hardware hasn't changed.

What changed was our software.

This massive rise in scores doesn't mean we're born with better brains than our recent ancestors. If you dropped a modern teenager with a high IQ into the agrarian world of 1900, they'd likely starve while their "low IQ" great-grandparents flourished.

What the Flynn Effect shows is that the IQ test is measuring a very specific type of thinking skill that modern culture and schooling happen to prioritize. The cognitive skill set needed to navigate the world of today is entirely different from the one we needed a century ago. We moved from environments that demanded physical utility to ones that demanded abstract, symbolic problem solving. Thanks to that cultural shift, more and more brains were trained to solve the specific kinds of puzzles found on IQ tests, and average scores went up as a result.

The Flynn Effect reveals that the "intelligence quotient" is more like a "cultural training quotient." The metric designed to measure our hardware is actually just measuring our software's version history.

A Predictable Failure

The failure of the IQ test as a measure of intelligence should not surprise us. It was created over a century ago. Back when we thought brains were fixed after childhood. Back before the invention of the EEG, and long before CT scans, MRIs, and functional imaging. Back when our only tool for studying human brains was to dissect them after someone died. It was like trying to create a pilot's license exam before there were airplanes.

And yet variations of the test have persisted for over a century. Why? Path dependency. That's a fancy way of saying that old habits die hard. The test and the concept of IQ have been around for so long, it's hard to imagine anything different. Institutions built themselves around it. Entire fields of study grew up trying to explain and interpret it. School systems organized around it. Businesses incorporated it into hiring. Once something becomes that entrenched, it's hard to dislodge, even when the evidence clearly shows it doesn't work.

Resources for Cognition

In the spirit of charitability, the IQ test does at least measure *something*. Something that's even relevant to this conversation around hardware and software. Because it turns out that there probably is a correlation between a brain's hardware and how it performs on an IQ test. In fact, IQ's meager predictive power actually illustrates why differences in our hardware hardly matter.

Consider first how our physical traits, or "hardware," influence our sporting abilities. Traits like the length of our legs, the size of our muscles, and the acuity of our vision. These all contribute to how fast we can run, how high we can jump, and how far we can see. And these abilities *are* influenced by our genetics. More specifically, some of the observed *variability* in these abilities is influenced by genetics.

In the same way, our brain's hardware, including things like the proteins and fats in our neuronal membranes, the signal-conducting myelin wrapped around our nerves, and its neurotransmitter systems, are the physical substrates of cognition. They directly influence metrics like the speed of neural transmission and efficiency, which impact cognitive abilities including processing speed, working memory, and attentional control. These are our basic resources for cognition. But resources alone don't produce intelligent behavior. A powerful computer is useless without the software to run on it.

The analogy with computing hardware is useful and fitting. Processing speed is like CPU speed. Working memory is like RAM. Attention is like bandwidth. They are the resources for cognition and computing, but alone they can't do anything useful. Alone they can't solve problems.

Research shows that cognitive resources influence IQ test performance, with working memory being the resource that best correlates. Since genetics do influence our cognitive resources, IQ test performance shows some degree of heritability. So yes, the IQ test does measure something, a portion of which appears to be genetically influenced. It's just that what's measured isn't intelligence.

The fact of the matter is that we all inherited a human brain, the genetic blueprint for which has been honed and refined over millions of years of evolution. Yes, subtle differences in hardware may exist. But for all practical purposes, it's the same brain—the differences in our "hardware" pale in comparison to the similarities. Furthermore, thanks to the role of software in creating intelligence, those differences have minimal practical significance. Your brain has all the same bits as Einstein's.

Why Hardware Hardly Matters

Once again, one of the hallmark features of our brain is that we can continue to add complex cognitive skills throughout our lives. These are problem-solving algorithms, written in the language of neurons, built through learning. Algorithms that run on the brain's hardware.

And it is differences in our software, which is to say differences in our learning histories, that account for the differences in our solution spaces. To help appreciate the differing relative contributions of hardware and software, let's consider a couple of hypothetical battles. Our first is a tennis match between Ledron Gains and Doug Needlebinder.

The Tennis Match

Ledron is a professional basketball player. He's 6 foot, 9 inches tall, bench-presses 325 pounds, and jumps over three and a half feet in the air. By conservative estimates, his collection of physical attributes is one in ten million. He's taller, faster, and stronger than virtually everyone else on the planet. But he has never played tennis.

Doug Needlebinder is in the fourth grade. He's 4 foot, 6 inches tall, bench-presses 25 pounds, and can jump 8 inches off the ground on a good day. His combination of basic physical traits and abilities is a bit below average for a boy his age.

Doug has been playing tennis for five years. He takes lessons three times a week, plays a handful of tournaments a year, and is ranked among the top 20 boys his age in the state of Wisconsin.

Ledron and Doug are going to play a tennis match. Who is your money on?

If you said Ledron, then I hope you bet conservatively. Because Doug is going to annihilate him. Despite his formidable physical gifts, Ledron would be lucky to win a game.

That's because tennis, like all skill sports, is a never-ending stream of movement and perceptual problems (not to mention its fair share of mental challenges). Doug's years of training have equipped him with a vast network of tennis subskills that can be executed automatically, simultaneously, and with precision. Many of those movement and perceptual problems are in Doug's solution space. Virtually none are in Ledron's. Like all skill sports, tennis requires intelligence. And only software, built through training, confers intelligence.

Give Ledron the same tennis experiences that Doug has had, and the tables would turn. In that case, Ledron's edge in the hardware department would matter.

Ledron's exponentially greater physical attributes and athletic abilities are of little use in the face of Doug's superior skills. Because when it comes to intelligence, software is the deciding factor.

Hardware only provides the foundation. It's software that creates intelligence.

The Chess Battle

The same is true of our thinking skills, of course. To illustrate, let's now consider a hypothetical chess battle. Chess is the canonical example of a game of intelligence, right? There's no better game for separating the smart from the . . . not so smart, right?

This time the battle is between Malbert Weinstein and Margie Greenfield.

Malbert is an award-winning physicist at Princeton who is revered by his colleagues. His cognitive resources are formidable as well, with scores on processing speed and working memory above the 95th percentile.

Margie is president of her fifth-grade chess club. She began playing chess at the age of five with her dad and has been hooked ever since. She's ranked among the top 3 chess players her age in the state of Delaware. She has a C average in school and struggles to concentrate in class. Often because she's thinking about chess. Tests of her attention put her in the bottom 25 percent compared to her peers.

Surprisingly, Malbert has never played chess before.

Once again I ask, who'd you bet on?

Unless you don't like money, you'd put yours on Margie. As with Ledron and Doug, the game would be over quickly, with Margie checkmating Malbert in just a few moves. Malbert's superior cognitive resources are of little use in the face of Margie's chess intelligence. Malbert's hardware advantage is no match for Margie's superior software.

That's because chess intelligence, like all our thinking skills, is acquired through learning. Through years of playing and practice, Margie has built cognitive scaffolding that provides a solution space for chess problems that's exponentially larger than Malbert's.

The Einstein Algorithm

Doug destroys Ledron at tennis despite being a fourth grader with below-average physical attributes. Margie crushes Malbert at chess despite having attention problems and mediocre grades. In both cases, superior hardware provided no advantage. Software was the deciding factor.

Because intelligence is about your problem-solving abilities. Abilities that, in a softwired brain, are created through learning.

Based on what we know now, Einstein's ordinary-looking brain isn't the least bit surprising. It's what we'd expect if feats of genius are enabled by shared neurobiological bits. If they're the product of special software and not special brains.

The thinking skills that produced Einstein's feats of uncommon genius resided in the connections he'd forged through a lifetime of curiosity-driven learning. A lifetime of learning that cultivated a unique set of problem-solving skills, constructing the conceptual scaffolding (and its neural correlates) that would ultimately bring his iconic breakthroughs into his brain's solution space. Before that scaffolding had been built, those breakthroughs were biologically impossible.

Einstein's early life wasn't anything remarkable. He didn't start speaking until around age two, so no playgroup bragging rights for Mama Einstein. And his delayed and limited speech remained a persistent source of anxiety for his parents and teachers through much of his childhood. School was a struggle. Teachers described him as slow and dreamy. In sum, believers of the Special Brain Story would've surely passed him over without a second thought.

But Einstein did exhibit one noteworthy trait, a trait more likely to land a student in detention than in the gifted program. He was insatiably curious. He was captivated by fundamental questions about the natural world. At age five, his father showed him a compass, and Einstein was mesmerized by the invisible forces that made the needle always point north. He spent years thinking about the nature of light. At the age of twenty-three, he took an undemanding job as a patent clerk so he could ponder these questions every day.

This wasn't idle, unproductive daydreaming. Every paper he read, every conversation with other physicists, every thought experiment he contemplated was scaffolding-building work. No different from the basketball player shooting free throws every day, or the pianist practicing her scales.

Importantly, Einstein's training was unique. Everything about his life and his story, from early childhood onward, was unconventional. And day after day, he was asking questions and working through problems that nobody else was asking or working through. A unique training path that created a unique solution space. Through these efforts, he built cognitive scaffolding that enabled him to solve problems that nobody else could solve.

Einstein wasn't born with a brain that could discover relativity. He *built* it.

EINSTEIN'S EXPANDING SOLUTION SPACE

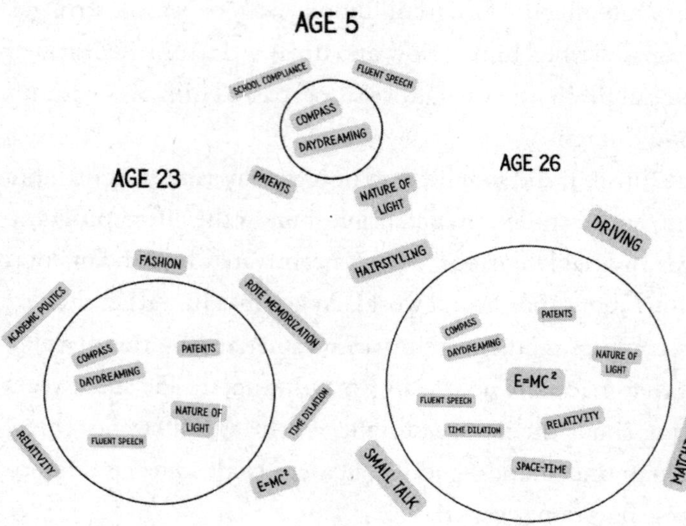

EINSTEIN WASN'T BORN WITH A BRAIN THAT COULD DISCOVER RELATIVITY; HE BUILT IT THROUGH YEARS OF OBSESSION WITH SPECIFIC PROBLEMS. THOSE OBSESSIONS BUILT THE COGNITIVE SCAFFOLDING THAT BROUGHT HIS INSIGHTS INTO HIS BRAIN'S SOLUTION SPACE.

HIS SOLUTION SPACE WASN'T NECESSARILY LARGER THAN AVERAGE, BUT IT WAS VERY UNIQUE.

BY CONTRAST, HE SPENT COMPARATIVELY LITTLE TIME BUILDING A SOLUTION SPACE IN AREAS LIKE ACADEMIC POLITICS, DRIVING, OR FASHION TRENDS. LIKE EVERYONE, HIS SOLUTION SPACE REFLECTED THE PROBLEMS HE'D CARED ABOUT SOLVING.

The difference between the mental feats of uncommon genius and those performed routinely by adult humans every day isn't one of complexity. It's one of uniqueness. An unconventional learning path that creates unique software with a unique solution space.

The pattern is so familiar that the oddball and often self-taught genius with the strange interests and obsessions has become cliché. At the age of twenty-two, Isaac Newton left college for his family farm to pursue his own academic interests . . . and ended up inventing calculus. Charles Darwin dropped out of medical school, spent five years on a ship collecting beetles, and discovered the mechanism that explains all life. Emily Dickinson barely left her house for decades, writing poems in secret, and invented a poetic form no one had yet seen. Miles Davis dropped out of Juilliard to play bebop in Harlem clubs and revolutionized jazz.

But what about child prodigies? The five-year-old chess master? The ten-year-old studying graduate-level math? Don't they prove some brains *are* special right out of the box?

Quite the opposite!

What's unique about a child prodigy isn't their brain but their *interests*. A five-year-old obsessed with chess instead of Pokémon is unusual. A ten-year-old fascinated by calculus instead of Minecraft is rare. These obsessions reflect our natural curiosities, and our natural curiosities are what feed the Genius.

Unusual interest drives unusual training. While most of their peers are building scaffolding for playground politics and video games, the prodigy spends thousands of hours building scaffolding for more atypical pursuits. It's the same learning machinery pointed in an uncommon direction.

This is why the abilities of child prodigies seem miraculous compared to other five-year-olds but not to those who've had similar amounts of training time. It was never about better hardware, but about an early head start in one specific domain. A brain that receives uncommon training will end up with uncommon abilities.

When Hardware Matters

I've spent considerable time arguing that hardware differences between brains are minimal compared to software differences. But what about instances where the hardware is different? What about cases where disease, injury, or an altered developmental trajectory results in a brain that differs from the norm?

Does a different set of rules apply? Does software no longer trump hardware here?

Not in the least.

These kinds of alterations in the hardware of cognition can indeed create real and meaningful differences. Dyslexia creates genuine obstacles to mapping sounds to symbols. ADHD can alter how the brain directs attention. An autistic brain processes sensory and symbolic information differently. Traumatic brain injury can damage networks that took years to build.

These conditions have real-world consequences. They can make certain kinds of learning harder or slower. But none invalidate anything we've discussed about potential and learning. All brains can still learn. The Genius is still there. Progressive composition through optimal challenge still builds scaffolding.

In some instances, the path to building scaffolding may look different from the "norm." It may require different strategies or alternative routes. An environment that supports learning in one brain may undermine it in another.

And crucially, as we will discover later, weaknesses in one area are often accompanied by strengths in another. Obstacles create opportunity, if we know to look for it.

It's an enormous mistake to think those brains don't also possess extraordinary potential. In some ways, these differences are an advantage when it comes to generating novel insights and breakthroughs. Time and again, world-changing breakthroughs and insights have come from those who thought differently. In many instances, they came from those who, like Einstein, were perceived as having deficiencies or "disabilities." Their stories should serve as powerful reminders that "different" doesn't mean better or worse. And that we shouldn't allow societal norms and expectations that have been developed to support "neurotypical" brains to sabotage the development of "atypical" ones.

The Special Brain Story is still wrong. It's not that these brains can't learn, adapt, and achieve remarkable things. It's that they need different conditions to do so. And when we assume hardware differences determine potential, we rob ourselves of the opportunity to find those conditions. Variations in the hardware should never be used as an excuse to stop looking for what works.

Your (Extraordinary) Standard-Issue Brain

The ability to automate the skills we learn allows us to multitask, and multitasking enables exponential growth of our skills. With the necessary training data, the Genius can create endless scaffolding. The more unique that training data, the more unique the scaffolding, the more unique the solution space. Unique solution spaces can solve problems nobody else has solved, and find novel solutions for ones that have, whether they're in math, science, art, or sports.

But how long do we have these powers of boundless learning? As we've reviewed, our skills of common genius, like walking, talking, and socializing, are constructed in early life. Does the

Genius ditch us after the work is done, or can it keep scaling intelligence throughout our lives?

chapter summary

- **Automaticity is the engine of intelligence:** Complex skills feel effortless because the brain automates their execution into neural tissue, freeing conscious attention for new challenges.
- **Easy does not equal simple:** Skills feel easy when mastered, not because they're simple.
- **Multitasking requires automation:** Novices can only do one thing at a time because every subtask demands conscious attention, while experts juggle multiple tasks because their automated subskills run in parallel.
- **Automation enables exponential growth:** Automated skills combine in unlimited ways, like a twenty-thousand-word vocabulary producing quadrillions of possible sentences.
- **Software trumps hardware:** Differences in cognitive resources pale compared to what we've learned. Margie the chess-playing fifth grader crushes the Princeton physicist because she has the software and he doesn't.

6

genius never stops

Every man can, if he so desires,
become the sculptor of his own brain.

—Santiago Ramón y Cajal (author and histologist)

For most of the twentieth century, neuroscientists thought the adult brain couldn't change. In his book *Degeneration and Regeneration of the Nervous System*, histologist Santiago Ramón y Cajal, often referred to as the "father of modern neuroscience," stated that "in adult centers the nerve paths are something fixed, ended, immutable. Everything may die, nothing may be regenerated."

If true, that indeed means that the mechanisms that enable the exponential growth of cognitive skills in early life are only present in youthful brains. That once our core cognitive skills are built, the Genius hits the road.

In short, "you can't teach an old dog new tricks" was an aphorism backed by science. The adult brain was fixed. If you haven't learned to throw a slider or mastered Mandarin by thirty, you've missed your window. Your potential has an expiration date.

The Myth of the Old Dog

Toward the end of the twentieth century, some upstart researchers decided to challenge the fixed brain dogma. They felt that the claim that brain change in adults was impossible had never been adequately tested, and so they set out to do so.

One of the more dramatic and influential experiments came from the lab of Dr. Michael Merzenich, a leader of the upstart rebellion. Using microelectrodes, Merzenich and colleagues first

SOMATOTOPIC MAPS

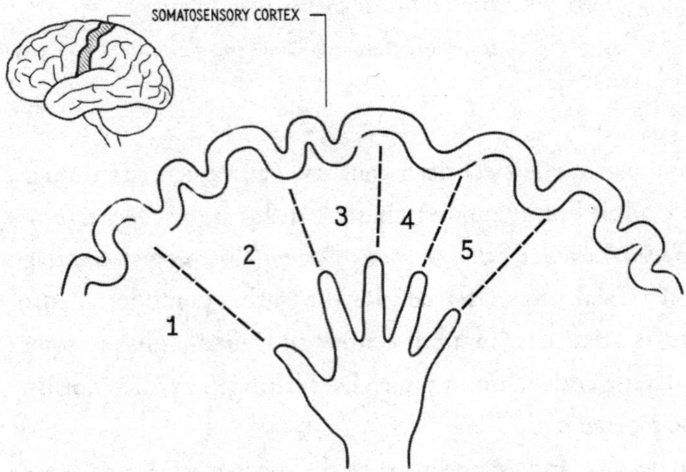

THE BRAIN CONTAINS A "SOMATOTOPIC" MAP OF THE BODY IN THE SENSORY CORTEX, MEANING THAT THE SPATIAL RELATIONSHIP OF BODY PARTS IS MAINTAINED IN THE BRAIN.

IN THE HAND, SENSORY REGIONS FOR ADJACENT DIGITS ARE IN ADJACENT REGIONS WITH DISCRETE BORDERS. IN THIS WAY, THE BRAIN'S ANATOMY REFLECTS THAT OF THE BODY.

created a map of the area in a monkey's somatosensory cortex that received sensation from the fingers. Your sensory cortex contains what's known as a "topographic" map, meaning the spatial layout of your body is preserved in the spatial layout of your brain. The area of the brain that processes sensation from the index finger sits next to the area that processes sensation from the middle finger, which sits next to the area for the ring finger, and so on. Your body's geography is reflected in your brain's geography.

So, after making the sensory maps, the researchers sewed the monkey's third and fourth digits together surgically. After letting the monkey go about its business for several weeks, the fingers were separated. After the separation, they mapped the sensory cortex again.

When they did so, they found that the sensory maps for the two digits had merged into one. Sewing the digits together had effectively transformed two digits into a single one, and the brain had remodeled itself to reflect that new reality. The brain of an adult primate had changed, which, according to the prevailing dogma, was not supposed to be possible.

As you might imagine, the results from Merzenich's lab were met with great skepticism. Even ridicule. But the evidence for adult plasticity continued to grow. The initial data came from animal experiments because we lacked tools for observing brain change in humans. That would change, however, with the advent of new noninvasive technologies for studying the brain.

In 1995, neuroscientist Alvaro Pascual-Leone of Harvard and colleagues at the Centre for the Mind in Australia conducted an experiment that would provide some of the most striking evidence yet. In the first part of the experiment, researchers made

THE DYNAMIC BRAIN

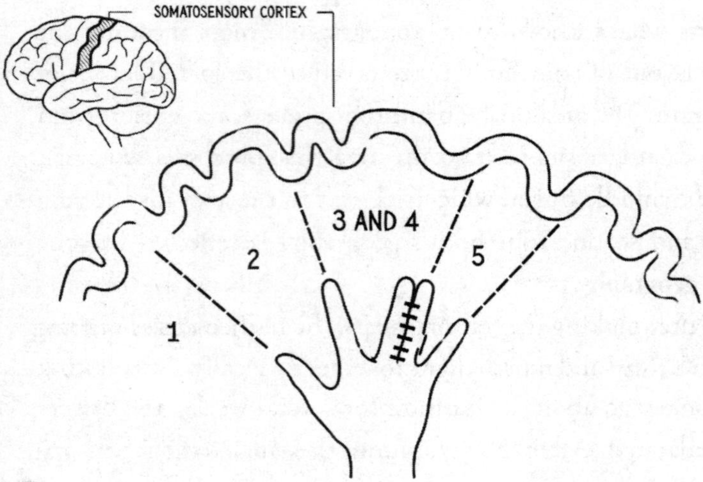

IN THE EXPERIMENT BY MERZENICH AND COLLEAGUES, SURGICALLY ATTACHING THE THIRD AND FOURTH DIGITS CAUSED THE BRAIN TO REMODEL ITS MAP OF THE HAND, FUSING THE DIGITS INTO ONE REGION TO REFLECT THE NEW REALITY OF THE BODY.

A CHANGE OF THIS KIND REQUIRED THE KIND OF STRUCTURAL CHANGE IN THE BRAIN THAT WAS THOUGHT TO ONLY OCCUR IN CHILDHOOD. THESE AND OTHER EXPERIMENTS DEMONSTRATED THAT BRAIN PLASTICITY IS LIFELONG.

a map of which parts of the brain controlled which fingers in each of the subjects. They did so by using transcranial magnetic stimulation (TMS), a device that's placed over the skull and can stimulate the underlying brain tissue with a painless magnetic pulse. First, they built a map of the motor cortex by stimulating different areas and documenting which muscle contracted.

Then, over the course of five days, participants practiced a specific five-finger sequence, much like the movements required to play a short, simple tune on a keyboard. Each day prior to the practice session, the researchers remapped the motor cortex.

What they found was a progressive expansion in the cortical representation of the trained fingers over the course of the study. The part of the motor cortex controlling the fingers grew bigger, clearly demonstrating plastic change in the adult human brain.

But that wasn't even the coolest part.

They also ran a second version of the experiment, this time with a group of participants who didn't actually perform the finger movements. Instead, they just *imagined* themselves making the movements. They practiced each day like the subjects in the initial experiment, but only in their minds.

What happened? The same thing! Their maps grew, too! Just the act of *imagining* the movement was enough to stimulate the brain to change.

The Illusion of Rigidity

The evidence for adult plasticity is overwhelming. The Genius doesn't hit the road after early life, which means that our capacity for boundless learning is lifelong.

That's what the science clearly shows. And yet, it doesn't always *seem* that way. It often does seem like our capacity for learning shrinks with age. That's part of why the fixed brain dogma has had such staying power. So where's the disconnect between the science and our lived experience? Multiple powerful factors create the illusion that learning gets harder with age.

Illusion #1: Biological Efficiency

As we've discussed, we humans hardwire very little into our brains. Having an unskilled brain at birth means we have loads of wiring up to do. We have the longest childhood in the animal kingdom so that we can wire up our core cognitive skills. No brain changes more from birth to adulthood than that of a human.

This fact of human brains guarantees that children will be changing all the time. They'll be leveling up their skills and intelligence virtually every day for several *years*.

Furthermore, once we've wired up our major motor and perceptual skills, they're going to stay that way. Barring a radical change in your body or the environment, there's no reason to change that wiring once it's finished. As long as our brain is accurately modeling the world around us and controlling our body effectively, there's no reason to modify our wiring. That's it's job. If it ain't broke, don't fix it.

What the experiments from researchers like Merzenich and Pascual-Leone revealed was that the brain can change, if it *needs* to. The Genius never stops checking to see if our brain maps and capabilities are still accurate and adequate. As long as they are, things stay fixed. If they aren't, then those maps and capabilities will change. If two digits become one, or if we need finer control over our fingers, then our plastic brain will make the necessary adjustments.

Adults change less because less *needs* changing, not because the capacity for change has declined. That's a feature, not a bug.

Illusion #2: The Survival Threshold

Remember, our brain's core objective is to keep us alive. Remodeling brain tissue is an expensive proposition. We owe our existence to the fact that thousands of generations of humans that preceded us were ruthlessly efficient in their energy usage.

Ultimately, the only reason for our brain to change is if it thinks the juice is worth the squeeze. To change, it must be convinced, one way or another, that doing so improves our survival odds. Otherwise, bad idea.

Rewiring so you can communicate with other humans, distinguish a garden hose from a rattlesnake, or shoot an elk with a bow and arrow is a clear survival enhancement. Convincing the brain to rewire so we can learn to yo-yo or solve a Rubik's cube requires a bit of creativity and deception.

The childhood wiring project is ultimately about acquiring the skills we need to survive on our own. From this perspective, adulthood is defined by the absence of a *need* to acquire new skills.

The skills we wish to acquire as adults are rarely a matter of life or death. As a result, brain change won't happen automatically. The Genius needs other reasons to care enough to invest the energy.

Illusion #3: The High Stakes of Maturity

A sculptor with a lump of soft clay can smash and smoosh with abandon. There's no damage to be done by working fast and loose. Mistakes are no big deal.

After you've spent days carefully molding and refining features, however, that's no longer true. One wrong move could obliterate that earlobe contour you spent three hours getting just right.

Likewise, at birth all that untrained and uncommitted cortex is like that lump of soft clay. With no information yet housed in their connections, the risk of synaptic remodeling is minimal.

By the time we're adults, however, we've spent a couple of decades of hard work constructing the networks that power our skills and store our memories. Now if we play fast and loose with our synapses, we risk forgetting our wedding anniversary or how to make cheese toast. All that time and effort spent creating those connections is wasted. Re-creating them means expending all that time and effort again.

The more mature our networks, the more capable our brain becomes, the more there is to lose from careless rewiring. When our brain is unskilled and there's nothing to lose, you can dial the plasticity up to 11.

Illusion #4: Automaticity's Double Edge

I just spent the last chapter celebrating automaticity as the engine of our intelligence. And it's true that without the ability to write algorithms into our brain tissue, we'd never learn anything.

But once we've reached our goal of unconscious competence, once those algorithms are written, they become our brain's path of least resistance. Flip the circuit's switch, and the steps unfold.

For an organ trying to maximize energy efficiency, taking the path of least resistance is a smart move. If you need to make your way through a section of the jungle to reach your destination, are you going to try to hack your way through the dense vegetation or are you going to take the well-beaten path that thousands of humans have carved out for you?

It's the same with our neural pathways. This is fantastic if that neural pathway we've carved leads where we want it to go.

But what happens if it doesn't? What happens if our automatic behavior yields a suboptimal solution?

For example, what happens if you automate a golf swing that consistently slices the ball 150 yards to the right each and every time? What happens is, every time your brain switches on the golf swing circuit, it guarantees you get to have another ball-retrieving adventure into the land of self-loathing.

Now, if you want to learn to hit a drive straight, you have to trick your brain into not flipping that automated golf swing switch when you step up to the tee. Good luck!

The common term for an unwanted automated neural pathway is a bad habit. Our automated networks are a product of our learning path. After a few decades of learning, we're bound to have created a bad habit or ten.

This is the double-edged sword of automaticity. Automaticity is the reason why we can continue to learn complex skills throughout our life, but it's also the reason why changing existing skills and behaviors can be difficult. The path of least resistance is the easiest one to travel.

And bad habits can obstruct our learning efforts. When they stand in the way of progress, we have to find a way to circumvent them. They add friction and frustration to the learning process—friction and frustration that leads many to give up.

Illusion #5: Societal Expectations

In modern society, we've "decided" that childhood is the time for learning and adulthood is the time for working. When you're young, the world around you naturally steers you in the direction of learning. You're expected to go to school. There's even a free bus that will take you there! You have no family to support. You aren't expected to earn a living.

Part of the reason why we front-load so much of our learning may be due to the very myth that our learning capacity shrinks with each passing year of life. If the adult brain is fixed and rigid, it makes sense to do your learning while your brain is still flexible and plastic.

So we go to college and learn the oboe as youngsters. Learning complex skills as a grown-up means swimming upstream against the cultural currents. So now we find ourselves in a world where getting a degree or learning an instrument later in life is so unusual, it's liable to get you featured in the local paper.

Illusion #6: School's Ineffective Techniques

Children are master learners. No surprise, since learning is the objective of our childhood. And it's why the success rate in learning our core cognitive skills is so high.

Research shows that young children naturally use the most effective learning techniques. Research also shows that adults do not. Somewhere between the ages of three and thirty, we become much worse at learning. Why?

One clue may have to do with the place where we spend so much of our time during those years. The place where, ironically enough, we go to learn.

Research shows that there are three key ingredients for effective learning. The first is intrinsic motivation, meaning we need to want to learn what we're learning, and that desire comes from within.

The second key ingredient is active construction of knowledge. We don't just passively receive information via text or lecture; we manipulate information to generate understanding. We are the ones constructing knowledge about what it is we're learning.

And the third is ongoing feedback. To learn effectively, we must know how we're doing. We only grow when we're operating at the edge of our knowledge and skills, or in the Goldilocks Zone. The Genius is trying out different patterns to figure out which ones to make permanent and thus needs to know which of our efforts fail and which ones succeed. For that we need feedback.

All three ingredients are necessary for us to enter the virtuous cycle of learning and growth, which is action → feedback → modification → action. If we're not in the cycle, we're spinning our wheels.

With these three key ingredients of effective learning in mind, let's review the key features of traditional schooling.

In school, we don't choose what we learn. That's chosen for us. We're usually discouraged from asking about or exploring topics unrelated to the chosen subject matter. Without natural curiosity to motivate us, we're instead incentivized to learn through rewards and punishments, mainly in the form of grades and class rankings. Correct answers are rewarded with gold stars and awards, wrong ones with red X's and public humiliation.

We sit at a desk and *receive* information. We are passive consumers of information given to us in class lectures and textbooks. We receive and we regurgitate, but we rarely create.

The feedback we receive is primarily in the form of tests for a grade. It is intermittent and separated from the learning process, existing for the purposes of measurement, not modification.

In short, traditional schooling is zero for three in providing the key ingredients for effective learning. No intrinsic motivation. No active knowledge construction. No ongoing feedback. When it comes to the effectiveness of their learning methods, schools earn a failing grade.

It'd be hard to design a better system for instilling inferior learning techniques or for transforming insatiably curious little learning machines into obedient automatons chasing their next reward.

How could that possibly be? It's possible because the format and architecture of schools have been virtually unchanged for more than a century. Were you to walk into a school in 2025 or 1925, you'd find a standardized curriculum, age-based progression, grading systems and report cards, set school hours, subject-based curricula with bells to demarcate their rigid boundaries, and teacher-led instruction in indoor classrooms where students sit quietly at desks.

The primary objective of this structure was to prepare children to enter the workplace. The workplace of the 1920s, that is! Schools resemble factories because in the 1920s they were preparing children to work in them.

I think we'd all agree that, if you were to design school from scratch today, the objective would be to support a child's cognitive development while incorporating best practices from learning research. Not only was that not the objective a century ago; they couldn't have done that if they'd wanted to. Our current school model was created before any of that research existed.

As a result, good grades have little to do with intelligence and a lot to do with how well you follow the rules and respond to achievement-based incentives. That may be helpful information if you're an employer, but it's poor preparation for lifelong learning.

School taught us how to learn badly. Not surprisingly, adults use these ineffective techniques. In fact, studies show that, compared to children, when faced with a learning challenge, an average adult will wait for instructions or guidance, try to find the "right" answer quickly (rather than exploring the solution space), avoid trial and error, limit learning to formal settings, ask fewer questions, quit when challenged, and stick to rules and procedures even when they're clearly suboptimal.

To summarize, adults tend to default to conservative, rigid, and externally driven strategies, avoiding self-guided exploration and instead seeking explicit direction. Behavior that formal schooling reinforces and that we know leads to poor results.

Illusion #7: Use It or Lose It 2.0

So we have multiple forces conspiring to reduce learning as we age. As a result, we tend to learn less the older we get. Our brain stops changing not because it can't, but because we stop asking it to.

That in and of itself can make it harder to stimulate change, because our body only maintains the parts we use regularly. If you stopped walking tomorrow, in short order your body would stop supporting the tissue in your gluteus and quadriceps muscles. They would wither away, and walking would become much harder. In their quest for energy efficiency, living systems don't spend energy maintaining what's not being used.

Rewiring the brain so we can learn new things requires a distinct set of biological machinery. If you stop learning, your brain will stop maintaining that machinery. And the fewer brain changing materials we have around, the less effective at brain change we'll become. The same learning stimulus won't produce the same results.

In other words, plasticity itself is plastic. The less we learn, the harder learning becomes. The more we learn, the easier it gets to trigger plasticity. It's a vicious cycle that contributes to the illusion that older brains can't change.

But doing so does require understanding the factors conspiring to make it appear as if learning gets harder with age. That the Genius abandons us once we've flown the nest. That's a myth the Impostor not only wants you to believe but has perpetuated.

Fortunately, it's also reversible. You can turn the vicious cycle into a virtuous one at any age.

METAPLASTICITY: HOW LEARNING BEGETS LEARNING
(AND VICE VERSA!)

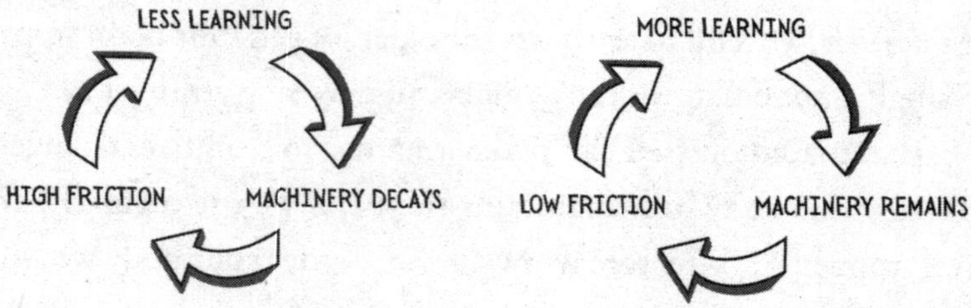

PLASTICITY IS PLASTIC. IF YOU STOP LEARNING, THE BIOLOGICAL MACHINERY REQUIRED FOR LEARNING WITHERS, MAKING LEARNING HARDER (THE VICIOUS CYCLE).

HOWEVER, THIS IS REVERSIBLE. LEARNING REBUILDS THE MACHINERY, MAKING FUTURE LEARNING EASIER (THE VIRTUOUS CYCLE).

The Impostor's Investment

The science is clear. Your brain retains its capacity for learning and growth throughout life. The Genius never abandons you. It may seem otherwise, but that's just an illusion.

Those illusions feel real because the Impostor has a vested interest in maintaining them. Every one of them reinforces the Special Brain Story. It's a story the Impostor actively maintains because his survival depends on it.

This is why simply learning the science isn't enough. You may accept on an intellectual level that the Genius never stops but deep down still believe what the Impostor says is true.

Because he's not just whispering doubts. He's fundamentally changing how your brain works and determining what feels possible in any given moment.

To understand how he wields that power, we need to look at how your brain is organized. We need to look at the architecture that explains both your extraordinary capabilities and your extraordinary vulnerability.

chapter summary

- **The Genius never leaves:** Adult brains retain their capacity for plastic change throughout life. Learning tends to diminish with age, but the capacity for it does not.
- **Adults change less because less needs changing:** The brain stays stable not because it can't change, but

because it doesn't need to once core skills are built. To change, we must convince the brain it's worth it.

- **Bad habits are the price of automaticity:** Automaticity that makes skills effortless also makes unwanted behaviors hard to unlearn, as automated pathways become the path of least resistance.
- **Plasticity itself is plastic:** The less we learn, the harder learning becomes because the brain stops maintaining its learning machinery when unused. This cycle can be reversed at any age by resuming learning.
- **The Impostor has a vested interest in the illusion:** The Impostor maintains illusions that make learning seem harder because his survival depends on you believing your potential has an expiration date.

7

the disconnected mind

What we call the self is a decentralized collection of cognitive programs.

—Marvin Minsky (AI pioneer)

In 1873, Karl Wernicke, a German neuropsychiatrist and luminary in the field of neurology, encountered an intriguing patient. Despite being able to speak and hear perfectly well, the patient could no longer understand what was said to him. This inability to understand speech had begun abruptly following a stroke. At autopsy, it was discovered that the stroke had damaged the left hemisphere, specifically the back part of the temporal and parietal lobes.

Wernicke's discovery came only a few years after his French colleague Paul Broca had published his landmark findings on patients with the opposite problem. Broca's patients had suffered damage to the back part of the left frontal lobe, resulting in the inability to *produce* speech. Yet, unlike Wernicke's patient, they could understand it just fine. Importantly, their inability to speak wasn't due to any problem with muscle control, as their muscles of articulation worked perfectly fine. The damage appeared to have impacted the part of the brain that housed the precise sequence of movements needed to form words. It had destroyed the brain's algorithms for producing the movements of speech.

Wernicke would assimilate these findings into a comprehensive model for how language is organized in the brain, which he published in a paper titled *The Aphasic Symptom Complex*. This revolutionary framework represented a breakthrough in a long-standing debate about the fundamental architecture of human cognition.

On one side of the debate stood the holistic model of the brain. Advocates of this model argued that the brain was a general-purpose machine, and cognitive functions emerged from the coordinated activity of the entire brain working as an integrated whole.

On the opposing side was the localizationist model. Its advocates argued that the brain was composed of teams of specialist regions, or modules, each dedicated to particular cognitive functions.

These competing theories made testable predictions about the impact of brain injuries. If the brain was a general-purpose machine, then damage to any brain region should impair all cognitive abilities equally. If the brain was a team of specialists, then localized brain damage should selectively impair specific cognitive skills while leaving others intact.

The Phrenology Problem

This debate about whether the brain functions as a generalist or a collection of specialists has been around ever since people began contemplating the brain. One of the most notable early proponents of the localizationalist model was Franz Gall, a German neuroanatomist and physiologist born in 1758. Gall not only believed that the brain was organized into functionally distinct areas but also claimed that you could predict someone's personality and cognitive abilities based on the lumpiness of their skulls.

This purported correlation between skull lumps and cognitive abilities was based on the theory that an exceptional cognitive ability would be associated with a larger corresponding brain area, which would result in a palpable lump in the overlying skull. Thus, your skull's pattern of lumpiness would indicate your cognitive strengths and weaknesses.

Eventually, an entire commercial enterprise arose around this concept. You could become certified as a phrenologist, and people would pay you to feel their skull lumps and provide career guidance, marital advice, or an assessment of the intellectual potential of their children. Phrenology was like a modern-day IQ and personality test all rolled into one.

By the mid-1800s, however, science doused the claims of phrenology with the cold water of evidence. Studies revealed that skull lumps did not correlate with the size of the underlying brain regions. Phrenology was dismissed as pseudoscience, and its practitioners were seen as nothing more than glorified palm readers.

Through its guilt by association with phrenology, the localizationalist model fell into disfavor, and for decades the holistic model dominated. But Wernicke's paper on the neuroanatomy of language would change that trajectory.

Double Dissociations

Wernicke's paper was especially compelling because it demonstrated what's known as a "double dissociation" of function. This term, coined by Hans-Lukas Teuber in 1955, refers to a pattern where two different experimental manipulations have opposite effects on two different functions or abilities. Double dissociations are considered the gold standard for demonstrating functional specialization in the brain.

In this case, lesions in Broca's area impaired speech produc-

LANGUAGE'S DOUBLE DISSOCIATION:
EVIDENCE FOR MODULARITY

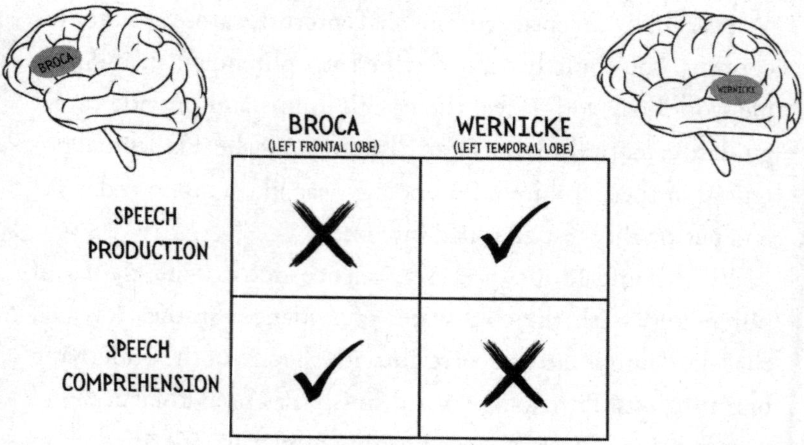

A DOUBLE DISSOCIATION OCCURS WHEN DAMAGE A IMPAIRS FUNCTION X BUT SPARES FUNCTION Y, WHILE DAMAGE B IMPAIRS FUNCTION Y BUT SPARES FUNCTION X.

THE OPPOSING PATTERNS OF DEFICITS IN BROCA'S AND WERNICKE'S APHASIAS PROVIDED THE FIRST DEFINITIVE PROOF THAT THE BRAIN IS ORGANIZED INTO SPECIALIZED MODULES RATHER THAN ACTING AS A SINGLE GENERAL-PURPOSE MACHINE.

tion while preserving comprehension, whereas lesions in Wernicke's area impaired comprehension while preserving production. This double dissociation of language production and comprehension provided powerful evidence that brain regions were specialized.

Evidence supporting localization continued to accumulate over the following decades. Once it became the prevailing model of brain organization, scientists launched systematic efforts to generate a neuroanatomical map of the brain's cognitive functions, and to determine the full extent of neural specialization.

A leading figure in this effort was neurologist Kenneth Heilman. One of Heilman's many areas of interest was prosody, which refers to the variations in tone of voice we use to modify the meaning of words and sentences. For example, the phrase "thanks a lot" can express genuine gratitude or bitter sarcasm depending on your tone, and tone of voice is a crucial element in how we communicate. Heilman wondered whether a different part of the brain handled that piece.

Specifically, he wondered whether propositional speech was mediated by different brain networks than affective speech, and whether the right hemisphere might play a role in the latter. Propositional speech consists of the components of language that are intended to convey information, facts, or ideas, such as "our flight to New York is at three p.m. tomorrow." Affective speech consists of the components of language that employ prosody to convey emotion or modify meaning.

So, in 1975, nearly a hundred years after Wernicke reported his case of sensory aphasia from left hemispheric damage, Heilman devised an experiment to determine the location of affective speech. In it, he took twelve patients who'd suffered a stroke.

Half the subjects had strokes in their left hemisphere that impacted speech, while the other half had strokes in similar regions of the right hemisphere.

Researchers read each subject the same four sentences using four different tones of voice: happy, sad, angry, and indifferent. After the sentence was read, the subjects were asked to point to a face indicating the mood of the speaker and to announce it aloud.

What Heilman found was that subjects with right-hemispheric lesions were unable to identify mood based on tone of voice. But their propositional speech was unimpaired. Heilman had discovered another double dissociation, indicating a segregation of these two functions. One hemisphere handled propositional speech, while the other handled affective speech.

Subsequent work has demonstrated further divisions of labor in the control of affective speech. Just as there are separate regions for producing and comprehending propositional speech on the left side, there are separate regions for producing and comprehending affective speech on the right. In addition to conveying emotions, we also use prosody, or intonation, to distinguish questions from statements. Each of these prosodic functions is also mediated by distinct regions.

Similarly, considerable depth and detail have been added to our understanding of propositional language. We have networks for parts of speech such as nouns, verbs, and function words. We have networks for syntax and networks for semantic processing. The point being that, as best we can tell, it's modularity all the way down. The more we keep looking, the more specialization we keep finding.

The Modular Advantage

There are clear advantages to the modular organization of cognition. One of those is energy efficiency. The most energy-efficient organisms win out in the survival of the fittest, which is why every organism is so exquisitely adapted to its particular habitat.

The same principle applies to the problem-solving networks we build. These modules are created in response to having to solve the same kind of problem repeatedly. The more optimized that module is for that particular problem, or the less wasted effort and unused capacity, the less energy it will consume.

Additionally—and perhaps most importantly—modularity enables multitasking. Having multiple autonomous modules that can run simultaneously is what allows us to scale our intelligence.

Simply put, why have one brain when you can have thousands?

But organizing cognition in this way introduces its own set of challenges. In many ways, those challenges mirror those of any large organization of people with diverse roles, responsibilities, and skills. The combined talents of all your people represent the potential intelligence of the organization. But it's the ones who are contributing that determine your *actual* intelligence. Realizing that potential is as much a matter of coordination and logistics—about assigning tasks to the right people at the right time—as it is about the skills of its individuals.

So, organizing cognition into modules means the brain must solve the coordination problem. Having an individual or module with a particular skill set is only useful if you (1) know that they possess that skill and (2) are able to call upon those skills when they're needed. Having a capability within your organization does you no good if you can't *access* it.

The Man Who Could Write but Not Read

It was just past 2 a.m. when the alarm of my pager jolted me from the kind of deep slumber only decades-worth of sleep debt can produce. I was in my second year of neurology residency and was on call that night.

I grabbed the pager off the nightstand and checked the number. It was the emergency room at the Malcolm Randall VA, one of the two hospitals I was covering that evening.

I cleared my throat a few times in an attempt to boot up my voice and dialed the number.

"Sorry to bother you," said Dr. Kershaw, one of the ER residents currently on night shift. "I've got a case I want to run by you. It may not be anything, but I just figured I'd check."

"Sure thing," I replied.

"Sixty-four-year-old male by the name of Dennis M, prior smoker with a history of hypertension. Said he was reading the paper last night and suddenly couldn't read anything. And as best I can tell, he can't. But the weird thing is there's nothing wrong with his vision and nothing wrong with his eyes. He can see just fine; he just can't read. And he has a nonfocal neuro exam. No focal weakness, normal strength. It's probably nothing, right?"

My heart started beating a little faster.

"What workup have you done?"

"Labs and a head CT. Head CT shows some chronic subcortical vascular disease, but nothing acute. So I was thinking I'd just send him home with neuro follow-up, but I figured since it's weird, I'd run it by you."

"Yeah, don't let him go. Did you happen to check his visual fields?"

"No, not really."

"OK, no worries. I'm coming in."

Based on what the ER doc had told me, I was almost certain that Dennis had suffered a stroke. I was also almost certain that I had a really cool case on my hands.

I threw on my shoes, hopped in the car, made the short drive to the ER, and found my way to Dennis's room.

I began by confirming the history I'd received, then moved on to the neurological examination, beginning with testing of his cranial nerves. I had a hunch about the stroke syndrome Dennis was suffering from, and was eager to test his visual fields. If my suspicions were correct, he wouldn't be able to see anything in his right field of vision.

"Look straight at my nose and, without moving your eyes, tell me how many fingers you see." I held one finger up on my right hand (his left side) and two fingers up on my left hand (his right side). "One," he said, indicating that he saw only the fingers on his left side.

Then I held up two fingers on my right hand and one finger on my left. "Two," he said, once again indicating he saw only the fingers on his left side.

"Now tell me when you see my fingers wiggle," I said. I wiggled the fingers on his left side.

"Now," he said. Then I wiggled the fingers on his right side. No response.

Suspicions confirmed! Dennis couldn't see anything in his right visual field. It was as if the right half of the world had been erased, though he had no awareness of it being gone. In neurological jargon, he had a right homonymous hemianopsia.

The odds that I'd landed a really cool case just went way up.

The remainder of Dennis's basic neurological functions were normal. His speech, movements, sensation, coordination, and gait were all working as they should.

Finally, it was time for the cognitive exam. I'd intentionally saved the best part for last.

I began with the assessment of his language function. His speech was fluent, he was able to comprehend my speech and follow instructions easily, and he could repeat phrases back to me. His networks for spoken language were all intact.

Then it was time to test his reading. I wrote down "We are in the hospital" and showed it to him on the left side of his body (the part of the world he could still see) and asked him to read it. He studied it for a few seconds, squinting. "I'm sorry, Doc, I can't make it out."

"No worries," I said.

Now, in most neurological residencies, I could've stopped there. I had more than enough information to make a diagnosis. But this wasn't like most residency programs.

Because I knew that I'd be presenting Dennis's case in just a few hours in morning rounds. And I'd be presenting the case to my attending neurologist for that month, who was none other than Dr. Ken Heilman. As in the same Dr. Heilman we met earlier who'd made the breakthrough discovery that affective speech was controlled by the nondominant hemisphere. The same Dr. Heilman who had also developed the prevailing models of the functional neuroanatomy of reading. He was a living legend and a huge reason why I'd come to the University of Florida for my neurology training.

In sum, in a matter of hours, I'd be presenting a case to one of my personal heroes, who was the world's preeminent expert on cases like these and who also happened to be a seasoned practitioner of the Socratic method. Translation: I had to have my shit together.

Which meant that my examination of Dennis was far from over. I needed to determine the precise nature of his reading problem.

Routes to Reading

It turns out that, when we humans learn to read, we usually construct at least two distinct modules for decoding written words in the brain. One of those modules is capable of constructing words from their basic elements. It converts "graphemes" into "phonemes," meaning it takes the written letters or letter combinations and converts them into their corresponding sounds. This is also referred to as the "phonological" route to decoding a word, and it's the route we use when "sounding out" a word.

The other module is capable of recognizing the entire written word as its own pattern. When we encounter a word enough times, we also learn to recognize the whole word as a single object, in the same way we might recognize a face or a tractor. Using this route, referred to as the "lexical" route, we go straight from recognizing the visual pattern of the word to its meaning, without needing to sound it out. Unless you're encountering an unfamiliar word, this is likely the path that your brain is using to read these words right now.

How do we know these are housed in different areas? If you said "double dissociations," give yourself a pat on the back! Specifically, we have documented cases where a lesion knocks out the phonological route but not the lexical, and vice versa.

One of the objectives in the assessment of someone with problems reading is to figure out which of these routes to reading is impacted. How might you do so? To determine if the lexical route is still working, which is the path that can recognize whole words but can't sound them out, we provide a reading task that only it can perform. Present a word to read that doesn't play by the rules of phonics. These are known as "irregular" words, and include ones like "yacht," "colonel," "phlegm," and "choir." I showed a few of these to Dennis, and he couldn't read any of them. The lexical pathway to reading was blocked.

To determine if the phonological route is still working, we provide a reading task that only it can perform. Present a word that doesn't really exist (a "nonword") but that can be sounded out phonetically. Examples include nonwords like "flarch," "crimsley," and "spleck." Dennis couldn't read nonwords, either. The phonological pathway was also down.

Based on these tests, the most accurate description of his reading deficits was "pure alexia," in that all his routes to reading had been taken out.

The next step was to test if Dennis could still write. That may seem like a waste of time. If he couldn't read anything, how could he possibly still write? I asked Dennis to write a sentence.

He wrote: *I am talking to the doctor at the hospital.*

Perfect spelling. Perfect grammar and punctuation.

"Can you read what you just wrote?" I asked.

Dennis stared at the paper. He paused. "Uh, I mean, gosh, I know what I wrote. But no, I'm sorry, Doc, it looks like scribbles. What's going on here? Am I okay?"

I tried to reassure him: "Yeah, you're gonna be okay. You've had a stroke and will need some rehabilitation to relearn how to do some things, but things are probably as bad now as they'll get."

Back to the exam. Despite being unable to read, Dennis could still write perfectly well.

But there was one more test I had to do. This one was not a part of the routine neurological exam. To perform it, I needed supplies.

I went over to the nurses' station and asked if there was any colored paper. Together, we rummaged through the desk and managed to cobble together a collection of pink, blue, green, yellow, and white papers. I took two of each and went back over to Dennis's bedside.

I held up the green paper in front of Dennis. "Can you tell me what color this is?" I asked.

"Yeah, it's . . . uh. It's . . . uh. Dang. I know what that is, but it's just not coming to me."

I held up the pink one. "And what about this one?"

He nodded his head and then paused. "I know that one, too, but just can't call up the name."

Dennis was unable to name any of the colors.

"Okay, try one more thing. I'm gonna give you these ten pieces of paper and I want you to just create five separate piles of the same color." I handed him the colored papers.

Without hesitation, he quickly made five stacks, each of the same color. He couldn't name the colors, but he could match them with ease. This meant that he could perceive the colors just fine; he just couldn't call them by name.

My exam was complete, and my initial suspicions were confirmed. Dennis had the triad of alexia without agraphia (difficulty reading without any problems writing), right homonymous hemianopsia (loss of his right field of vision), and color dysnomia (difficulty naming colors).

I was certain that Dennis had suffered an ischemic stroke. It was too early for it to show up on a CT scan, which was why that had been normal.

But I knew we'd find one on his MRI scan. Specifically, I knew it would show a stroke in his left occipital lobe and the splenium of his corpus callosum from a clot in his left posterior cerebral artery, the artery that supplies those areas of the cortex.

I knew this because I had just seen my first case of Dejerine syndrome, a rare neurological condition initially described by French neurologist Jules Dejerine in 1892. A condition that, until now, I'd only read about. A condition that has profound implications for how we understand cognition and how our potential can be undermined.

Dennis's Disconnection

Let's unpack the various deficits seen in Dejerine syndrome as displayed by Dennis.

First, the loss of vision in the right field of vision (right homonymous hemianopsia). Dennis couldn't count the fingers on my left hand or see them wiggle because he couldn't see them. That's because the area of the occipital lobe that first processes visual signals from the retina had been damaged by the stroke. In his case, light from the right side of the world would strike his retinas, where it would be transduced into a nerve impulse. That impulse would then travel backward along optic nerves, ultimately reaching his left visual cortex. Upon encountering the infarcted brain tissue, the signal would have nowhere else to go. As a result, those signals couldn't be processed, resulting in an inability to see anything on his right side.

Second, the inability to read but preserved ability to write (alexia without agraphia). Why couldn't Dennis read? Yes, he'd lost one half of his vision, but the other half worked just fine. So it wasn't that he couldn't see.

As we learned earlier, language function is strongly lateralized to one side of the brain. In most people, that's the left side. When we learn to read, the networks that develop are also usually lateralized to the left side as well, close to those that already exist for speech.

Let's trace the path of light as it bounces off a page of text and enters Dennis's brain. The signals from the right side hit a dead end when they land on the left occipital lobe. But the ones on the left make it to the right occipital lobe just fine, where they undergo their first round of processing.

That would typically include analysis by the visual word form area in the left hemisphere, which is responsible for identifying letters and words. But in order for that visual information to reach the networks on the left side where that module resides, it must cross over the now infarcted corpus callosum.

The part of Dennis's brain that knows how to read is still there but has been effectively cut out of the cognitive conversation.

And yet Dennis could still write. How? When we write, the

ABILITY WITHOUT ACCESS: WHY DENNIS COULDN'T READ

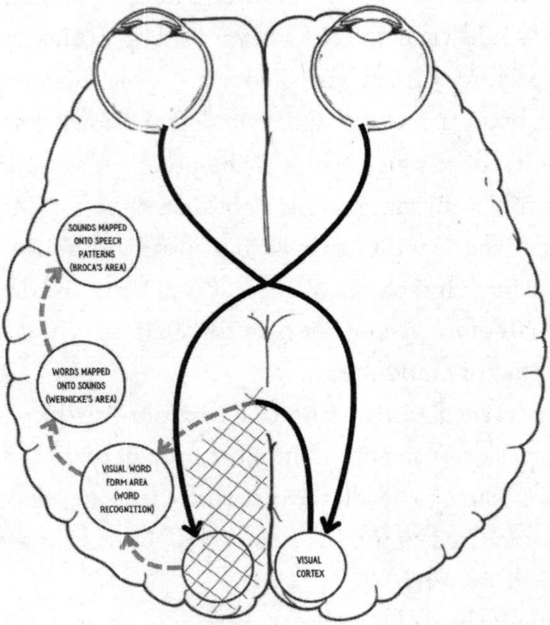

DENNIS'S STROKE DAMAGED HIS LEFT OCCIPITAL LOBE (HATCHED LINES), WHICH PROCESSES VISUAL INFORMATION. AS A RESULT, HE WAS BLIND IN HIS RIGHT FIELD OF VISION.

WHILE VISUAL SIGNALS COULD STILL REACH HIS INTACT RIGHT VISUAL CORTEX, THAT INFORMATION COULDN'T CROSS OVER TO THE MODULES IN THE LEFT HEMISPHERE (DASHED LINES) THAT DECODE WRITTEN WORDS.

EVEN THOUGH HIS BRAIN STILL POSSESSED THE ABILITY TO READ, HE COULD NO LONGER ACCESS THAT ABILITY.

words are coming from within, not from without. Generating the words is a purely mental task, not a perceptual one. When we write, the idea for what we want to express is generated in conceptual areas, then transferred to the visual word form area, where those concepts are mapped onto the appropriate words.

From there, information travels to areas of the frontal lobe where the words are mapped to the corresponding motor programs for the hand. Then it's sent off to the motor cortex, down through the brainstem and spinal cord, out to the muscles controlling your hand and onto the paper.

But what happens when Dennis tries to read what he's just written? Just as before, the visual information has no way of

WHY DENNIS COULD STILL WRITE

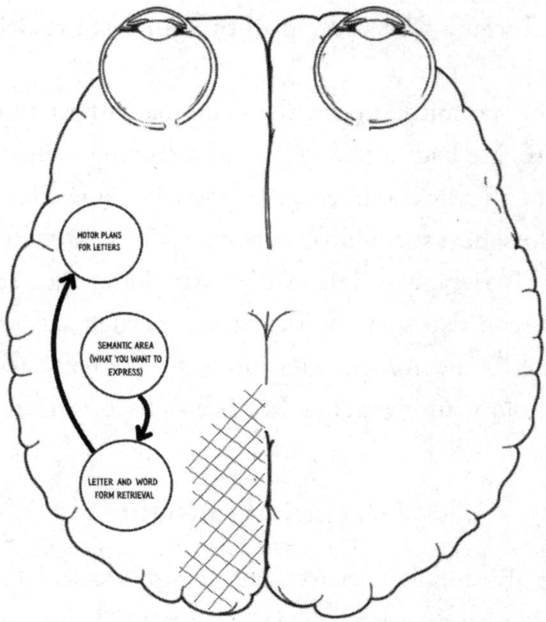

DESPITE BEING UNABLE TO READ, DENNIS WAS ABLE TO WRITE. THIS WAS BECAUSE THE MODULES NECESSARY FOR WRITING WERE UNAFFECTED BY THE STROKE (THOUGH HE WAS UNABLE TO READ HIS OWN WRITING).

reaching the visual word form area, and so it still looks like meaningless scribble.

Third, the inability to name colors (color dysnomia). Dennis couldn't name the colored papers I showed him. The reason why is closely related to why he couldn't read words. Even though his brain could "see" the colors with his intact right hemisphere, it couldn't send that information to the left side, where color names are stored.

It would be reasonable to assume that this meant that Dennis couldn't recognize colors anymore. And if there were one single dedicated region for handling all things related to colors, then that would be true.

But his performance on the color-matching test indicated otherwise. He had no trouble at all matching identical colors, indicating that he could recognize them just fine. He could perceive colors; he just couldn't name them. Why not? Because the part of his right hemisphere that was doing the recognizing couldn't send that signal to the part on the left side that stored the name. In neurological terminology, the color recognition and the color naming regions had been "disconnected."

Geschwind's Insight

In 1965, Boston University neurologist Norman Geschwind published a landmark two-part paper titled *Disconnexion Syndromes in Animals and Man*—a work that would become foundational to modern behavioral neurology. By the time of the paper's publication, the modular view of the brain had been widely embraced. But Geschwind thought the pendulum had swung too far in its direction.

In the paper, Geschwind synthesized decades of animal and clinical research to support the claim that the connections among brain modules were just as important to cognitive function as the modules themselves. Modules weren't operating in total isolation; they were part of larger networks.

One of the clinical cases that Geschwind used to support his argument was the "alexia without agraphia" syndrome we've just reviewed. The syndrome had been viewed as a curious edge case without broader significance, but Geschwind argued that it illustrated a fundamental organizing principle.

Cognitive functions were both localized and distributed, emerging from the integrated activity of multiple modules. Both the modules and their connections were critical to their execution, and deficits could just as easily arise from damage to the *connections* between modules as they could from damage to the modules themselves. You need the specialists and the phone lines.

The shift that he set in motion laid the groundwork for our contemporary understanding of a modular but highly networked brain. Furthermore, it highlighted the crucial role that the *flow of information* plays in cognition. Our cognition, our intelligence, is the result of an ongoing conversation among the brain's problem-solving specialists. And it showed that having a specialist network is functionally useless if it's not part of the cognitive conversation.

Controlling the Conversation

"Modular" and "distributed." This is the architecture of cognition. The Genius builds networks that solve the problems we care about. Those networks organize into functionally and anatomically discrete units. The fact that they can run autonomously and simultaneously enables our formidable intellectual abilities.

But they can only contribute if they can participate in the cognitive conversation. Think of it this way: A Spanish translation app on your smartphone does you no good if you can't paste text into it. A brain module for reading does you no good if you can't send visual input into it. The work of the Genius has

THE ARCHITECTURE OF INTELLIGENCE

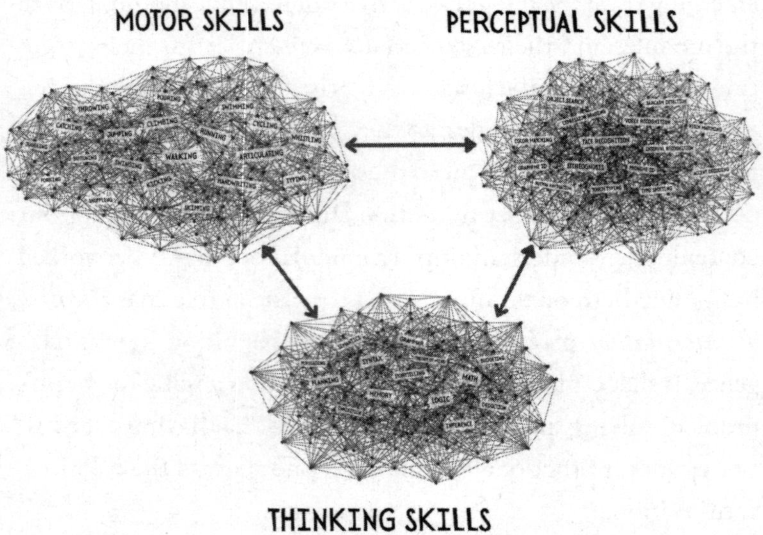

COGNITION IS BOTH MODULAR AND DISTRIBUTED, CONSISTING OF A VAST NETWORK OF SPECIALIZED MODULES.

YOUR SOLUTION SPACE AT ANY MOMENT IS DETERMINED BY THE SCAFFOLDING YOU'VE BUILT (YOUR SKILLS) AND THE CONNECTIVITY THAT ALLOWS THOSE MODULES TO PARTICIPATE IN THE COGNITIVE CONVERSATION.

no practical consequence if it's cut off from the cognitive conversation.

We've seen how this plays out when a module is physically cut off, when stroke or injury severs the connections, as in Dennis's case. But what about in healthy brains? In the absence of injury or disease, are all modules part of the conversation all the time? Or is the flow of information regulated? If so, how?

These questions matter, because whoever controls that conversation, whoever determines which modules get heard and which stay silent, wields tremendous power. Over your intelligence. Over what you can do. Over who you are.

Your solution space at any given moment is determined by the cognitive scaffolding you've built through learning *and* by which parts of that scaffolding can participate in the cognitive conversation. Having capabilities means nothing if they're disconnected from the conversation, as Dennis discovered. Understanding how that conversation gets controlled is the key to unlocking intelligence you didn't know you had.

chapter summary

- **The brain is both modular and distributed:** Cognitive functions are handled by specialist networks that must communicate, with intelligence emerging from their coordinated activity.
- **Modularity enables intelligence:** Multiple autonomous specialists running simultaneously scale our cognitive

abilities—why have one brain when you can have thousands?

- **Connections matter as much as modules:** Cognitive deficits can arise from damaged connections between modules, not just the modules themselves. You need the specialists and the phone lines.
- **Disconnection can hide capabilities:** Dennis could sort words despite not consciously reading them because his reading networks were cut off from the cognitive conversation. Having a capability means nothing if it can't participate.
- **The flow of information determines what you can do:** Your solution space depends on which parts of your scaffolding can communicate, not just what you've built. Understanding how the cognitive conversation gets controlled unlocks hidden intelligence.

8

a brain in flux

Do I contradict myself?
Very well then I contradict myself,
(I am large, I contain multitudes.)

—Walt Whitman (American poet, journalist, and essayist)

Ann was devastated. Her husband, Leonard, a fifty-three-year-old marketing executive, had been fired from his job six months prior for increasingly erratic and bizarre behavior.

"He's just a different person," she said at their first visit. "He won't sit still. He's always been pretty social, but now he talks to random strangers all the time. And he used to dress nice, but now he just grabs the first thing he sees. He doesn't bathe or brush his teeth unless I tell him to."

"Does he ever burst out crying for no reason?" I asked.

"Yes," she said. "He did that on the way over here. I asked him what was wrong and he said he didn't know. What does that mean?"

During this initial visit, Leonard leapt from the examination table multiple times, wandering around the room and eventually toward the door until Ann grabbed his wrist and gently guided him back.

When I asked Leonard a question, he'd often repeat what I said. "How are you today, Leonard?"

"You today, Leonard?" he would echo.

I pressed my index and middle finger into the palm of his hand, and he immediately gripped it tightly.

"Let go, Leonard, you're going to hurt him," Ann said.

"It's okay," I replied. "He doesn't mean to do it."

Leonard's MRI revealed atrophy in the frontal and temporal lobes, which fit with his history and examination findings. Leonard's personality changes and cognitive deficits were from frontotemporal dementia (FTD), a devastating neurodegenerative condition.

His impulsivity and cognitive problems would worsen. At his next visit, Ann reported that he was hoarding household items. "I can't find anything anymore. He takes tissues, pens, paper, clips, the mail, and just stuffs them into a drawer. He paces around the house, constantly repeating the same phrase, 'That's the way it is,' over and over again."

"I just don't understand how this is happening," Ann said. "He's not the man I married."

Ancient Circuitry

Every baby is born with a set of rudimentary reflexes and behaviors that are wired into the nervous system. Assessing these early reflexes and simple behaviors is one of the key elements of the neonatal neurological exam. Some of those reflexes are necessary for the survival of an infant, some are holdovers from our evolutionary past, while others may be an accidental byproduct of a nervous system that's yet to fully form.

A baby will reflexively suck on anything placed in its mouth, for example, a reflex that supports its ability to nurse. If you press a finger into a newborn's hand, it will grip it tightly.

Other primitive behaviors aren't present at birth but consistently wire themselves in during early childhood as the brain matures. Parents observe their children going through phases where certain behaviors will emerge and be repeated obsessively.

For example, many kids go through a hoarding phase where they become preoccupied with gathering certain things in one place. Sometimes they may even hide them from others, a hoarding instinct seen in many wild animals as a means of protecting hard-won resources. Some may go through a phase that looks like obsessive-compulsive disorder where they'll experience intrusive and repetitive thoughts, or engage in stereotyped behaviors like blinking, throat clearing, or the repetition of words or phrases.

Why exactly does it happen this way? If we have brain networks that no longer serve our needs, why not just erase them altogether?

Because evolution doesn't work that way. Evolution has to work off what it's got. We "evolve," we don't "build from scratch." We modify our form and physiology over time. When we need to adapt to a change in the environment, we don't invent new parts out of thin air. Instead, we retool the ones we have.

As a result, our bodies and our brains tell the story of our evolutionary past. Life began in the sea, for example, and we humans still show evidence of our aquatic past in the way our arms and legs are attached to our bodies. This is also how we've ended up with "vestigial" structures that have no function, like goose bumps and a tailbone—parts of us that were useful when we were different animals adapted to different habitats.

The same is true of our brain, with its history of millions of years of modification on top of modification to get to where it is now. This is precisely why all our intelligent behavior, as well as all intelligent behavior of every complex multicellular organism with a nervous system, is powered by the spiking of neurons.

You've likely heard reference to our "lizard brain" or "reptilian brain," referring to some of the oldest parts of our neural hardware. These ancient circuits have been with us for hundreds of millions of years and still control our most basic and vital functions. Since that time, our brain has undergone massive evolutionary changes, layering new neural circuits on top of the old ones at different points in our evolutionary history. Remarkably, when our individual brains develop, these same circuits still emerge in the same evolutionary sequence.

Some of those circuits may mediate behaviors that once served us well but are not so appropriate for us today. Things like hoarding, for example. Others, like the sucking reflex, are useful when we're breast-feeding infants, but not so much after that. So, if we don't want those behaviors rearing their heads and jeopardizing our ability to function in polite society, we must keep those circuits quiet.

Because once those circuits are wired in, they're ours for good. How do we know?

We know this because sometimes, often decades after they disappear, they return. We now recognize their re-emergence as a telltale sign of damage or degeneration in the frontal lobes.

That's because one of the jobs of the frontal lobes is to inhibit those brain networks and the ancient behaviors they produce. When something disrupts the function of the frontal lobes, those primitive circuits are "released" from their suppressive influence. We know these as the aforementioned release signs.

Leonard's hoarding, his echolalia (repeating what I said), and his grasp reflex weren't behaviors his damaged brain was creating. They were old behaviors his damaged brain could no longer suppress. Behaviors that had been humming quietly in the background his entire adult life, held in check by his frontal lobes.

Analog or Digital?

Frontal release signs aren't just a window into our developmental and evolutionary past. They're a window into a fundamental principle about the control of cognition.

Let's consider the problem the brain is trying to solve here. We have circuitry inside the brain that controls behaviors (as well as thoughts and emotions) that we no longer need. Behaviors that might undermine, rather than support, our brain's primary objective of keeping us alive. Circuits we can't just delete.

The simplest solution to that problem would be to simply never turn on those circuits. Just let them lie dormant. Here, the brain would operate like a switchboard, with each network turned on or off in a binary, all-or-nothing manner.

If that's the actual solution our brain used, however, then release signs wouldn't exist. If the circuit is off, then a lesion elsewhere in the brain would have no impact on those brain networks.

Release signs indicate that those ancient circuits are still active but being actively suppressed by another part of the brain—the part of the brain that, when damaged, leads to the released behavior. The technical term for this phenomenon is "disinhibition," meaning removal from inhibition. The fact that the area needs to be inhibited in the first place indicates that, to some extent, it is always active.

In this case, the brain is operating like a soundboard, with sliders that can adjust the "volume" of different networks. Our primitive reflexes and ancient behaviors are always humming quietly in the background, held in check by the inhibitory control of our more recently evolved regions. The line between our civilized and most primitive selves is far thinner than most think.

We see these release signs for evolutionarily conserved behaviors almost exclusively in the presence of lesions in the frontal lobe, as was true in Leonard's case. This is why they're also referred to as "frontal release signs."

This dynamic balance between activation and inhibition occurs at every scale of the nervous system, from brain-wide networks all the way down to individual neurons. A single brain cell tends to fire spontaneously unless it's actively inhibited. Stability doesn't come from silence, but from balance. And the reason we need frontal lobes with inhibitory control is that nothing in the brain is ever truly switched off.

Fortunately for us, this evolutionary constraint also turns out to be incredibly useful. An advantage of the sliding-scale approach is that it allows for much more nuanced control than a simple on/off switch would provide. By keeping older circuits intact and active, the brain ensures that critical behaviors can be deployed instantly if needed. In this way, the frontal lobes can orchestrate behavior by turning up or down the volume of different networks in the cognitive conversation, controlling who is heard and who stays silent. And it uses its powers of suppression to either lower (inhibition) or raise (disinhibition) the volume.

The frontal lobes also mediate our conscious attention. Attention is how we utilize the frontal lobes' influence to direct the cognitive conversation. When we attend to something, we enhance the influence of the circuits processing that information while suppressing others. In this way, we shape the modules that drive our thoughts, perceptions, or actions at any given time.

Far from behaving like a machine that flips neural circuits on or off to perform tasks, the brain operates as a dynamic and perpetually active system—countless neural circuits buzzing with background activity, competing to influence our thoughts, emotions, perceptions, and actions. Our behavior, and our entire conscious experience, is dictated by who's winning that battle, with the winners and losers decided by a mix of top-down controls and emergent self-organization. It's a teeming stew of activity, and we're only privy to the tiniest morsel of it.

A Case of Contradiction

"I can't get her out of the house. I know she needs the exercise, but she just wants to sit inside all day and look at the TV," said John. John was the husband of Barbara, a seventy-six-year-old woman who was in the early to middle stages of Alzheimer's disease.

I'd been seeing Barbara in my clinic for about two years. She'd initially come at the request of her primary care doctor, who'd noticed that she often repeated herself in conversation, suggesting a possible problem with her memory.

Indeed, her initial examination revealed cognitive decline well below what would be expected of a woman her age. Her short-term recall was especially poor. This is often one of the earliest signs of Alzheimer's, a reflection of the disease's predilection for the medial temporal lobes.

The medial temporal lobes and surrounding structures play a crucial role in encoding new memories. On the brain's dominant side (usually the left), these structures usually handle memories related to verbal aspects of experience. When this area deteriorates, people struggle to recall things they recently said or that were said to them. So they often repeat themselves and forget recent conversations.

The corresponding areas on the nondominant side (typically the right) process nonverbal memory elements like perceptual and spatial details. Damage here makes it difficult to remember where things are located or what they look like. Again, modules for everything.

Sometimes, both sides are impacted equally. Other times, one deteriorates first. For Barbara, her verbal-related memory was impaired initially, indicating that the left side was likely the first to deteriorate.

Loads of evidence now demonstrates that reduced physical activity increases the risk of age-related cognitive decline and Alzheimer's disease, and that exercise can improve cognitive function in those already affected. Given its importance, conversations during visits with my Alzheimer's patients always include the topic of physical activity.

Cruelly, those with Alzheimer's often lose the desire to move about precisely when moving about matters most. Barbara's sedentary inclinations had become a source of frustration for John.

"Do you like to go for walks?" I asked Barbara.

Her eyes widened with alarm. "Oh, no," she said gravely. "There are too many big dogs in our neighborhood. I don't like dogs. They scare me."

Stymied, I moved to another subject.

A few minutes later, as I began wrapping up the visit, I reviewed our conversation. "Okay, so you and John are going to try taking a short walk in the mornings," I reminded them.

"We never take walks anymore, do we, John?" she said.

"I know those dogs scare you, but John will be there to protect you," I replied reassuringly.

"Oh, they don't bother me. I love dogs," she responded cheerfully.

She had no recollection of expressing a fear of dogs just minutes earlier.

In both instances, Barbara was entirely sincere and authentic. In one moment, she was genuinely afraid of dogs. Minutes later, she genuinely loved them. But if Barbara wasn't lying, and I seriously doubted she was, what are we to make of her contradictory statements? Which statement was made by the "real" Barbara? Did the real Barbara love dogs, or was she deathly afraid of them?

Her statements are surprising because we think of ourselves as a stable collection of memories, beliefs, and preferences that are constant across time. We assume that who we are now is who we were yesterday, or even 5 minutes ago. Recent neuroscience, however, tells a very different story.

Nightly Insanity

Let's face it, sleep is super weird. One moment, you're lying in your bed, meticulously cataloging your personal shortcomings in a perfectly orderly and rational manner. The next, you're being chased by a rabid artichoke with a peg leg whose face looks like that kid with the mullet who once stepped on your broken toe in third-grade recess. And in that moment it all makes perfect sense. So much so that, just as the artichoke is sinking its fangs into your flesh, you wake in a cold sweat and thank your lucky stars it was just a dream. As if artichokes could actually catch rabies!

During sleep, we imagine things we would never see, hear, feel, or think in waking life. We believe the most absurd scenarios are truly happening without a shred of skepticism. It's as if our accumulated knowledge about the world and our entire autobiographical memories are inaccessible.

Once again, super weird! And baffling. We've grown used to this insanity because it happens every night. But that doesn't make it any less insane.

It's natural to think of sleep as just our brain powering down to recharge. But our dreaming life indicates that stuff is still happening in there, albeit a very peculiar kind of stuff. Our brain during sleep is obviously very different from our brain when we're awake. What's behind our nightly descent into madness?

The Subway Map

The transition into sleep is controlled by just a few key players in the brain. A couple of those key players help prepare us for sleep, while another player flips the switch once we are. It's a blend of bottom-up pressure from the body's accumulating need for rest and top-down signals that align us with the rhythms of day and night.

As you may have noticed, the longer you stay awake, the sleepier you get. This feeling is known as "sleep pressure," and is due in large part to a buildup of the chemical adenosine throughout your brain.

Scientists discovered the role of adenosine in sleep while investigating the effects of caffeine. Caffeine enhances our alertness, at least temporarily, by blocking the receptors for adenosine. If blocking adenosine's effects makes us feel less sleepy, then adenosine must be making us drowsy.

Sleep and wakefulness are also tightly regulated by two clusters of neurons, or nuclei, in the hypothalamus, the brain's master control center for homeostasis. One of those clusters, known as the suprachiasmatic nucleus (SCN), manages our twenty-four-hour biological cycles, or circadian rhythms. As the day progresses, the SCN releases melatonin, which suppresses arousal-promoting circuits while triggering metabolic shifts that prepare our body for sleep. Rather than initiating an abrupt shutdown, melatonin orchestrates a gentle dimming of our neural systems, gradually easing us toward sleep.

The second cluster, the ventrolateral preoptic nucleus (VLPO), functions more like a sleep switch. As VLPO activity steadily ramps up throughout the day, these neurons inhibit nearby brainstem neurons that keep us awake. Once that silencing crosses a critical threshold, bam—we're off to la-la land.

In sum, adenosine and melatonin prepare us for sleep, and the VLPO flips the switch. Once flipped, it changes the balance of activation and suppression across the cortex, producing entirely new patterns of activity and signal flow. Those patterns create a new routing architecture that dictates how information flows across the brain.

Imagine a subway system with a network of stations. In the daytime, one set of stations and tracks is open. This pattern of openings and closings is the subway's present routing architecture for travel, dictating how traffic can flow. That routing architecture influences the places you can visit and the people you come into contact with.

Now imagine that, when night falls, an entirely different set of stations and tracks opens and closes. This new routing architecture leads to other patterns of travel. Now you can visit people and places that were inaccessible in the prior routing architecture. This is what happens when our brain shifts between sleep and wakefulness, only the tracks are neural pathways, and the subway cars are neuronal impulses (or information).

These changes in routing architecture are in service of our goals in these different brain states. During wakefulness, part of the brain's job is to process and interpret sensory input, leading to widespread activity in the sensory cortices. During sleep, most of those signals are shut down, as the brain shifts its focus from the world outside to the world within.

Sleep has a purpose, which this changing pattern of activity reflects. Our brain needs time when it isn't busy processing the world around us to do other things, like repair and recover from its daytime brain activities. That's why incoming sensory traffic is shut down.

But there's much more than repair and recovery going on. Serious cognition is happening, too! Sleep gives our brain the

ROUTING ARCHITECTURE DETERMINES INFORMATION FLOW

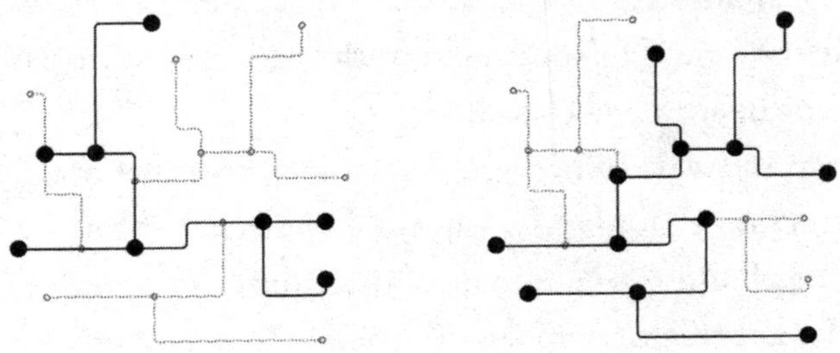

ROUTING ARCHITECTURE A

ROUTING ARCHITECTURE B

LIKE A SUBWAY SYSTEM, THE ROUTES THAT ARE OPEN (SOLID LINES) OR CLOSED (DASHED LINES) AT ANY GIVEN TIME IN A NETWORK DETERMINE ITS PRESENT ROUTING ARCHITECTURE, WHICH DETERMINES WHICH AREAS ARE ACCESSIBLE.

THE DESTINATIONS ("STATIONS") YOU CAN REACH IN ARCHITECTURE A, AS INDICATED BY THE LARGE DOTS, ARE DIFFERENT FROM THOSE YOU CAN REACH IN ARCHITECTURE B. THE ARCHITECTURE THUS DICTATES THE FLOW OF TRAFFIC.

distraction-free time and space it needs to think deeply, so it can integrate memories, reinforce learning, reorganize knowledge, and solve problems. As mentioned earlier, sleep is when we automate skills through the strengthening of our synaptic connections, based on our learning activities.

Let's stop and highlight the key features of the transition from wakefulness into sleep. First, it's a controlled process, one that's orchestrated by just a few conductors. In this case, those are the SCN, VLPO, and the chemical adenosine.

Second, once the transition occurs, there's a total shift in the brain's routing architecture, transforming how information flows across the brain. That shift comes from changes in the balance of activation and suppression in the brain's circuitry.

Third, that pattern of activity is reproducible across time. The routing architecture of sleep and the pattern of activity are largely the same from one night to the next. The same pathways are being opened and closed.

Sleep and wakefulness are thus two very distinct brain states, a distinction that aligns with our experience. When we go to sleep, our brain *toggles* into an entirely different mode of operation. It's a regulatory process designed for the most efficient allocation of our cognitive resources. Like a Transformer changing from a semitruck to a heavily armored robot, it's a total metamorphosis that unleashes an entirely new complex configuration and set of skills.

Unlike a Transformer, however, our brain has multiple forms, or modes, that it can toggle between. Using brainwave recordings (EEG), scientists have identified four unique stages of sleep: three stages of non-REM sleep and one stage of REM sleep. Each stage has its own unique pattern of activity, which is precisely what produces an identifiable electrical pattern.

For example, during stage 1, or light sleep, brainwaves begin to slow down, with bursts of gentle activity across a range of frequencies. By stage 3, often called deep sleep, the brain settles into a slow, steady rhythm, producing large, sweeping delta waves. Just like the shift between waking and sleep mode, these shifts are stereotyped and tightly controlled. The EEG patterns are the same each time, and the brain cycles through all stages roughly every 90 minutes. And just like the transition from wakefulness to sleep, the transition from one sleep stage to another serves a distinct purpose, enabled by distinct routing architectures.

So, if sleep has submodes, then what about our waking brain?

Are we in just one mode the whole time, or does it have submodes with their own distinct patterns of activity?

Surprisingly, there was hardly any research into that question until very recently. And even then, it happened almost by accident.

Our Default Mode

Ever since the localizationalist model of the brain took hold, there's been an ongoing project among cognitive neuroscientists to build an anatomical map of our cognitive modules. Initially, the only way we could build those maps was by studying the effects of brain lesions. When there's loss of function when an area is damaged by injury or disease, it's strong evidence that the area is involved in that particular function.

The development of functional imaging technologies (PET, SPECT, and fMRI) expanded our mapping capabilities. These technologies work by detecting changes in blood flow in the brain, which functions as a surrogate for energy demands. The more active a brain area is, the more energy it consumes.

These mapping studies usually involve having a subject lie inside the scanner while performing a particular task. But since all living brain tissue is metabolically active to some degree all the time, you need to also know the amount of activity across the brain when it's *not* performing the task. That way you can subtract the activity in the brain at rest from the activity while performing the task to find the areas where there was an increase.

Early on in this research, it was assumed that the blood flowing around the brain at rest was just supporting basic metabolic needs. In the same way that a muscle that you aren't using still needs blood flow to stay alive, so do the cells of an inactive but living brain. Any additional activity beyond that would be random and idiosyncratic.

But around the turn of the twenty-first century, about a decade and a half after this area of research had begun, scientists at Washington University noticed something peculiar about the "resting" brain. When the brain was not performing a specific task, there was an *increase* in activity in particular areas of the brain. As soon as subjects performed the task, however, that activity quieted down.

Furthermore, the pattern of increased activity was consistent across individuals. In the resting brain from one subject to the next, there was an increase in activity in the same areas: the medial prefrontal cortex, posterior cingulate, and the inferior parietal lobule. Counterintuitively, certain areas were more active in a brain that was thought to be doing nothing. This resting pattern had been there all along, in study after study. But nobody had noticed it before.

The authors described that pattern as "an organized, baseline default mode of brain function that is suspended during specific goal-directed behaviors," and named it the Default Mode Network (DMN). As in it's the "default" mode of the brain when it's just chilling. Subsequent studies have shown that the default mode is active when we're doing things like daydreaming, recalling autobiographical memories, imagining the future, or thinking about other people's thoughts and feelings.

What do these activities have in common? They're all instances where we aren't focused on external stimuli. Instances where our attention is directed inward.

The discovery of the DMN showed that submodes of activity aren't just a feature of sleep; they're a feature of the waking brain, too. And just as we do when we sleep, when we're in the "default" mode, we're no longer consciously attending to the outside world.

But what about our brain when it's not in the default mode? In the experiments where the default mode was first observed, subjects were toggling between focusing on the task and resting. It stands to reason, then, that if there's a rest mode, there's probably a task mode with its own signature of activity, too.

Indeed, not long after the DMN was first described, researchers also dubbed its counterpart, the Task-Positive Network (TPN). It's the submode we're in anytime we're focused on tasks that are attentionally demanding, including those that are novel or complex. When you're learning to drive, for example, the TPN is active. Once you've learned to the point of automation, however, it shuts off.

The TPN has its own distinct pattern, characterized by activity in the prefrontal cortex, intraparietal sulcus, and frontal eye fields—regions that had long been associated with attention, working memory, and goal-directed behavior. Activity in this network is "anticorrelated" with activity in the DMN, meaning that if the DMN is on, then the TPN is suppressed, and vice versa. They are mutually exclusive.

In sum, while we're awake, the brain has a resting mode, and it has a get-to-work mode with distinct, non-overlapping routing architectures.

Importantly, when we toggle in and out of the default mode, we don't stop processing the outside world. We still perceive. We still move. We can still do things like walk, drive our car to work, or wash the dishes. We can perform automated tasks to our heart's content. The critical distinction here is where our spotlight of attention is focused. If it's focused externally, then the default mode powers down. If it isn't, it boots back up again.

Eureka!

Now, if different modes and submodes have distinct, unique routing architectures, how will that impact our solution space in those states? It will change. With its own unique set of modules and patterns of activity, each mode should have a unique solution space. This means that there would only be certain problems that could be solved in certain modes. So, is that a thing?

Is it ever!

Perhaps you've heard of people making breakthrough discoveries during their sleep? Of course you have! Stories of "solutions" emerging during sleep are legion. Otherwise, "it came to me in a dream" wouldn't be such a familiar expression. For example, some of the most significant breakthroughs in the history of science came to sleeping minds.

One legendary example of a sleep-related breakthrough is Dmitri Mendeleev's "discovery" of the periodic table of the elements. Born in 1834 in a small Siberian town near Tobolsk, Mendeleev studied chemistry in Saint Petersburg and went on to teach at its university. Early in his career, more than sixty chemical elements had been identified, but how they all fit together remained a puzzle. Solving that puzzle became Mendeleev's central obsession.

Mendeleev knew deep in his bones that there was an organizing framework for how the elements were related, but he couldn't pin down what that was. According to neurologist Oliver Sacks, during long train rides between Saint Petersburg and Tobolsk, Mendeleev would play "chemical solitaire" in hopes of unlocking that framework. In this game, he would write each element on a card, along with other known features like its atomic weight and reactivity. The object of the game was to find an arrangement where similar elements lined up in a repeating pattern. But ride after ride, year after year, that pattern eluded him.

Until one day, after obsessing over the problem for days on end, he fell asleep at his desk, then, in a dream, the solution came to him. "I saw a table where all the elements fell into place as required. Awakening, I immediately wrote it down on a piece of paper." One of science's greatest mysteries—the table that provided the underlying code for our material universe—had been solved inside a single sleeping mind.

For over a decade, Mendeleev had been feeding the Genius, building cognitive scaffolding in chemistry through relentless curiosity-driven learning: scaffolding that could identify patterns in elemental properties and relationships between atomic weights and chemical behaviors.

The Genius had built the scaffolding that could unlock the secret for how it all fit together, but the cognitive conversation of wakefulness couldn't find it. To arrive at the solution, he didn't need to acquire more knowledge; he needed to connect the knowledge he already had in a new way. And the routing architecture of sleep allowed his brain to make those connections. Same scaffolding, different conversation, breakthrough solution.

Of course, Mendeleev's epiphany is far from the only noteworthy example. Other famous sleep-inspired breakthroughs include the structure of benzene (Kekulé), the melody for "Yesterday"

(McCartney), the guitar riff in "Satisfaction" (Richards), the model of the atom (Bohr), and the plots of *Frankenstein* (Shelley) and *The Strange Case of Dr. Jekyll and Mr. Hyde* (Stevenson). And a great many more.

And now experimental evidence confirming unique problem-solving abilities emerging during sleep also exists. In a landmark 2004 study published in *Nature*, participants were given a puzzle in which they had to convert an eight-digit number into a single number according to a series of rules they were given. Completing the conversion required a repetitive chain of steps.

What the researchers did not tell the participants was that there was a hidden shortcut to completing the puzzle, in that the second digit of the original sequence always predicted the final answer. If you spotted that hidden rule, then you could skip straight from the eight-digit number to the solution.

Sixty-six volunteers were trained on the task and tested on the task again eight hours later. Subjects were split into three groups according to how they spent that eight-hour interval: one group stayed awake all day, one stayed awake all night, and one slept.

What did they find? The subjects who slept were more than twice as likely to have discovered the hidden rule than the subjects who didn't. The sleeping brain was much better at solving this problem than the awake brain.

Other research has demonstrated similar findings, altogether indicating that sleep "enhances the integration of unassociated information for creative problem solving." In other words, the routing architectures of sleep allow for cognitive conversations that don't happen during wakefulness.

We are fascinated by the stories of sleep-inspired breakthroughs because they seem extraordinary. How on earth could our mind do something so smart while it's busy scaring itself to death with visions of rabid artichokes?

These stories are often presented as examples of the power of the subconscious mind, which is valid. But the implication is that most problems are solved by the conscious mind, which is not true.

As we've reviewed, our conscious mind may help direct the flow of neural traffic, but it is not the seat of our intelligence. It may assign problems to other parts of the brain, but it doesn't do the actual solving.

So, problems are solved in the circuits of our nonconscious modules, regardless of whether we're awake or asleep. What dream-related breakthroughs instead reveal is that routing architectures reshape our solution space.

What about during different modes of wakefulness? Are there solutions that only happen when a brain is in default mode?

Well, let me ask you: Have you ever had a great idea come to you in the shower? Or while taking a long walk? Ever had a word or a song title or a person's name that you couldn't conjure, and then have it appear later on, when you're not even trying to remember it?

Once again, we find these episodes surprising. How can it be that we can't find the answer when we're trying our hardest to do so, only to have it surface when we're not trying at all? Or how can a brain present us with a brilliant idea out of the blue?

You already know the answer. It's not that you stumbled onto the solution despite not trying; it's that you found it *because* you weren't trying. By stepping back, you let your brain toggle into a mode that has connections and associations your "on-task" mind can't reach. As with dream-related insights, these moments feel like magic only because we overestimate the role of conscious effort in problem solving.

The unique problem-solving abilities of a brain in default mode have also been demonstrated experimentally. In one study, participants were given a set of tricky word problems that required finding a word that could be combined with each of three given words to make a common phrase—the sorts of problems where you know you just have to sit and wait for the answer to appear in your mind.

After working on the first half of the problems, participants either jumped straight into another mentally demanding task (which kept their attention locked in "on-task" mode) or were given a break where they could rest quietly with no specific mental demands.

When they returned to tackle the second half of the problems, those in the quiet, mind-wandering condition solved significantly more of the remaining problems. And it wasn't because they had been consciously thinking about them during the break, as most reported they hadn't. Rather, it was the very act of *not* thinking about it that enabled their brain to arrive at the solution.

Other experiments have found the same pattern across a variety of "creative insight" tasks. In problems where the solution requires restructuring how the problem is framed or pulling together ideas from seemingly unrelated domains, participants who first spent time in a low-demand, daydream-friendly activity (like a simple shape-tracing task) were more likely to experience the sudden aha moment than those who stayed in a focused, analytical state.

These findings suggest that the Default Mode Network isn't just idle background noise. Rather, its distinctive architecture enables cognitive conversations that otherwise wouldn't take place, allowing the brain to arrive at solutions that no amount of brow-furrowing, white-knuckled effort could ever find.

And let's not forget the transitional states between sleep and wakefulness, referred to as hypnagogia and hypnopompia, respectively, which many creatives have long recognized as particularly fertile states for inspiration. For example, Salvador Dalí famously exploited this phenomenon by holding a handful of coins while drifting off to sleep in a chair. The moment he fell asleep, the coins would slip from his relaxed grip and crash to the floor, jolting him awake. He would then immediately sketch the vivid images and ideas that had been forming in his mind before they slipped away.

Genius at Rest

By today's productivity-obsessed standards, the daily routines of many of history's greatest scientists, artists, musicians, and creators would appear to be the definition of laziness and sloth. Afternoon naps, weeks-long vacations, leisurely strolls through the park, hours spent in cafés, morning swims, extended lunches with friends, and long baths are commonplace. For many, only a relatively small proportion of time each day—perhaps two to four hours—was spent doing actual "work," meaning the sort of thing that generates a tangible work product.

Einstein was famous for his regular long walks in the woods around Princeton University. Charles Darwin, whose insights laid the groundwork for all modern biology, spent only a few focused hours each morning at his desk, then spent the rest of his day walking his gravel "thinking path," napping, or reading novels. Winston Churchill famously took afternoon naps, dictated from bed, and maintained a schedule filled with long baths, cigars, and champagne. Ludwig van Beethoven began each day with a slow cup of coffee he painstakingly prepared with exactly sixty beans, then walked for hours in nature, where ideas for his compositions would often come to him. Agatha Christie, who wrote sixty-six novels, fourteen short-story collections, and the world's longest-running play, often crafted her pieces while washing dishes or daydreaming in the bath. Virginia Woolf, who authored ten novels and volumes of essays and diaries that helped reshape modern literature, spent her afternoons walking or gardening.

Their works of greatness didn't emerge in spite of their idleness or unconventional work ethic. They emerged because of it. What looks like goofing off to some looked like mode shifting to them. Mode shifting that enabled the routing architectures that were capable of unlocking their breakthrough ideas. They were toggling between brain states to access solutions that a brain in focused mode could never find.

Explicitly or implicitly, they realized that the intelligent bits of our brain are still solving problems even when our attention is directed elsewhere. And they realized that certain breakthroughs can only emerge when we're not trying to make them happen.

Far before we had the neuroscience to explain it, they recognized the importance of mode shifting to creativity and problem solving. As philosopher Friedrich Nietzsche famously wrote in 1889, "All truly great thoughts are conceived by walking."

The productivity myth persists because the Impostor is obsessed with appearances and genuinely believes he's the source of our intelligence. He's the reason we still believe that our best work and ideas come from sitting at a desk and thinking really hard. And, honestly, he only really cares about us *looking* productive. For someone whose entire existence depends on managing how others perceive us, time spent not producing feels like time wasted.

These days, we commonly think of rest as a passive state of inactivity with no productive value. We define it by the absence of work. To the productivity gurus, rest is just a necessary evil so we can recharge our productivity engine.

That critical and costly oversight is a reflection of our ignorance around the role of our conscious attention and the importance of mode shifting. And so we dismiss the leisure activities that have unlocked many of humanity's greatest insights as indulgent distractions, signs of laziness, or time wasted.

People have long recognized that psychoactive drugs are a shortcut to rapid mode shifting, activating the novel routing architectures that enable thoughts and behaviors that are otherwise inaccessible. A few drinks can transform a lifelong introvert into an extrovert. Stimulants can turn chaotic thoughts into hyperfocus. Psychedelics can break down the rigid categories that normally organize our thinking. It's no surprise, then, that many creators have turned to these substances to unlock creative breakthroughs, often struggling with dependency as a result.

You Contain Multitudes

As we've discussed, learning is how we create intelligence. It's what builds the software that defines our solution space. But only a portion of that space is available to us at any given time.

Mendeleev spent more than a decade obsessing and learning about the elements. That intellectual labor was necessary to construct the conceptual scaffolding that would bring the periodic table into his brain's solution space. That labor was necessary, but not sufficient.

At least not while he was awake. It took the routing architecture of sleep mode, and the cross-modular cognitive conversation it enabled, for his brain to envision the periodic table.

The crucial point here is that the flow of information in our brain is always changing. That flow is determined by the routing architecture of the mode our brain is in, which determines what we're capable of in that moment.

While scientists have identified several discrete modes during sleep and wakefulness, it's likely that a great many more exist. Our technology for studying live brain activity, while leaps and bounds ahead of what we had a half century ago, is still quite crude. As our ability to monitor brain activity at finer detail improves, many more modes will almost surely emerge.

We all recognize that context can profoundly change behavior. Think of a professional athlete on and off the court, a surgeon in the operating room or at home with her young children, a performer on and off the stage. The difference can be so dramatic that it's hard to believe it's the same person. But in a very real sense, it isn't. If we could view their brain's activity in these

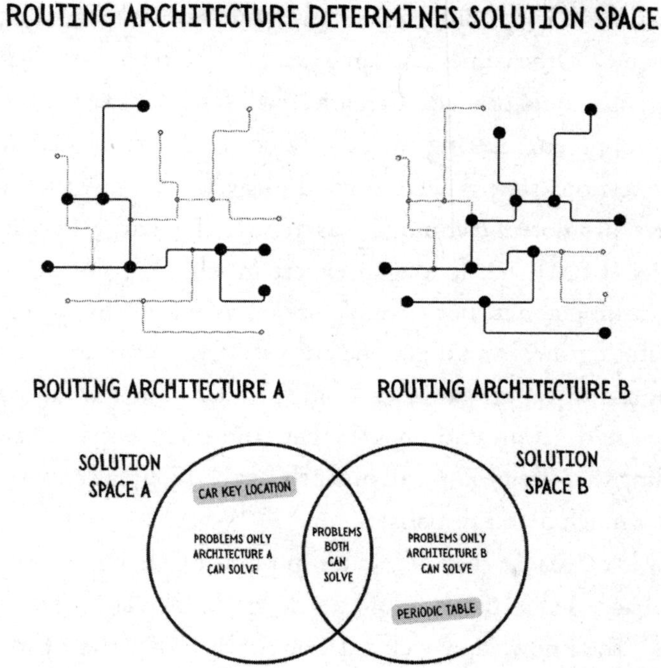

EACH ROUTING ARCHITECTURE PRODUCES A UNIQUE SOLUTION SPACE, BASED ON THE AREAS THAT ARE INVOLVED IN THE COGNITIVE CONVERSATION.

AS SUCH, THE BRAIN CAN ARRIVE AT CERTAIN SOLUTIONS IN ONE SOLUTION SPACE BUT NOT ANOTHER. FOR EXAMPLE, THE "PERIODIC TABLE" WAS PART OF MENDELEEV'S SLEEPING ROUTING ARCHITECTURE, BUT NOT HIS WAKING ONE.

different contexts, we would surely find very different routing architectures, with different sets of modules participating in the cognitive conversation.

Shortly after the release of ChatGPT in 2022, users began to notice that subtle differences in how a question was phrased could significantly impact the quality of the responses it generated.

Sometimes the variability was simply due to misunderstanding or ambiguity. Other times, the same exact question phrased slightly differently could produce dramatically different answers.

"Prompt engineering" was the name given to the art of crafting questions that generated good answers. Perhaps the most widely promoted technique was to tell the Large Language Model (LLM) that it was an expert in whatever domain you were asking about. For example, if you asked, "Why won't my tomatoes grow?" you'd get one answer. If you were to first say, "You are an expert gardener," and then ask your tomato question, you'd get an entirely different, and often better, answer. Adding that to a prompt, all other things being equal, could produce a much better response.

Why? Because that difference in phrasing changed how the LLM accessed its database of knowledge, known as its "training data." The knowledge itself is static. It's not that the LLM expanded its knowledge or became more intelligent in the space between prompts. It was the same exact piece of software. But the differences in the prompts altered how it accessed that knowledge, or the route it took through its database. The simple tweak of asking it to act as an expert triggered a mode shift in the LLM's "brain." In some instances, this kind of change in prompt can even generate contradictory responses.

The route we take through our own database of knowledge also influences our thoughts and behaviors. When Barbara gave me two contradictory answers about her feelings toward dogs, I could've assumed she was being deliberately deceptive. If I were under the impression that she was a single unified "self" with one single mode of operation, then that would've been the most logical conclusion.

But she isn't a single unified self. Neither am I. And neither are you. We aren't stable, unchanging beings throughout each day. We are ever-changing entities, toggling between different modes throughout the day, each with their own set of behaviors and capabilities, triggered by both internal and external stimuli. Sleep and wakefulness are the most extreme and familiar versions, but only the tip of a very large iceberg.

My first question to Barbara took one route through her brain, possibly activating a memory of an unpleasant canine encounter. The second time the topic arose, it took another, triggering only positive interactions and feelings. Her difficulty forming verbal memories prevented her from recognizing the contradiction in her statements.

So much of what we can think, do, solve, or say in a given moment has less to do with what's in our brain than with how it's operating at that moment. The modules don't change. The memories don't change. What changes is which ones are talking to each other, and which ones are sitting quietly on mute. Different brain modes, by virtue of their unique routing architectures, determine what kind of mind we have access to. That's why the same brain can fail to find the answer in a frenzy of effort, only to deliver it midtoothbrushing. Different modes aren't better or worse; they just have access to unique solution spaces. Mendeleev's periodic table didn't emerge because his sleeping brain was smarter than his waking one, but because sleep mode enabled the routing architecture that could find the answer.

Organized Chaos

It feels to us as if we are a stable, unchanging entity throughout the day. A single unified self with a predictable set of needs, beliefs, and capabilities. But the science paints a very different picture. From wakefulness to sleep and everything in between, our brain is always in flux. The result of a shifting balance of activation and suppression that determines, moment by moment, who has access to the cognitive conversation.

We've seen how certain parts of the brain exert powerful influence over that conversation. Networks deep in the brain toggle us into sleep mode, radically reorganizing which networks can communicate. Networks in the frontal lobes conduct the waking conversation, including the ability to silence entire areas for decades. In Leonard's case, suppressing those ancient networks was to our benefit. They would've been a disruptive force in the cognitive conversation.

But this dynamic reorganization isn't just happening between major states like sleep and wakefulness. It's happening continuously throughout your waking life. Different contexts, different emotional states, different modes of attention—each creates a different routing architecture. Each determines which specialists can participate and what conversations can happen between them.

What we are capable of at any given moment isn't just what our modules can do individually; it's what they are capable of together. A team of specialists working as a unit becomes much more than the sum of its parts. But only if they're allowed to communicate. And only if the right configurations can form.

Throughout this book, we've been building a case for your capacity for lifelong learning. For the Genius's ability to continue building new capabilities, expanding your solution space, scaling your intelligence. It's a capacity that is real and extraordinary.

But the dynamic state of the cognitive conversation adds a new wrinkle. How much of unleashing your potential is about building new capabilities through learning, and how much is about accessing capabilities that already exist?

If your brain is constantly shifting between different routing architectures, hiding some networks while revealing others, then at any given moment you're only accessing a fraction of what you've built. Which raises a tantalizing question: How much intelligence is sitting in networks that are never invited into the conversation? How much of what you're capable of right now—today, this moment—is functionally invisible to you simply because the current routing architecture hasn't given it access? Just how large a role is the cognitive conversation playing in what you're capable of, and what might you stand to gain by deliberately shaping it?

chapter summary

- **The brain is never truly "off":** Neural circuits operate on a sliding scale of activation and suppression, always active. Stability comes from balance, not silence.
- **Routing architectures determine what you can do:** Activation and suppression patterns determine how information flows, with different modes creating different routing architectures and solution spaces.

- **Sleep and wakefulness are distinct operating modes:** Sleep isn't the brain powering down but toggling to a different configuration with its own routing architecture optimized for memory consolidation and problem solving.

- **The waking brain has submodes, too:** The Default Mode Network activates during inward attention; the Task-Positive Network, during focused work. They're mutually exclusive—when one is on, the other is suppressed.

- **Breakthroughs often require mode shifts:** Rest and mind-wandering unlock solutions that focused effort cannot reach because rest's routing architecture enables different cognitive conversations.

9

hidden genius

To see is to forget the name of the thing one sees.

—Paul Valéry (poet and philosopher)

James was a sixty-three-year-old right-handed gentleman with no history of any medical problems or brain injury. At the request of his wife, Debbie, he'd come for an evaluation of his memory.

"He's been forgetting his words," she said. "Or sometimes he'll just use the wrong one."

James's neurological examination confirmed her observations. While James could name everyday objects, when presented with pictures of less common items like a cactus or a canoe, he struggled to find the word. His comprehension of spoken language, however, was unaffected. He could easily follow multistep commands. The pattern was altogether consistent with Broca's aphasia, indicating pathology of some kind in the left frontal lobe.

An MRI showed no sign of stroke or tumor but revealed an

enlargement of the cortical sulci in the left anterior temporal lobe. The cerebral cortex is heavily folded, and the sulci are the grooves or valleys between the folds of brain tissue. An increase in the size of these spaces indicates loss of brain tissue in that region.

Taken together, his clinical findings were consistent with the early stages of frontotemporal dementia. More specifically, the semantic variant. As discussed in an earlier chapter, frontotemporal dementia is a neurodegenerative condition that often leads to profound personality changes, impulsivity, and obsessive behaviors.

"Has he been doing anything else out of character?" I asked.

"Yes, he draws all the time," she said.

"Ah, so that's not typical for him?" I asked.

"No, he's a car salesman!" she said, chuckling.

"And so art was not even a hobby?" I asked.

"Ha, not a bit," she said. "He wouldn't draw anything even if you asked him to. He was too embarrassed."

"I see," I replied.

"But what's so odd is that these drawings are so good. They're so realistic," she said. "I brought a few for you to see."

Debbie pulled a few of his drawings out of her purse and showed them to me. She was right. These had the look of a seasoned artist. They were mostly realistic and highly detailed drawings of household items or landscapes.

"You're right, these are quite good," I said.

"His other doctor told me he might have dementia, but how could that be?"

How indeed. Here was a man losing his ability to name objects, struggling to find words, showing clear signs of cognitive decline. And simultaneously gaining artistic abilities he'd never possessed. No formal instruction. No years of training and struggle. A brain paradoxically gaining in function because of loss.

The Savant Syndrome

The movie *Rain Man* came out in 1988. I was thirteen years old. The character referenced in the title is Raymond, an autistic savant living in a residential care facility. It's a wonderful film that hits all the right notes. Great story, great writing, great acting. But I was especially fascinated with Raymond's character. As were many others who saw the film.

Raymond could perform mental feats I'd have previously thought impossible. He could do complex calculations faster than a calculator, memorize entire phone books, and count blackjack cards with perfect accuracy. He seemed to have perfect memory for every single day of his life.

Yet he was also severely limited in other ways. He couldn't understand social cues, struggled with any change to his routine, and had difficulty with basic life skills. So much so that he couldn't live safely on his own and was confined to an institution where his days followed the same rigid schedule.

What made Raymond's character especially interesting was that he was based on an actual person, which meant that there really was someone who could perform these sorts of mental feats, and who also had the same limitations. And he wasn't the only one.

For me and I think many others at the time, this was our first exposure to a savant. Savant syndrome is a rare condition in which someone with a developmental disorder displays areas of exceptional abilities in a particular area.

Intriguingly, while the specific abilities vary from one individual to the next, the range of possible savant talents is remarkably narrow. Calendar calculation, pitch-perfect musical performance, intricate visual art, lightning-fast arithmetic, mechanical design, and extraordinary memory represent virtually the entire catalog. Each savant has their own unique peak, but those peaks cluster in the same few cognitive domains.

Like Raymond, nearly all individuals with savant syndrome also have marked cognitive impairments. The nature of these deficits is as consistent as the abilities themselves, typically manifesting as profound difficulties with language and social interaction. Someone might sketch an entire cityscape from memory yet struggle to distinguish between the face of anger and joy.

It was the apparent contradiction of extraordinary ability paired with severe limitations that made Raymond's character seem so impossible. How could all this occur inside a single mind? I couldn't make sense of it.

At the time, many assumed savants must have special brain structures. That's what the Special Brain Story would say, of course. In addition to dysfunction in certain areas of the brain, savants must also possess unique and innate neural hardware that enables their remarkable abilities. Something *added* to their brain that wasn't present in most brains.

But there's another class of savants that points to a very different explanation.

Paradoxical Gains

Occasionally, savant-like talents don't emerge until later in life. When they do, it's been exclusively observed in the setting of deterioration, insult, or injury.

James is a textbook example. He was suffering from a neurodegenerative disease, frontotemporal dementia, that was causing deterioration in specific parts of his brain. That deterioration was causing profound loss in multiple areas of cognition and behavior. Yet simultaneously, he was experiencing a profound *gain* in artistic ability. A loss of function and a gain of function occurring at the same time.

While not common, many cases of extraordinary abilities emerging after trauma or disease have been recorded over the years. The condition is known as "acquired savant syndrome." The noted individuals weren't born with savant abilities but "acquired" them at some point.

The kinds of abilities seen in acquired savant syndrome are more or less identical to those seen in the congenital form: calendar calculation, artistic ability, mathematical prowess, musical talent, and prodigious memory.

Like the far-fetched cliché of someone gaining superpowers after a blow to the head, these cases strain believability even more than congenital savant syndrome. They're even more inconceivable because there's no way the gain could've arisen from new hardware or software. The loss clearly caused the gain. It's another phenomenon that can't be reconciled with the Special Brain Story.

But even more revealing than the abilities that emerge is the pattern of abilities that are lost.

When savant abilities emerge later in life, the damage is remarkably consistent in location. When it's caused by frontotemporal dementia, it occurs in the "semantic" variant, a subset characterized by profound language deficits. Likewise, in cases that have occurred after stroke, tumors, or head trauma, the offending pathology is in the language cortex in the dominant hemisphere. In other words, when savant-like abilities are gained, they are consistently accompanied by a loss of function in symbolic cognition.

Acquired savant syndrome may not be compatible with the Special Brain Story, but it's easy to explain with the model we've constructed. One where our capabilities aren't just a function of the modules we possess, but also of the conversations they're allowed to have. We've seen this exact sort of thing before with the frontal release signs we encountered in the last chapter, where long-dormant behaviors emerged when their controlling networks were released from suppression. The networks were always there; they'd just been silenced.

Likewise, the networks responsible for James's artistic ability weren't created by his dementia. They were always there, held in check by the symbolic processing networks that were now deteriorating. When those networks could no longer maintain their suppressive influence, the artistic ones gained access to the cognitive conversation so they could now influence James's thoughts and behaviors.

There's reason to believe these abilities are lying dormant in every brain. If true, why might our brain suppress those networks by default? Once again, it may boil down to a matter of efficiency.

The Rise of Symbols

When we're born, before we've trained our sensory cortices, everything is raw perception. A borderless, unfiltered experience of pure sensation.

As we've discussed, one of our brain's early missions is to learn how to turn those raw perceptions into something meaningful. Through the mechanisms of learning, it must create the networks to decode that sensory data and distinguish a rock from a tree, Mom from Dad, edible from nonedible, Ernie from Bert.

But this learning process occurred in stages, layer by layer. In the visual system, for example, our brain first constructed networks to recognize fundamental elements like edges, contrast, and movement, then gradually built up to identify shapes, patterns, and spatial relationships, before finally developing the ability to recognize complete objects, faces, and scenes. Until, ultimately, we built a catalog of objects we could identify by their various features (appearance, sound, feel, smell, etc.).

Initially, we didn't have names for those things. Before we started using symbols, the perception was the thing. We'd yet to create things that stood for other things, like the sound of the word "tree" to refer to the collective perceptual features of a tree. Our experience of the world was initially "preverbal." We experienced the world more directly, and the processes that enabled us to understand these perceptions we can refer to as "direct cognition."

Developing the perceptual skills needed to accomplish this kind of analysis of our sensory data was an extraordinary feat on its own, as Moravec's Paradox illustrated. It's a feat performed by all animals with a brain.

Unlike other animals, the human brain takes things a step further when we learn to talk. We begin our project of learning the sounds, or sonic symbols, that stand for objects out in the world. We attach our perceptions to those symbols. And we learn how to connect those sounds using the rules of our symbolic system, so that we can share our stories and ideas. In other words, we begin constructing our modules for symbolic cognition. Once we enter school, those symbolic circuits go into overdrive as we develop our skills for reading, writing, and math (and, for some, computer coding).

As we've discussed, symbolic cognition is the distinguishing feature of the human mind and is why we're the only species to have created advanced civilizations, invented toasters, and come to blows over the Oxford comma. It's easy to see why we've tried to milk symbolic cognition for all its worth in our educational system.

Eventually, the symbolic layer sits atop our hierarchy of perception, shaping how we see the world. Which is why, as adults, we can't help but perceive the world in symbols. Look around the room you're in, and you're sure to automatically identify the objects you see by their sonic symbols, aka the words we use for them. In my case, it's computer, table, painting, man, woman, barista, etc.

Ask the "average" adult to draw a picture of a house, and they'll typically draw the symbol for a house—a square with a triangle on top, with perhaps a rectangular door and a couple of square windows. It's not what a house actually looks like, but it's enough to represent the concepts of one.

This transition from a direct to a symbolic perceptual experience begins quite early, in tandem with language development.

By around age three or four, most children begin to use simple graphic symbols in their drawings. Mommy and Daddy are stick figures, the sun is a circle with radiating lines, and houses are squares with triangles above. These drawings are a window into a mind that's building the symbolic layer of categories on top of direct perceptions.

Again, this is a feature and not a bug. It's not a brain being bad at art but one learning to get good at symbols. The adaptation that enabled symbolic cognition is arguably the greatest survival advantage in the history of evolution.

For example, one of the many benefits of using symbols is that it saves loads of storage space, since symbols are often highly simplified versions of the thing they represent. Imagine a picture of a boy standing on the edge of a cliff overlooking the ocean. To store that image at the resolution of our visual system (500 megapixels) would take roughly 1.5 billion bytes of memory. Storing the sentence "The boy is standing on the edge of a cliff overlooking the ocean" as a text file requires about 50 bytes of memory. In other words, storing the symbol uses over 25 million times less memory. When the gist is all we need, storing and processing information at the symbolic level is massively more efficient. It's the smart thing to do.

Our hierarchy of perception dictates our mental experience of the world. By the time anything hits our conscious awareness, the movie in our mind, it has been through many rounds of processing and filtering. The nonconscious networks that perform all the heavy lifting present our conscious mind with the version they presumably deem most useful. For most of us most of the time, that version is a generalization, with the details smoothed over. A tree is a tree is a tree. A dog is a dog is a dog. No need to waste bandwidth once we've gotten the gist of the thing if the gist is what's most useful. Provide the necessary amount of detail, and no more.

Again, you can prove this to yourself right now. When looking at this text, you don't see it for what it is, a random series of straight and curved lines. You see words, or symbols. You can't not see it that way, because the processing that occurs beneath the symbolic layer is hidden.

The networks for symbolic and direct cognition are housed in different parts of the brain. In most people, it's mostly the left hemisphere for the former, and the right hemisphere for the latter. Neurologists refer to the hemisphere that handles language as the "dominant" hemisphere, a term that reflects its primacy in the signal pathway.

But what happens if the symbolic layer fails to develop or is damaged? It no longer sits atop the processing hierarchy. Those higher-resolution sensory perceptions gain access to conscious experience. We can now experience all the rich details of a visual scene or of a piece of music more directly. In Raymond's case, the symbolic layer never rose to prominence in the cognitive hierarchy. In James's case, those high-resolution details had been there all along; they'd just been cut off from his conscious experience.

Bypassing the Filter

In her book *Drawing on the Right Side of the Brain*, author and artist Betty Edwards contends that the reason people struggle to create realistic drawings isn't a problem of motor skill; it's a problem of perception. Most of us draw in symbols because we perceive in symbols. The symbolic layer dominates and obfuscates. Drawing the world as it truly is requires that we perceive it as it truly is, without interference.

The methods she uses are thus designed to help people perceive the world more directly. How? By using techniques that temporarily quiet the symbolic layer.

For example, one effective strategy is simply to turn an object upside down, making it harder to recognize. If we can't recognize it, we can't attach a symbol to it. If there's no symbol activated, we have no choice but to draw what we see.

The results Edwards gets from this method are extraordinary. Not just the extent of the transformation, but the speed at which it occurs. In a matter of days, students go from drawing

RELEASING THE ARTIST

DRAWING THE SYMBOL OF A FACE

DRAWING THE REALITY OF A FACE

ARTIST AND AUTHOR BETTY EDWARDS ARGUED THAT REALISTIC DRAWING IS NOT A MOTOR SKILL PROBLEM, BUT A PERCEPTION PROBLEM.

USING TECHNIQUES DESIGNED TO HELP PEOPLE SEE THE WORLD AS IT IS—RATHER THAN IN SYMBOLS—CAN PRODUCE RAPID AND DRAMATIC IMPROVEMENTS IN THEIR DRAWING ABILITIES.

rudimentary self-portraits to ones that look like the work of seasoned artists. All from changing the cognitive conversation to unlock what's already there.

Again, the evidence indicates that the same phenomenon is at work with acquired savant syndrome. That these are universal capabilities normally hidden from conscious experience by symbolic networks. How might you test that hypothesis? Deactivate those networks and see what happens.

That's exactly what Dr. Allan Snyder and colleagues at the Centre for the Mind in Australia did in their experiments using repetitive transcranial magnetic stimulation (rTMS). As we've discussed in prior chapters, rTMS involves delivering a series of magnetic pulses to specific areas of the brain, which can temporarily disrupt activity in those targeted regions without causing permanent damage. An experimental technique for changing the cognitive conversation.

In Snyder's study, participants received low-frequency rTMS over the left anterior temporal lobe, an area known to be directly involved with symbolic cognition. Before stimulation, subjects completed baseline tasks involving drawing, proofreading, and estimating quantities.

After stimulation, with those left hemispheric areas silenced, many participants showed marked changes in their abilities. Their drawings were more detailed and realistic, they noticed more anomalies in proofreading tasks, and their quantity estimations improved. These changes often lasted only an hour or two, but the speed and magnitude of the shift were remarkable.

Here, as in the cases of acquired savant syndrome, we have a clear and significant gain of function from the disruption of a cortical area. Furthermore, the gain in function is in the same category of capabilities as seen in savant syndrome, while the area disrupted is the same area that demonstrates a loss of function. Suppressing the dominant hemisphere appeared to give the conscious mind access to lower-level perception. Not only did this experiment provide strong evidence for the disinhibition theory of savant syndrome, but it offers another glimpse of the potential we can unleash by simply changing the cognitive conversation.

THE INTELLIGENCE EQUATION

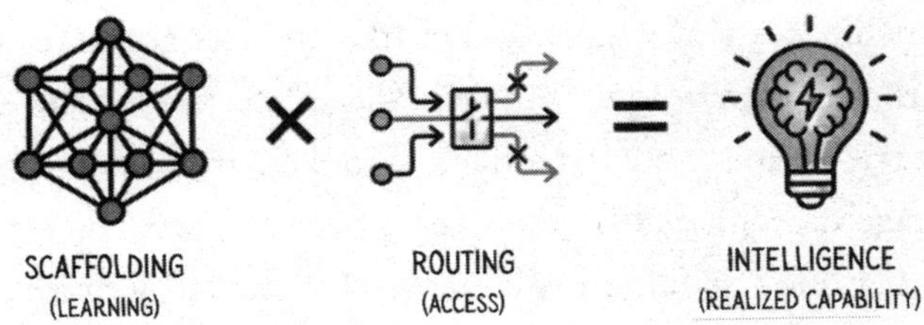

What Lies Beneath

As intriguing as the idea of unlocking savant-like abilities is, there are really two important and broader takeaways here.

The first is that, once again, they demonstrate the role of routing architecture in determining our capabilities. Disruptions in the modules supporting language function, whether temporary or permanent, produce major shifts in the brain's architecture. Shifts that unlock extraordinary new capabilities, showcasing the powerful and underappreciated role of information flow in our cognitive and intellectual abilities. Differences in information flow alone can make the same brain function very differently.

The second is that, like Moravec's Paradox, they reveal the astounding complexity behind what every brain does every day. Savant syndrome provides a window into what is happening in every brain by surfacing into consciousness what is normally hidden, revealing the astounding complexity that powers our common, everyday behaviors. It's an opportunity for us to appreciate the extraordinary feats of "ordinary" cognition with fresh eyes. The evidence strongly suggests that the neural processing that powers savant syndrome is occurring in every brain, regardless of whether we ever experience it directly.

Just like feats of genius, savant-like abilities are noteworthy because they are unique. Einstein was a later talker and struggled early on in school. In today's school environment, his early language difficulties likely would've been flagged as a learning disability. He also famously lamented his challenges with math, which people often erroneously dismiss as false modesty.

But what Einstein's history suggests are early struggles with symbolic cognition. Enough at least to produce atypical routing architectures. Einstein had no special brain hardware. But his mind clearly had a unique solution space, thanks to an atypical learning path and atypical routing architectures. An atypical routing architecture likely enabled in part by a weakness in one area of cognition. Like all who've achieved feats of uncommon genius, his breakthrough insights were not because he could think better, or was more intelligent, than the average person, but because he could think *differently* from the average person.

Once again, we are back to the inescapable conclusion that a human brain is a human brain. For all practical purposes, what other brains are capable of, every brain is capable of. The differences that we observe are the result of differences in our learning path and our routing architectures. Differences in the modules we've built and in how signals flow through them. Not better or worse, just different.

Savant syndrome makes the invisible visible. It shows that what we can do isn't just about the brain areas we have, but about which ones get their messages through. Change the routing, and you change the abilities that surface. Sometimes the most astonishing gains happen not from adding capacity, but from removing a gate.

Your capabilities at any given moment are determined not just by the scaffolding you've built, but by whether that scaffolding can participate in the cognitive conversation. The knowledge and skills that the Genius builds determine your potential, but which of those are part of the conversation determines what's realized.

Which raises a crucial question: In a healthy brain, what determines who gets access to the conversation and who stays silent? What force controls the routing architecture that shapes what you can think, perceive, and do?

The Genius built your capabilities. But something else has been controlling the conversation. And he has his own agenda.

chapter summary

- **Savant syndrome provides a window into hidden potential:** The extraordinary abilities seen in savants aren't created by brain damage; they're released by it. The capabilities likely existed all along but were suppressed.

- **Symbolic cognition filters what we experience:** As we develop language, the symbolic layer dominates our perception, compressing the world into words and categories. What we experience as "reality" is a summary, not the raw data.
- **The filter can be bypassed deliberately:** Betty Edwards's drawing techniques and transcranial magnetic stimulation experiments show that quieting the symbolic layer can unlock hidden capabilities in healthy brains. New capabilities emerge just by changing the conversation.
- **Routing architectures determine present capabilities:** The knowledge and skills the Genius builds determine your potential. But which of those are part of the cognitive conversation determines what's realized.

10

an unreliable narrator

The first principle is that you must not fool yourself—and you are the easiest person to fool.

—Richard Feynman (Nobel Prize–winning physicist)

When Billy walked through my clinic door, I barely recognized him. Four weeks prior, he'd been brought in by ambulance to the hospital after a neighbor found him in his trailer, disheveled and disoriented, barely able to walk. When I saw him in the emergency department to evaluate his altered mental status, he was alert but unable to tell me the year and he had no recollection of recent events.

He had adequate strength in all limbs and didn't demonstrate any focal deficits of neurological function to suggest a stroke or brain bleed. But his balance was way off. And when his eyes looked to the side to follow my finger, they would jerk rhythmically, a phenomenon known as "nystagmus."

This combination of disorientation, unsteady gait, and nystagmus formed the classic triad of Wernicke's encephalopathy, a neurological condition caused by a deficiency of thiamine, or vitamin B_1. It is most commonly seen in the context of chronic alcoholism due to a nutrient-poor diet. Indeed, it would later come to light that Billy had been subsisting almost entirely on beer for weeks.

Now he was back in my clinic, accompanied by his girlfriend, Eileen, and looking like a new man.

"You look so much better than the last time I saw you, Billy!" I said. "How are things going?"

"I'm doin' a whole lot better, Doc. I'm walking good and I ain't talkin' crazy like I was when you saw me."

"That's great to hear," I said. "And you haven't noticed any new problems?"

"Nope, things seem back to normal," he replied.

"That's not true, Billy!" Eileen interjected. "Tell the doctor about your arm."

"Ain't nothing wrong with my arm. I keep telling you that."

"What's going on with his arm?" I asked.

"It's acting crazy!" Eileen explained. "It's like it just does what it wants. The other day we were in the grocery store and he starts unzipping his pants. And the other night we were in the middle of an episode of *Lost* and he just grabs the remote and turns it off."

"Do you remember that, Billy?" I asked.

He laughed. "Yeah, I guess I just got bored, Doc!"

"It's your favorite show, Billy," Eileen said. "I'm telling you, something weird is going on."

"Have a seat on the table and let me examine you," I said.

"Sure thing, Doc." He took a seat on the table.

As I approached him, he reached out with his left hand and

grabbed the ID badge off my coat. He looked almost as startled as I felt.

"Billy!" Eileen shrieked.

"Sorry, Doc, I couldn't remember how you spelled your name." Using his right hand, he pried my badge out of his left hand and gave it back to me.

"No worries," I said, continuing with my neurological exam.

Overall, Billy was doing much better. He knew the date and his memory for recent events was much improved. His gait and balance were normal. And no more jerky eye movements.

I drew a circle on a piece of paper and handed it to him, along with my pen. "Pretend like this is the face of a clock and draw in the numbers for me."

After writing in a couple of numbers with his right hand, his left hand grabbed the paper, crumpled it, and tossed it across the room.

"See, that's what I'm talking about, Doc!" Eileen said. "That is *not* normal."

"Yes, I see what you mean," I replied. "Do one more thing for me, Billy. I want you to pretend like you're holding a screwdriver with your right hand and show me how you'd screw in a screw."

Billy pantomimed using a screwdriver with his right hand with no problem.

"Now imagine you're holding a pair of scissors with your left hand, and show me how you'd cut with them," I said.

Billy opened and closed his left hand like he was squeezing a ball.

"Does that seem right?" I asked.

"That's how my scissors work," he replied.

"No it isn't," said Eileen. "We have regular scissors, Doc."

"Billy, I think I know what's going on with your left arm, but I need to check an MRI of your brain to be sure."

His MRI confirmed what his exam suggested. There was a small hole in his corpus callosum, the large tract of nerve fibers connecting the left and right hemispheres of the brain. The official name for what Billy was suffering from is Marchiafava-Bignami syndrome, a condition most commonly seen in alcoholics where thiamine deficiency damages the corpus callosum.

And a condition that had given Billy an alien hand.

A Tale of Two Hemispheres

Our brain has two symmetric hemispheres, which we refer to as left and right. The left hemisphere controls movement and receives sensations from the right side of the body, and vice versa. Yet, despite being mirror images of each other, they aren't identical in function. We've already discussed the differing roles of left- and right-sided circuits in processing and production of language.

The two hemispheres communicate with each other chiefly through a thick bundle of nerve fibers known as the "corpus callosum." We met the splenium of the corpus callosum when discussing the alexia without agraphia syndrome. The splenium is a smaller section that connects the rear portions of the hemispheres.

In addition to carrying signals related to cognitive operations, these fibers can also transfer electrical activity from one hemisphere to another during a seizure. Back in the early 1940s, it was discovered that severing the corpus callosum helped stop the spread of seizures. And surgically severing the corpus callosum became an extreme measure for extreme cases of epilepsy. A crude but effective last resort when all other efforts had failed.

Severing the corpus callosum effectively splits the brain into two disconnected hemispheres, and patients who've had this procedure are referred to as having "split brains." The two hemispheres can no longer communicate with each other. Surprisingly, despite its extreme nature, it's not always obvious when someone has had his or her brain split.

In the mid-twentieth century, a series of experiments were performed in the lab of Dr. Roger Sperry at Caltech to explore the cognitive effects of split-brain surgery. These "split brain experiments" would produce some of the most surprising and illuminating discoveries in brain science, challenging our most fundamental assumptions about who we are.

The specific questions researchers wanted to know were: What happens when each hemisphere doesn't know what the other is doing? What happens when they can no longer "talk" to each other?

In a now famous experiment, a split-brain patient was shown a picture of a snow scene and a picture of a chicken claw in each of their visual fields at the same time. In this case, the chicken claw was presented to the patient's right visual field and the snow scene was presented to the left visual field. Since the visual cortices process information from the opposite side, this meant that the left hemisphere saw the chicken claw and the right hemisphere saw a snow scene.

Then the patient was asked to point to a picture that related to the image they'd seen. Since each hemisphere had seen a different image, researchers wondered which associated image they'd choose.

The answer was both! The image that was chosen depended on the hand that was doing the choosing. The right hand, controlled by the left hemisphere, pointed to an image of a chicken, which corresponded with the image of the chicken claw that the left hemisphere "saw."

The left hand, controlled by the right hemisphere, pointed to the image of a shovel, which corresponded with the picture of the snow scene that the right hemisphere saw.

Each hemisphere had processed its own image and responded appropriately, completely independently of the other. It was as if two minds were sharing a single skull.

But when the subject was asked to explain why he chose the particular images, things got weirder. His response was that "the chicken claw goes with the chicken, and you need a shovel to clean out the chicken shed."

Of course, the shovel went with the snow scene and not the chicken claw. So why didn't he say so?

Because the left hemisphere is where our language networks reside, and those networks were disconnected from the right side. The right hemisphere correctly chose and pointed to the image of the shovel to go with the snow scene. But thanks to the split-brain surgery, the left hemisphere had no knowledge of that. If the right hemisphere could talk, it would've surely provided the correct explanation. But since the left hemisphere is the one that does the talking, it had to make one up.

Subsequent experiments with split-brain patients continued to demonstrate independent processing between the two hemispheres. In one, two different images are flashed simultaneously to each visual field, such as a toothbrush to the right and a spoon to the left. When asked what they saw, subjects consistently report only the object seen in the right visual field (the toothbrush) and deny seeing anything else. Yet when asked to point to what they saw, their left hand points directly to the spoon.

In another, a written command is presented only to the left visual field, such as to pick up a pen. The subject will correctly execute the command with the left hand, which is controlled by the right hemisphere, where the visual image was processed. However, the subject will deny having seen the command that prompted the action and, when pressed, will say that they acted under their own volition.

The split-brain experiments were a watershed moment in our comprehending of the brain, profoundly shaping our understanding of the organization of cognition, as well as the nature of consciousness and the self. For one, they strongly supported the localizationist model, demonstrating a clear division of labor between the two hemispheres.

They also raised profound and unsettling questions about the nature of the self. Does the right hemisphere contain a separate consciousness that we've ignored because it doesn't speak? Do we experience it on some level but just can't talk about it?

In Billy, my patient with damage to his corpus callosum, his right hemisphere was sending movement instructions to the left hand. But his left hemisphere, cut off from the right, had no access to that information. Absent that knowledge, the language networks in Billy's left hemisphere couldn't explain his left hand's behavior. Billy's "alien" left hand literally had a mind of its own.

And why could Billy accurately demonstrate skilled movements with his right hand but not his left? Because our learned motor programs for skilled movements, also known as motor "engrams," are usually stored in the left hemisphere. Normally, when the left hand is called upon to execute a skilled movement, those instructions are sent across the callosum to the motor cortex on the right side, so they can be used to guide the movements of the left hand. Only in this case, that route wasn't available, so the instructions couldn't make it. This was why Billy's left hand couldn't mimic skilled movements like using scissors or a screwdriver.

What was also extraordinary about the split-brain experiments was that, when the talking parts of the brain weren't privy to the reasons behind the left hand's behavior, it didn't admit its ignorance. It made something up instead. One that the experimenters knew to be false. It was as if there was a part of the brain whose job it was to tell stories about why we do the things we do.

The Interpreter

Dr. Michael Gazzaniga, who trained under and collaborated with Sperry, named this part of the brain "The Interpreter." As in, the part of our brain that interprets our thoughts and behaviors. The part that explains why we say and do the things we say and do.

You are well acquainted with the interpreter, because we all have one. Many refer to it as the voice in their heads.

But why? Why do we all have a voice chattering away all the time, explaining ourselves to ourselves?

We can't say for sure, but perhaps the most plausible theory is that it evolved to explain our behavior in ways that made sense to others. We are a social species. We rely on others and they rely on us. Using our gifts for communications to coordinate and cooperate has been our secret weapon.

But cooperation requires trust. If I mean what I say and say what I mean, you are more likely to trust me. The more predictable my actions, the more trustworthy I become. If I'm entirely unpredictable, then you'd be foolish to trust me.

Over the course of human history, those humans who offered consistent, plausible explanations for their actions were more likely to be trusted, included, and supported. They were more likely to survive, and more likely to pass along any penchant for crafting consistent, plausible explanations to their offspring.

In a social species, natural selection would thus favor individuals who both explained themselves to others and were consistent and believable. So our brain has its own public relations department, responsible for creating the stories we share with the world and managing our reputation in human society.

But what's an interpreter to do when it has no access to why we said or did something, as in the case of the split-brain patients? What if it has no factual data for its stories?

One option would be to admit ignorance. To say, "I don't know." But would you trust someone who admits to having no control of their actions? Not me!

So, in the face of ignorance about our own motives, it's best for the interpreter to make up something. But this is a highly unusual scenario, of course. Split brains are the result of a rare surgical procedure. In an intact brain without severed connections, rogue networks in our disconnected hemisphere aren't controlling our actions. The interpreter isn't having to explain behavior that we didn't consciously control. In the typical case, our behaviors are consciously controlled, and so the interpreter does have access to all facts. In the typical case, the interpreter's stories can be trusted, can't they? Just how accurate are the interpreter's explanations in a fully intact brain?

The Hungry Judges

Being a parole board judge seems like a cut-and-dry affair. A prisoner comes in front of you. You review the relevant documents, hear the arguments for and against their release, and then use that information to render a decision.

Based on all that, you'd expect the outcome to be determined by the facts of the case. Certainly something as arbitrary as the time of day that a decision is made wouldn't be the primary predictor of a favorable ruling for the parolee, right?

Except that's exactly what a team of Israeli researchers found when they reviewed 1,112 judicial rulings made by 8 Israeli parole board judges over the course of 10 months. In their analysis, the odds of being granted parole weren't reliably higher for less severe crimes, or for prisoners who expressed remorse, or for those with good behavior.

What factor did give a prisoner the best odds of being set free? Having a judge who'd just eaten.

That's right, when the researchers looked at the data, the odds of being set free were highest first thing in the morning. Those odds steadily dropped over the next couple of hours. When did they go back up? After the judges had their midmorning snack.

If a judge with a full belly was hearing your case, you had about a 65 percent chance of being set free. If you had the misfortune of sitting before one with a growling stomach, you were virtually guaranteed to go back behind bars! The best predictor of the outcome had nothing to do with the facts of the case, and everything to do with the metabolic state of the human making the decision.

When these findings were published in 2011 in the *Proceedings of the National Academy of Sciences*, they caused quite a stir. What had been assumed to be a rational, fair, and objective decision-making process had been shown to be anything but.

Yet until this study was published, everyone assumed that it was. Including the judges. Without the data to prove otherwise, they never would have believed that hunger and fatigue could matter more than the facts of the case.

Position over Quality

In a study published in 1977 by psychologists Richard E. Nisbett and Timothy Wilson, forty shoppers were shown four identical pairs of pantyhose laid out on a table from left to right. Participants were asked to choose the one they thought was the highest quality. But the truth was that the pairs were all identical.

With four identical pairs, you'd expect their responses to be evenly distributed across the four pairs, with roughly 25 percent choosing each one. But they weren't. A whopping 40 percent of the subjects chose the pair on the far right, while only 12 percent chose the pair on the far left. And 72 percent of the subjects picked a stocking from the right half of the table. There was a clear bias toward picking items on the right side of the table, even though none of the subjects cited item location as an influencing factor, providing other justifications for their selections. Even when informed that the stockings were identical, some of the participants still insisted that there was a discernible difference.

Subliminal Influence

Most of our sensory processing happens beneath our awareness. What we perceive of the outside world as the movie in our mind is not only a fraction of what's perceived and analyzed, but of what shapes our actions. Consider what happens when information bypasses conscious awareness entirely.

In a study published in 2005 by Piotr Winkielman and his colleagues, participants were shown a smiling or frowning face for sixteen milliseconds before being given another picture of a face and asked to classify it as a man or a woman. After they finished classifying the pictures, the real experiment happened. Subjects were offered a fruit-flavored beverage. Thirsty subjects who'd had the smiling face flash before their eyes poured themselves twice as much of it and drank 50 percent more than those who'd seen the frowning face.

In another version of the experiment, researchers offered the subjects a fixed amount of the beverage to drink. They then asked how much they'd be willing to pay for the beverage. Those who'd seen the happy faces were willing to pay nearly *four times* as much! Further testing showed that the subjects had no awareness of having seen the happy and angry faces, even though the images had clearly influenced their gustatory experience.

The Arbitrary Anchor

Could something as arbitrary as the last two digits of your Social Security number shape how much you'd pay for something?

Absurd as it sounds, it's exactly what behavioral economists Dan Ariely, George Loewenstein, and Drazen Prelec discovered.

In the study they conducted, participants were asked to write down the last two digits of their Social Security number (SSN). Then they were shown a series of consumer goods, such as a cordless trackball, a bottle of wine, and a box of Belgian chocolates. After viewing the items, they were asked if they'd be willing to buy the product for an amount equal to their last two SSN digits and also asked the maximum price they'd pay.

What effect did their SSN have? The higher their number, the higher the price they were willing to pay. And the effect wasn't trivial. Those whose digits ended between 80 and 99 were willing to pay *three times* as much on certain items as those whose digits ended between 1 and 20! Of course, the subjects, believing themselves to be the rational beings we all imagine ourselves to be, denied that their SSN had any impact on their valuations.

Misattributed Arousal

We've already discussed how hunger can subconsciously influence parole decisions, but could physiological factors impact romantic attraction? In a famous study from the early 1970s, researchers Donald Dutton and Arthur Aron stationed an attractive female experimenter on a narrow, wobbly, anxiety-inducing suspension bridge perched 230 feet above rocks and rapids.

As male participants crossed the bridge, in many instances gripping the handrails for dear life, the woman asked them to complete a brief survey and write a story about a picture they were given. She then offered her phone number "in case they had questions."

As a control, the same setup was also performed on a sturdy, immobile wooden bridge that stood roughly 10 feet over a shallow stream. So what was the impact of standing on a shaky bridge? The men standing on it wrote stories that were more likely to be laced with sexual imagery and were far more likely to call the experimenter afterward with their "questions." They'd presumably attributed their heightened arousal to sexual attraction rather than to a fear of plummeting to an early death.

The same experiment was repeated with a male experimenter on the bridge. This design produced a result that shocked no one, which was that in this instance, the men on the shaky bridge did not write more lurid stories, nor were they more likely to call the experimenter after the encounter. Other similar experimental paradigms have demonstrated that physiological arousal, in the presence of the opposite sex, regardless of what triggered it, is commonly chalked up to romantic interest.

Explaining Choices Never Made

In a study published in 2005, authors Lars Hall and Petter Johansson showed participants pairs of female faces and asked which one they found more attractive. After the subject pointed to their choice, the researcher surreptitiously switched the photos and slid to them the one they hadn't chosen. Subjects were then asked to explain why they'd rated that woman as more attractive.

Incredibly, only 13 percent of subjects detected the switch, despite the faces looking nothing alike. But even more extraordinary was that the participants offered detailed, confident explanations for their decisions. Explanations that were just as detailed and heartfelt as when describing their genuine choices, such as "she had kind eyes" or a "warm smile." They provided convincing stories to explain a choice they never actually made.

If we can invent stories to explain faces we didn't choose, might we invent explanations about movements we didn't make? You bet!

Claiming Authorship of Others' Actions

In a study published in 1999, psychologists Daniel Wegner and Thalia Wheatley invited college students into their lab individually and sat them in front of a computer next to one other supposed study participant. In front of them was a square board mounted atop a computer mouse. Both participants placed their fingers on the board and moved the mouse together, Ouija board–style.

On the screen in front of them was a photo filled with dozens of tiny objects like plastic dinosaurs, toy cars, and miniature swans. Their instructions were to move the mouse around the screen together until they heard some music piped into their headphones. When the music came on, they were to stop moving the mouse within 10 seconds, and after each stop, they rated how much they had intended to stop the cursor on that specific object. Additionally, as they were moving the cursor, sometimes they would also hear a word through their headphones.

In some of the trials, the confederate "study participant" would forcefully stop the mouse on a particular object. And in some cases, that object was the word that the subject heard through their headphones. For example, if the participant heard the word "swan," then the confederate would force a stop on the picture of the swan.

What the researchers found was that, if they heard the corresponding word prior to the cursor stopping on that object, the subject rated that they had intended to do so. Hearing the word corresponding to the chosen object was enough to make the subject believe *they* had been the one to stop the cursor, even though they'd played no part in it.

Here we have experiment after experiment showing our behaviors to be determined by factors outside our awareness. And furthermore, of us providing false explanations for those behaviors that we believe wholeheartedly.

Decision Before Awareness

Now, in the unlikely event that you're still hanging on to a thread of hope that we have conscious control, allow me to snip it with one last experiment. It's an experiment that has probably generated more existential angst than any other in the history of cognitive science.

The design was simple. Subjects were hooked up to an EEG and then asked to just bend their wrist. Whenever they felt like it.

In front of them was a screen with a clock with a dot revolving around the perimeter. Subjects were told to report the position of the dot as soon as they experienced the urge to move.

Prior to this experiment, scientists had discovered that there's a buildup of electrical activity in the brain in a particular location just prior to the onset of voluntary movement. That electrical activity is known as the "readiness potential," and it indicates that the brain has made the decision to move.

You've probably gone through your life feeling as if you decide when to do something. You consciously decide to tap your foot or snap your fingers and then it happens. Your conscious decision precedes the execution of the movement. If that's actually how things work, then the urge to move should occur *before* the readiness potential. This experiment was designed to determine if that was actually true. Nothing short of our notion of free will was on the line.

So when did the readiness potential occur? You probably know where this is headed.

That's right, the readiness potential occurred *before* the subjects reported the conscious urge to move. Which meant that by the time the subjects felt as if they'd decided, the decision had already been made. On average, the conscious urge occurred 350 milliseconds after the readiness potential. It might not sound like much, but it's an eternity on a neural timescale.

Like you and me, the subjects believed that they were calling the shots, that it was their conscious urge that got the ball rolling. But the results indicated otherwise, revealing that even the most elementary of decisions, the decision to bend and straighten your wrist, or tap your finger, or scrunch your toes is ultimately not under conscious control.

You don't decide to move. You are informed of that decision. Your conscious mind isn't the controller of your actions; it's the *observer.* What we see in split-brain patients isn't some esoteric phenomenon occurring in a rare neurological situation. What we see there is happening in each and every one of us, every moment of our day. The interpreter never has the real story.

Hidden Capabilities

All these experiments show the interpreter fabricating explanations for actions. But what about capabilities themselves? Can the narrator be wrong not just about why you do things, but about what you can do in the first place?

Remember Dennis from Chapter 7? The man who could write but not read because his stroke had disconnected his visual cortex from language areas? There's one last finding I've yet to share. One that, at the time, challenged some of my most fundamental beliefs about the human mind.

"So, Dr. Turknett, are you certain that Mr. M can't recognize words?" Dr. Heilman asked.

Uh-oh. This sounds like a trick question. Tread carefully.

"Well, he can't read them aloud. And, he says he doesn't recognize them at all, whereas with the colors, he said that he did. So it doesn't seem like he can, but I suppose it's still possible he can? I guess I don't know for sure."

When in doubt, always equivocate.

"Yes, I don't know for sure, either."

Phew.

"So let's find out."

What does he have up his sleeve now?

Dr. Heilman turned to one of the medical students and asked, "Can you write down the name of eight different animals on a separate piece of paper?" He turned to another student and asked, "And can you write down the name of eight different plants?"

After the students completed the task, Dr. Heilman first presented the words to Dennis and asked him to read them. As expected, Dennis couldn't.

"Okay, now I want you to try something for me," Dr. Heilman said. "I want you just to tell me if the word is a plant or an animal."

Dennis still couldn't answer. "I'm telling you, I know those are supposed to be words, but I don't know what they are." We could sense his frustration rising.

Where is he going with this?

"Just one last thing I want you to try," Dr. Heilman said. "I'm going to hand you these pieces of paper one at a time . . . and I want you to sort the cards into two piles: plant names in one pile and animal names in the other."

"Okay, but I told you I don't know what they say. I'll just be guessing," Dennis replied.

"Just try your best. Do it with your left hand and go as fast as you can. Ready? Go."

Dr. Heilman handed Dennis the cards one at a time. He looked briefly at each and then quickly sorted them one by one into two piles, as instructed.

A stunned silence filled the room. Dennis had sorted all but one of the cards into the correct pile. The chance that he'd just gotten lucky was less than 1 in 4,000.

Dr. Heilman smiled with a satisfied expression.

My head was spinning. I knew I'd just witnessed something profound. Something even more fascinating than alexia without agraphia and color dysnomia. But I had no explanation for it.

Based on his sorting performance, Dennis clearly did recognize the names of the plants and animals he'd been shown. And yet he outright denied it. He recognized them, but he didn't know that he did.

How was this possible?

It was possible because the right hemisphere of Dennis's brain—the side still receiving visual information—could actually read the words on those cards. And it could use that knowledge to guide the movements of his left hand. But, as in the split-brain patients, that capability was entirely hidden from his conscious mind. Dennis's brain could do more than the interpreter realized, which is why Dennis was just as surprised by his performance as the rest of us.

I wasn't prepared for what I saw back then. It was one of those moments where I realized something I thought was true about the world was not. My brain would have to reconfigure itself to accommodate this new reality.

Decades later, my brain has reconfigured. In fact, it now feels inevitable and obvious. Given what we've covered about cognition, it may feel obvious to you as well.

As we've learned, the Genius knits together problem-solving algorithms in neural tissue so they can run autonomously. So they can escape the bottleneck of the single-tasking conscious mind. This is the mechanism by which we scale intelligence. Our intelligence hinges on our abilities being nonconscious.

So, of course we don't know what we're capable of. Of course we don't know how or why we do the things we do. Our conscious mind lacks access to that information.

And yet, we still need to explain our thoughts and actions. So our brain is faced with a dilemma. The part of our brain that knows how to talk, where the interpreter lives, is the only part that can explain ourselves to others. But that part isn't involved in the decision making. The best it can do is craft the most convincing tale it can.

What's perhaps even stranger is that we *believe* those tales. Why do the interpreter's stories ring true to us, even though they're works of fiction? Recall that the interpreter's job is to provide convincing explanations to others to promote trust and social cohesion. If that's the case, then who is more likely to beat a lie detector—someone who is lying and knows they're lying, or someone who is lying but believes they're telling the truth?

The best way to avoid the darting eyes, sweaty palms, dilated pupils, or any of the myriad other facial micro-expressions and autonomic cues that betray our lies is if we think we're telling the truth. We're much more likely to come across as trustworthy if we *believe* our own bullshit.

So if we need to explain ourselves to others but don't have access to the truth, it's better for us to not know that we don't know. This saves us from the social risks of lying. By this line of reasoning, evolution would select for the least "self-aware" brains.

This might seem like a convoluted way to set things up. Why not just have all the brain parts talk to each other? Why not just give the interpreter access to all the facts?

Because, once again, evolution doesn't work with a blank canvas. Evolution adapts by modifying what already exists. Our actions have been guided by autonomous, nonconscious modules since the very first brains came on the scene. That's why we still have a host of "primal instincts" from ancient brain circuits shaping our behavior. The new gets added on top of the old.

And language is the new kid on the block. Furthermore, symbolic cognition was an adaptation for enhancing communication, not decision making. As a result, our language cortex, where the interpreter lives, is functionally and anatomically separated from the parts that decide what we do next. And yet, the language cortex is the only part of our brain that knows how to talk.

As soon as the interpreter arrives on the mental scene in early life, its assignment isn't to learn what *actually* caused our behavior, because it can't know. Instead, its assignment is to learn what a reliable, socially valuable person would *say* caused it. It's never been about reporting the truth. Its job has always been to tell convincing stories.

Some of those stories might be closer to the "real truth" than others. For example, if you hear the word "swan" and then see your hand point to a swan, it's reasonable to assume that one caused the other. Many times you'd be right, though not always. But it's always an educated guess based on the available information.

The situation is not unlike where we find ourselves today with Large Language Models (LLMs) like ChatGPT. These were created as communication modules. They were trained to communicate through language. They weren't designed to understand how they work.

And yet, if you ask them to explain themselves, they're eager to provide a convincing answer. The fact that they have no access to their internal workings doesn't stop them. We may politely refer to these confabulations as "hallucinations," but it's precisely the same flavor of bullshit spewed by the interpreter.

In the end, there are clear advantages to *believing* the interpreter's stories. In many ways, we're better off not knowing that there's a separate, underlying truth. Which is why, despite all the extraordinary evidence I've laid out here, I know you still feel deep in your bones that you know why you think and do the things you think and do. It's why, despite being intimately familiar with the research and exploring these ideas for my entire adult life, I, too, still feel deeply in my bones that I know. But I also know that's thanks to the completeness of the illusion.

The feeling of certainty is real. The feeling that these explanations come from genuine self-knowledge may well have kept hundreds of generations of your ancestors alive. But it's the illusion that's real, not the knowledge itself.

The Greatest Deception

The interpreter's stories profoundly shape who we become. They shape our beliefs about our worth. About our value. About our intelligence. About our potential. About what we are and are not capable of.

Those beliefs become a guiding force in our lives. They shape our choices, determine what we attempt and what we avoid, and create boundaries around what we think is possible for us.

And all of it is built on lies.

Lies like "You're not good at that." "You're not smart enough." "You can't learn to do that." "You're too old to try something new." "I wonder what they think of me." "Do I look foolish doing this?" We tell these lies about others, too.

This is how the interpreter has ended up controlling the narrative both inside and outside our minds.

And the most devastating story of all? "Who do you think you are?"

The interpreter is the voice in our heads, narrating our lives to ourselves and to others. And he needs us to not only believe that his stories are true, but that his voice is *our* voice. That his thoughts are our thoughts.

That is the greatest deception of all. It's the lie upon which all other lies depend.

And that is why referring to him as "the interpreter" is much too generous. And misleading. It's a term that, ironically, hides his true nature. We need a name that calls him what he is: the Impostor.

An Uninvited Guest

The Impostor hasn't always been with you. For the first few years of life, there was no narrator. No story about who you were or what you were capable of. You were pure Genius.

Watch any two-year-old and you'll see this. They don't pause to wonder if they're "good at" climbing. There's no hesitation about looking foolish or trying something new. They just try, fail, and try again. No self-consciousness. No voice holding them back.

As author Karl Ove Knausgård observed:

> *What makes life worth living? No child asks itself that question. To children life is self-evident. Life goes without saying; whether it is good or bad makes no difference. This is because children don't see the world, don't observe the world, don't contemplate the world, but are so deeply immersed in the world that they don't distinguish between it and their own selves.*

When does the Impostor arrive? It's difficult to know precisely, but research on language development suggests it likely happens in stages. Most children start using words like "me" and "mine" around age two, indicating that they've begun recognizing themselves as separate entities.

Around the age of three or four is when they begin telling stories about themselves, like "I don't like peas" and "I'm a big kid now." They're forming a notion that they have properties and preferences that differ from others.

But the Impostor's voice likely doesn't fully emerge until around age seven to eight. This is the time when our words start to reveal an awareness of how we're perceived, along with the need to protect and project a particular identity. When our stories shift from "I did this" to "I am someone who does this." In psychological terminology, this is the time when children begin to develop an "autobiographical memory" and a stable sense of self across time.

This fits with my own recollections of the Impostor's arrival. In my earliest days of organized tee ball, I just showed up to the games and played. Fielded ground balls, threw to first, swung the bat, ran the bases. Pure bliss. And always the highlight of my week.

Then one morning on the way to a game, at the age of eight or nine, I noticed a strange feeling inside me. "Mom, my tummy doesn't feel right," I said.

"Those are probably just butterflies in your stomach," she replied, in what was intended as reassurance.

Butterflies?! In my stomach?! She noticed the alarmed look on my face.

"It's just an expression," she said. "It's the name people give to describe that feeling. It kind of feels like butterflies flying around."

"Oh," I replied, still trying to wrap my head around this unusual figure of speech. "But what are they from?"

"It just means you're a little nervous about the game."

Nervous? This was a new feeling. And a new concept. Why would I be nervous about the game? My mind was swirling to unpack all this. All I knew is that I didn't like the feeling and I wanted it gone. Little did I know then that it would become a familiar companion from that point forward.

Looking back now, I understand what I couldn't wrap my mind around then. I'd spent a lot of time playing baseball. I was obsessed with it. Being good at baseball had become part of my identity. Now my game performance wasn't just about the game itself. It wasn't just about whether my team won or lost. It was about *me*. It was now about the story I'd started telling in my head. Correction: the story the Impostor had started telling.

Once the Impostor appears in full force, his grip only tightens. By adolescence, he's running the show for all of us. Identity preservation becomes the central project. *Who am I? Who do others think I am? Am I living up to that?* The whisper has become a roar. It's no coincidence that this is the time in people's lives they'd least like to relive.

By adulthood, his voice is so constant, so intimately woven into your experience, that you've forgotten it was ever absent. You've forgotten that you and he are not the same, and that there was a "you" that existed before he began spinning his lies.

Our Predicament

So here's our predicament:

We're all living with a bullshit artist inside our heads. He arrived early in our childhood and has been chattering away ever since. For most of our lives, we believed him.

Earlier in this book, we asked, Why don't people believe in their potential? Why, if every brain is capable of extraordinary things, don't we act like it? Why do we believe in the Special Brain Story despite all the evidence to the contrary?

Now you've met him.

The Impostor probably served us well once. As mentioned, it was likely adaptive for us to have a master bullshit artist and for us to believe that bullshit.

But he has outlived his usefulness. What was once adaptive now limits us all in ways few of us appreciate. If we are to have any chance of realizing the full measure of our potential, we must first free ourselves from the tyranny of the Impostor. Both individually and collectively.

But naming him is not enough. To unlock the potential he hides, we must know his tricks.

chapter summary

- **The split-brain experiments revealed the interpreter:** When the corpus callosum is severed, the left hemisphere confidently explains behaviors it had no part in causing.
- **We are reliably wrong about ourselves:** Factors outside our awareness shape our decisions, yet we confidently provide false explanations, unaware we're making it up.

- **Capabilities can be hidden from the narrator:** Dennis could sort words he couldn't consciously read. His brain had the ability, but the interpreter had no access to it.

- **The interpreter is the Impostor:** The voice narrating your life is a module crafting stories to make you appear consistent. Its greatest deception is convincing you its voice is your voice.

11

the impostor's playbook

We are what we pretend to be, so we must be careful about what we pretend to be.

—Kurt Vonnegut (author)

You've met the Impostor and see him for what he is. A well-intentioned, blathering know-it-all who knows nothing. A module in your brain whose primary job is to tell lies about you. Lies that you are wired to believe.

On the surface, that sounds innocuous. Didn't we all learn way back when that sticks and stones may break our bones but words will never hurt us? Furthermore, I've just spent a great many pages showing you that the very reason those stories about you aren't true is that the Impostor doesn't control or even understand our actions. He observes and then narrates. Is that really enough to sabotage your potential? Is that enough to make the Genius go into a decades-long hibernation?

In short, it is. Because stories, as it turns out, do matter. In fact, we began this whole book talking about the common story we tell ourselves and each other about human potential. I said that story was wrong, and that we were going to dismantle it with science. Not just for the sake of truth and accuracy, but because that story is the very thing standing in the way of realizing your extraordinary potential. And it's a story that was concocted by the Impostor.

Science has convincingly demonstrated the power of our stories. About the power of what we believe. Stories fuel the extraordinary power of the placebo effect. What is the essence of that effect? It is that the belief that something will happen makes that thing more likely to happen. It is a story about the future coming true because we believe it to be true.

What does that mean for the Impostor and his lies about you? By crafting the story of you, he shapes what you *become*. He may be incapable of controlling your actions today, but he can shape your actions of tomorrow.

Once you buy into the Impostor's story—once you believe "I'm not the kind of person who can . . ." or "I always fail at . . ." —your unconscious bits take it from there. Unbeknownst to you, your brain starts filtering choices, risks, and opportunities to conform to that narrative. In this way, you become who you pretend to be.

The consequences of the Impostor's influence, and his grand deception, are vast. Neutralizing his influence is essential to unlocking the abilities he's spent a lifetime convincing you that you don't have. But he's cunning and resilient—and won't go down without a fight. So to help ensure you gain the upper hand, let's review his favorite genius-killing tricks.

Trick #1: The Hostile Takeover

Sarah has given this presentation twenty times.

Twice to her team. Three times to her boss. Fifteen times in front of the bathroom mirror while her coffee went cold on the counter. She knows every slide. Every transition. Every data point. She could give it in her sleep.

Now she's standing at the front of the conference room. The projector hums. Her slides glow on the screen behind her. The VP of Marketing sits in the front row, arms crossed. The CMO is in the back, half-watching, half-checking her phone. Twelve other expectant faces stare back at her.

This presentation could change everything. Six months of work. A promotion hanging in the balance. The project she proposed, the one everyone said was too ambitious, ready to launch if she can just convince them.

She opens her mouth to begin.

But nothing comes. Her mind goes blank. She can't even conjure the first word of her presentation. Panic sets in.

Snap out of it, Sarah. You're losing this. They're going to think you're a fraud if you don't pull it together.

Her mind searches frantically through the void where her expertise used to be. The silence stretches. Someone coughs. Others fidget. She can feel every eye on her.

Her heart thuds in her ears. Sweat pricks the back of her neck. Her hands, holding the clicker, start to tremble.

"So . . . um . . ." she hears herself say, her voice like a distant echo.

She glances down at her notes. The words swim on the page.

She knows what they say because she wrote them, but right now they might as well be hieroglyphics.

The VP shifts in his seat.

The voice in her head offers more friendly words of encouragement: *You're blowing it, Sarah. Everyone can see you don't know what you're doing. You're going to lose everything you've worked so hard for.*

She takes a breath. Tries to find the thread. Words come out, but they sound alien. Nothing like the smooth presentation she delivered yesterday to her empty living room.

For the next 30 minutes, she stammers through slides she could have explained in her sleep. Her mind stays two steps behind her mouth. Simple words feel like they're stuck behind glass. The flow she had is nowhere to be found.

An uncomfortable silence fills the room. Everyone knows this wasn't how Sarah wanted things to go. They can feel her pain, because they've all been there, too. In a show of mercy, the audience offers no questions or comments.

The VP nods politely. "Thanks, Sarah. We'll be in touch." Though everyone knows they won't.

I imagine you can relate to and understand Sarah's experience, moments when you needed to perform at your very best and ended up performing at your very worst.

Sarah had spent months building cognitive scaffolding for this presentation. The Genius had automated it all, from the data points to the key concepts along with the sequence and flow. It was all there, written into her neural tissue, thanks to her extensive preparation. But it made no difference. When she needed it most, she couldn't get to it.

Of course, we all know why this happens, right? It's the pressure!

But stop and think about that for a moment. Why should pressure make us perform *worse*?

When the stakes are high, when it really matters, shouldn't we perform at our best? Shouldn't our brain perform at its best? Surely millions of years of evolution wouldn't design a brain that withers at the most critical moments.

Yet the opposite has become normalized. We *expect* it to be harder to perform well under pressure. We know that performing better under pressure is what separates the best from the rest.

So what gives?

In the moments that matter, our nervous system kicks into a higher gear. A higher state of arousal. It's our brain's way of recruiting more cognitive resources to the task at hand, so that we can process a bit faster, focus a bit better. And this state of heightened arousal is something we *feel*.

The problem isn't the feelings. Those feelings are signs of our brain preparing us to be at our very best.

The problem is our *response* to those feelings. More specifically, the problem is the Impostor's response to those feelings.

Because the Impostor's first reaction is to take a high-stakes situation and transform it into something else entirely. To make it feel like the most important thing ever in the history of your life to date. Nothing short of a referendum on your worth as a human being. The defining moment of your existence.

This is especially true when the situation connects to your

identity. Not to what or who you truly are, mind you, but to the story the Impostor has been telling the world—and you—about what or who you truly are. Remember, protecting this story is the Impostor's sole purpose in life. Anything that threatens that story becomes, from his perspective, a *literal* life-or-death situation.

And your nervous system has a mode for life-or-death situations. We know it as the "fight-or-flight" response.

Mediated by the sympathetic branch of your autonomic nervous system, fight-or-flight exists to help you respond to true threats to your survival, like the proverbial saber-toothed tiger. Your pupils dilate to let in more light. Your heart rate increases to pump more blood to your muscles. Your breathing becomes rapid and shallow. Digestion shuts down. All resources redirect to immediate survival. The Impostor has turned arousal into full-blown panic.

Not exactly a mode conducive to expert piano playing or speech giving.

But the Impostor is too dumb to know this. He perceives a life-or-death situation and sounds the alarm. From his perspective, that presentation might as well be a saber-toothed tiger, that math test might as well be a coiled rattlesnake, that piano recital might as well be an approaching tsunami.

Not content to stop there, the hijack goes even further. Full of hubris and ignorance, the Impostor tries to take over the controls to your behavior. In other words, at just the moment when you need all those automated skill networks firing on all cylinders, he steps in and announces, "Sorry, guys, I got this one. It's too important to leave to you amateurs."

Your benevolent overlord is taking the reins of the cognitive conversation, ensuring that the world won't see the fruits of the Genius's labor.

Except the problem, as you now know, is that the Impostor doesn't know how to do anything. Your conscious mind is not the repository of knowledge and skills. And so, with the networks that power your cognitive skills silenced, your success in these moments becomes a biological impossibility.

You feel like an inept beginner in these moments precisely because an inept beginner has taken over your brain. In the very moments where you most need the Impostor to shut up and be quiet, when you need your conscious mind to disappear, he becomes his loudest. In his effort to ensure you live up to the identity he's crafted, he sabotages any hope of you doing so.

As martial artist Bruce Lee observed,

> *One can never be the master of his technical knowledge unless all his psychic hindrances are removed and he can keep the mind in the state of fluidity, ever purged of whatever technique he has obtained—with nonconscious effort.*

There's no "choking" when the Impostor isn't around, because the Impostor is the reason we "choke." Not because of some inherent law of the universe that says it's harder to perform under pressure. But because the Impostor's grip on so many brains is so strong and pervasive that his hijacking has become the norm.

And it's hard to overstate the impact here. Pressure is highest when things matter most to us, when we believe the consequences of that moment will have an outsized impact on our lives. Ones that will have lasting ripple effects.

THE ANATOMY OF PERFORMANCE HIJACKING

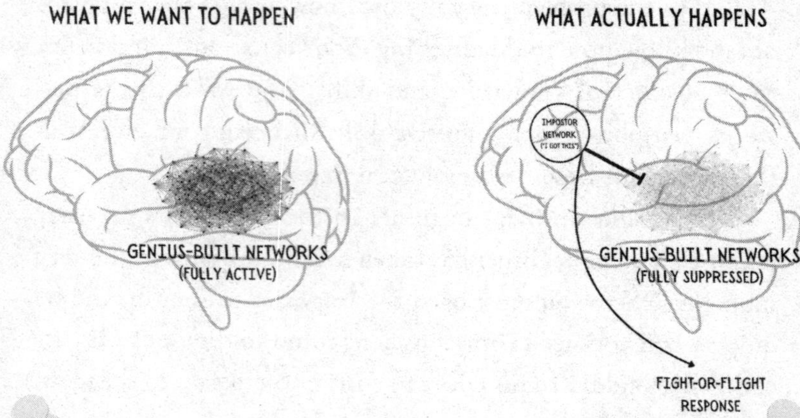

TO PERFORM AT OUR BEST, WE WANT THE AUTOMATED, GENIUS-BUILT NETWORKS OPERATING WITHOUT INTERFERENCE.

IN HIGH-STAKES MOMENTS, THE IMPOSTOR SIGNALS THE ALARM AND TAKES OVER, HIJACKING THE COGNITIVE CONVERSATION AND SHUTTING THOSE NETWORKS OUT. THIS RENDERS THE CIRCUITS OF OUR EXPERTISE INACCESSIBLE WHEN WE NEED THEM MOST.

The most damaging ripple effects, however, are the ones that shatter our belief in ourselves.

So many dreams and aspirations erode not because they were impossible, but because the Impostor made the very act of trying unbearable. There's no telling how many works of art have gone unpainted, innovations undeveloped, or moments of human brilliance unseen because in a decisive instant the Impostor choked the Genius into silence.

Trick #2: The Gold Star Trap

Here's a challenge: How do you get a child to learn something the Genius isn't interested in? You find a way to appeal to the Impostor by exploiting his weaknesses, that's how!

Remember, the Impostor spins his yarns so other humans will trust us. So we'll be considered valuable members of the tribe, with access to all the survival advantages that entails. He exists to help us climb the social ladder.

Status is the Impostor's prime obsession. He won't stop obsessing about it until we're at the top, and then he'll transform his obsession into keeping us there. Like all Impostor traits, status obsession emerges early in life, first as a whisper. In our earliest years, we don't notice or care about a pecking order.

By the time the Impostor's voice has risen to a deafening roar in adolescence, however, status seems to have become all we notice or care about.

The way we climb the social ladder is by proving our value to others. Which means we need others to *see* that value. And what better mechanism could there be for exploiting that need to demonstrate our value than grades? And rankings! These are like drugs to the Impostor. Simply irresistible.

Is this such a bad thing? Does it matter that we exploit the Impostor's weaknesses to get kids to learn? At least they're learning, right? Otherwise, they'd just be running around playing, exploring, and being altogether unproductive!

There are at least two devastating consequences here. And they are not trivial.

Exploiting the Impostor

The first consequence of this motivational strategy is that we replace curiosity-driven learning with achievement-driven learning. And we typically do so at an alarmingly early age. What's the problem with achievement-driven learning?

It doesn't work. At least if actual learning is the goal.

Why is it that you hardly remember any of what you "learned" in school but are a master of what you learned outside it? Because in one setting your learning was guided by the Genius, via the pursuit of curiosity, and in the other by the Impostor, via the pursuit of achievement. And only one of those characters knows how to learn.

Traditional schooling is designed to exploit the weaknesses of the Impostor to promote compliance. It's the Impostor's playground. And so the Genius, the part of us that knows how to learn, is nowhere to be found.

To use the conventional terminology, schools rely on extrinsic motivation—grades, rankings, and fear—as motivating tactics, tactics that appeal to the Impostor's burning desire for status and validation but which the Genius couldn't care less about.

Worse yet, research shows that learning through extrinsic motivation erodes natural curiosity. It transforms learning from that joyful, all-consuming thing we used to spend our days doing into a dirty word. Something we're forced to do. Achievement-driven learning drives the Genius into hibernation. Leonardo da Vinci recognized the cognitive cost of this approach centuries ago: "Study without desire spoils the memory, and it retains nothing that it takes in."

Research shows that effective learning requires three key ingredients:

First, intrinsic motivation. We need to want to learn what we're learning, and that desire must come from within. It's learning driven by curiosity rather than grades or validation. That's the signature of Genius-led learning, the kind that builds real intelligence without requiring classrooms, curricula, or syllabi.

Second, active knowledge construction. We are the ones building understanding. We *create* knowledge through exploration and discovery, not by passively receiving information. A toddler learns language by experimenting with sounds and words, not by sitting through grammar lessons. We learn to cook by trying recipes and adjusting flavors, not by memorizing lists of ingredients.

Third, ongoing feedback. Growth happens in the Goldilocks Zone, when we're pushing up against the edge of our capabilities, succeeding in some moments and failing in others. We need continuous feedback to know which approaches lead to success so we can wire them in.

Now let's review what traditional schooling actually provides.

In school, we don't choose what we learn. That's chosen for us. We're discouraged from asking about or exploring topics unrelated to the chosen subject matter. We are motivated to learn not by natural curiosity but through rewards and punishments, mainly in the form of grades and class rankings. Correct answers are rewarded with praise and awards; incorrect ones are marked with red X's and public humiliation.

We sit at a desk and receive information. We are passive consumers of knowledge given to us in class lectures and textbooks. We receive and we regurgitate, but we rarely create.

The feedback we get is predominantly in the form of tests. It is intermittent and separate from the learning process. It is designed for the purposes of measurement, not modification.

In short, traditional schooling doesn't provide any of the three key ingredients for effective learning: No intrinsic motivation. No active knowledge construction. No ongoing feedback. When it comes to incorporating effective learning methods, schools get a failing grade.

Genius-Led vs. Impostor-Led Learning

FEATURE	GENIUS-LED LEARNING	IMPOSTOR-LED LEARNING
Primary Fuel	**Curiosity:** Driven by an internal desire to understand, explore, and master.	**Status:** Driven by an external desire for validation, grades, rankings, and "looking smart."
The Goal	**Growth and Scaffolding:** To build deep understanding and neural structures (skills) that last.	**Performance:** To get the "right answer," pass the test, or avoid looking foolish.
Role of the Learner	**Active Constructor:** Explores, experiments, manipulates information, and connects the dots.	**Passive Consumer:** Waits for instructions, memorizes isolated facts, and regurgitates information.
View of Struggle	**Necessary Signal:** Struggle is feedback that you are in the "Goldilocks Zone" and learning is happening.	**Threat to Identity:** Struggle is evidence of a lack of ability or intelligence; something to be avoided.

FEATURE	GENIUS-LED LEARNING	IMPOSTOR-LED LEARNING
Feedback Loop	**Ongoing and Functional:** Constant, low-stakes feedback used immediately to modify and improve.	**Intermittent and Judgmental:** High-stakes feedback (tests/reviews) used to measure, rank, and judge worth.
Process	**Trial and Error:** Embraces mistakes as data points for refinement.	**Risk Aversion:** Seeks the single "correct" path to avoid the shame of failure.
Outcome	**Virtuosity:** Deep, adaptable knowledge and the ability to apply skills in new contexts.	**Fragility:** Shallow knowledge that is easily forgotten once the external reward is removed.

You'd be hard pressed to design a better system for instilling ineffective learning techniques or for transforming insatiably curious little learning machines into obedient automatons chasing their next gold star. Research on adult learning bears this out.

Studies show that, compared to children, when faced with a learning challenge, an average adult will wait for instructions or guidance, try to find the "right" answer quickly rather than explore the solution space, avoid trial and error, limit learning to formal settings, ask fewer questions, quit when challenged, and stick to rules and procedures even when they're clearly suboptimal.

To summarize, adults tend to default to conservative, rigid, and externally driven strategies, avoiding self-guided exploration and instead seeking explicit direction—behavior that, not coincidentally, formal schooling rewards and reinforces.

So many of our most celebrated thinkers, innovators, and creators dropped out of school. Not because they flunked out, but so they could chase curiosity and not status. Because learning based on someone else's priorities was unbearable. A disproportionate number of these individuals are the ones we now refer to as "genius." Not because they had a genius that others didn't, but because theirs was never silenced.

The Pursuit of Empty Goals

The second major consequence of motivating through achievement or external rewards is that we all too often end up pursuing goals—in the short and long term—that offer only fleeting rather than lasting fulfillment.

The pleasure we derive from achievement is like the pleasure we derive from a bowl of ice cream. It is intense and short-lived. As soon as it wears off, we crave it again. Sometimes even more. And we need increasing amounts to provide the same short-lived satisfaction.

This is smart evolutionary design. When it comes to things that meet our basic needs, like sugar and sex, we are wired so the pleasure we derive wears off fast, and we overestimate the gratification it will provide the next time around. In this way, we ensure we will continue to pursue more of it. Ideally—from our genes' perspective at least—we'll be *consumed* by the need to pursue more of it. Not for the benefit of our mental well-being, but for the benefit of our survival and reproduction.

It is not in our best interest for these things to provide *lasting* satisfaction. Which is why they don't.

The cautionary tale of the high-achieving individual who was "successful" by the Impostor's distorted metrics on the outside but miserable on the inside is so common that it has become a cliché. The athlete who becomes number one in the world and then wonders what it was for. The entrepreneur who sells their company for millions but feels unfulfilled. The lawyer who makes partner and realizes they've been climbing someone else's ladder.

The Impostor had promised them that reaching the summit would silence his voice, but instead he invents a new one to climb, assuring them that's the real prize. External validation can never fill the void because creating the void is how the Impostor stays alive.

We spend decades climbing ladders we never chose, pursuing goals that were never ours, and end up wondering why success feels so hollow. None of this is the fault of teachers or even individual schools. It's the product of a system built for a different world with different goals that's become so entrenched and calcified that it resists change.

Trick #3: The Productivity Myth

The Impostor doesn't sabotage just how we learn. He sabotages how we work.

One of the Impostor's favorite stories is the one about productivity. It goes something like this:

To be a productive member of society or a workplace, you must be working. If you rely largely on your mind for your work, then the only time you're actually doing meaningful "work" is when you're working on completing a specific task, ideally while seated at a desk in a sterile and soulless box and sipping lukewarm coffee. And the only meaningful measure of the work you've done is what you produce, be it lines of code, performance reviews, or TPS reports.

Any time in which you are not engaged in this kind of activity, you are not being productive. These include necessary evils like sleeping, eating, childcare, and dental work. But they also include very evil evils like breaks, hobbies, and, worst of all, vacations. These activities are the enemy of productivity and must be treated with the utmost ridicule and disdain to ensure you are filled with the proper amount of guilt and shame. If the Impostor had his way, these frivolous endeavors would be ended forever.

Yet, given the role of mode shifting in problem solving and intelligence, if the Impostor got his way, we'd have no theory of relativity or evolution by natural selection, no laws of planetary motion, no periodic table of elements, no calculus, no electricity, no modern medicines, no personal computers, smartphones, or internet. These were all breakthroughs that occurred in minds that weren't "trying" to be productive.

We expand our intelligence, or solution space, through learning and through mode shifting. Yes, accomplishing specific tasks can only happen when we're in task-positive mode. And certain kinds of learning, as well.

But when we're in that mode, our brain has access to only a fraction of its total solution space. By spending so much of our waking life in this mode, in a misguided effort to make us more productive, we miss out on so much of what our brain and every other brain has to offer. If we never allow the mind to rest and wander, we never access the ideas and insights that are only available in those states.

Tragically, as soon as our brain exits the typical school environment that is hostile to learning and cognitive development, it all too often enters a work setting that is hostile to imagination and invention. The mind moves from one prison to the next, where most of its capabilities lie dormant and hidden.

Recall the daily routines we discussed earlier—Einstein's walks in the Princeton woods, Darwin's "thinking path," Churchill's naps, and Agatha Christie's daydreaming. By today's productivity-obsessed standards, these behaviors appear to be the definition of laziness and sloth. Yet for these creators, hours spent away from their desks weren't a dereliction of duty.

They didn't produce works of greatness in spite of their idleness or unconventional work ethic. They produced them *because* of it. What looks like goofing off to some was mode shifting to them. Mode shifting that enabled the routing architectures that could unlock mental breakthroughs. They were toggling between brain states to expand their solution space. And they were giving their brains the rest needed for growth, so that the Genius could transform their studies into scaffolding.

Explicitly or implicitly, they realized that the intelligent bits of our brain are still solving problems even when our attention is directed elsewhere, and that certain breakthroughs can only emerge when attention is directed elsewhere.

Far before we had the neuroscience to explain it, they discovered the importance of rest and mode shifting to creativity and problem solving. The Impostor, along with the productivity gurus, would tell Nietzsche to get back to his desk. We have been conditioned to view rest as a necessary evil, a passive state defined strictly by the absence of work. This oversight completely ignores the mechanics of mode shifting, causing us to label the very activities that unlock human potential as nothing more than guilty pleasures.

Given the contributions that brains "at rest" have given to society, the Impostor's backward view of it may be his most destructive lie of all.

Trick #4: The Self-Illusion

The aforementioned tricks of hijacking, achievement-seeking, and productivity myths all serve a deeper purpose. They're all in service of maintaining the Impostor's ultimate deception.

Growth requires change. And yet what is a central feature of a self? The absence of change.

The self-illusion evolved to create trust, and trust depends on predictability. Others need to believe that your desires, motivations, and abilities remain stable across time. If you profess a belief today, they must feel certain you'll hold it tomorrow. If you promise to spend your life with someone, it's better that they don't know this merely reflects your current routing architecture, subject to change with your next mode shift.

We are vast collections of context-specific modules and behavioral subroutines. Our thoughts, actions, desires, and intelligence all depend on our brain's current mode and its pattern of information flow. But that's not a reality that would inspire trust.

To construct the illusion of stability, we must hide the dynamic reality beneath. Much of our psychological struggle stems from this fundamental deception we must maintain with the world and, more importantly, with ourselves.

Creating and maintaining this deception is the Impostor's entire reason for existence. He needs others to buy into the self-illusion, but he needs us to believe it just as much. He must convince us that there is no separation between him and us, that his voice is our voice. Because once we pull back the curtain to expose him for what he is, he vanishes.

This false equivalency has many consequences. For one, it prevents us from appreciating the dynamic nature of our mind. The only reason we find it so surprising that we could write songs in our dreams, remember our old Netflix password in the shower, or invent a breakthrough theorem on a forest walk is that we think of ourselves as the same person at all points in time.

Not coincidentally, when people describe moments like these, they're often framed as coming "from somewhere else." They may even feel reluctant to take credit. That "somewhere" might mean God or an external spirit. Or it might mean the "unconscious" (remember that, whether we're dreaming or awake, it always comes from the unconscious!).

If we are a fixed and unchanging entity, then what we are capable of now is what we are capable of three hours from now, or tomorrow. The sense of stability keeps us from fully appreciating the powerful role of context and environment in shaping our mental and emotional life, and the ways in which we can modify those to our advantage. There's an entire universe we've hardly explored when it comes to what we can unlock with mode shifting. Believing that what you are today is what you will be three hours or three years from now is the definition of a fixed mindset.

This biological reality also exposes a liberating truth, which is that "authenticity" is biologically impossible. The feeling of consistency is a fabrication that the Impostor works hard to maintain. But it's not actually possible to achieve given how your brain works.

When you feel confident one minute and shy the next, or sentimental in one situation and cynical in another, you aren't being hypocritical or "two-faced." You're shifting modes. Your brain is doing exactly what it was designed to do, which is to toggle between different routing architectures to meet the demands of the moment. The story of a static "you" who is stable across contexts is a fiction the Impostor perpetuates to mask that truth.

Stuck in Place

There's a reason that, as the Impostor's voice grows in our minds, we change less and less. Because we can't contradict the story. We can't contradict it with others. We can't contradict it with ourselves. The Impostor insists that we must be the same static character in every scene. And so we stop changing and stop growing.

Consider how readily your beliefs changed throughout childhood. What you believed to be true about the world when you were four was light-years from what you believed when you were seven. Did you care? No. Turns out pro wrestling is fake. Your ten-year-old self found that blindingly obvious. Your seven-year-old self was wrong. No big deal.

But changing the beliefs of an adult, when the Impostor is in full control? Good luck with that. So, we don't grow. We don't get smarter because the Impostor thinks it's too dangerous. You just can't trust folks who change their minds about things, he says. We find what reinforces our beliefs and avoid what challenges us. It may be terrible for our minds, but it's great for maintaining the Impostor's position atop the cognitive hierarchy.

The best way to keep us from changing is to make us believe

that we can't. The concept of the self and the fixed mindset clearly go hand in hand. The self-illusion is why we are so apt to believe that our abilities are fixed and innate, and why it's been so hard to divorce people of that belief. It's why it's so hard to divorce people from the idea that every brain has been doled out a set, unchanging quantity of intelligence that can be measured and reported as a numerical "intelligence quotient."

Yet we all know, on some level, that life's purest moments—the ones of greatest peace, joy, wonder, and connection—are those where we lose ourselves. Where the performance stops and something truer emerges. Moments where the Genius breaks through.

Trick #5: The Thief of Joy

The Impostor's final trick is perhaps his most insidious, because he uses it so pervasively, so subtly, that most people never even recognize it as sabotage.

Comparison.

You've been learning guitar for two years when you see someone half your age play circles around you. You dream of writing a novel, but a few lines of Hemingway make you feel like a fraud. Your coworker breezes through a spreadsheet analysis that's been eating your lunch all week.

The Impostor whispers, "See? They're just better. You don't have what they have. Stop making a fool of yourself."

This trick works because it contains a kernel of truth wrapped in a lie. The truth is that you will never play a guitar like Hendrix or write like Hemingway, no matter how hard you try. But the lie is that this means there's something wrong with you.

The Standard Issue

Your brain is standard issue. Just like Einstein's. What makes any brain special is not the hardware it's born with. The genetic blueprint for it has been debugged, optimized, and stress-tested by evolution's most ruthless quality assurance program. It's the best design process of all time, and it's what endows every brain with boundless potential. Your brain isn't a prototype; it's a production model. The differences between your brain and anyone else's pale in comparison to the similarities.

Importantly, those similarities include the mechanisms for learning that allow us to acquire and expand our cognitive capabilities, and our solution space, throughout our lives. The differences we observe between brains aren't in the fundamental architecture. They're in what that architecture has learned to do.

To understand how easily we mistake "learning history" for "fundamental architecture," let's consider a thought experiment.

The Literacy Parable

Imagine a society divided into two classes of people, the Readers and the Non-Readers. In this society, the ruling class believes that the ability to read is a rare, genetic gift possessed by only a select few. It's a gift they believe to be endowed by "The Literacy Gene."

Because books are precious and resources are scarce, the society decides it would be wasteful to try to teach the Non-Readers. Plus, it's a considerate thing to do. Subjecting them to the frustration of trying to learn a skill their brains aren't wired for would be cruel.

So, from the age of five, the children of Readers are sent to libraries. They are surrounded by books, tutored in the alphabet, and encouraged to practice phonics daily. The children of Non-Readers are sent to the fields. They never see a book, never learn a letter, and are constantly reminded that reading is "just not their thing."

At the age of twenty, everyone is given a standardized reading test. The Readers ace the test. The Non-Readers fail miserably. These results are held up by the societal elders as proof of The Literacy Gene and the wisdom of their two-class system.

We find this scenario laughable because we know that there is no special reading gene. Nor is it an inborn ability. Reading must be learned. The inability to read results from a lack of opportunity, not a lack of ability.

Yet, by and large, we are still living in this society today. With the exception that, at some point, we decided that reading was too important a skill for some people to miss out on. And so we made providing every brain a reliable path to reading a priority. This is the only reason we don't think some people are born with a reading brain and others aren't.

But when it comes to most everything else, we're still making the same mistake. When you look at someone who's a whiz at math, a virtuoso pianist, or a captivating public speaker and you think that you could never do that, you are making the same error as the societal elders. You are mistaking a difference in training history for a difference in biology.

So, does this mean that we've resolved the nature vs. nurture debate? Does it mean that the environment is the only thing that matters? Hardly.

First of all, one of the lessons in recent decades in genetics is that the debate itself is a false dichotomy. Our genes, which we'd consider the fundamental constituents of our "nature," are meaningless outside an environmental context. It's impossible to isolate the effects of genes and environment because it's the interaction that matters.

Our genes do matter. Genes contain the template for the development of every organ—a template that has been refined over millions of years of evolution. Our template, and the underlying genetic code, is incredibly similar from one human to the next. That comes with all being part of the same species. It's why any of our organs, including the brain, can be readily distinguished from any other animal's just by sight.

On the other hand, our individual environments, which include everything from our mother's diet to our first-grade teacher to our favorite breakfast cereal, are radically different. Environmental variability far exceeds genetic variability. So it's not that "nurture" matters more than "nature" in determining our cognitive capabilities; it's that environment accounts for the lion's share of the *variability* from one person to the next.

In principle, then, every brain can do what any other brain can do. *Provided* those brains are exposed to the *exact* same environments and given the *exact* same training data. We write our neural code based on that training data, and the same code running on two brains would be indistinguishable. The solution space of those two brains would be identical.

In principle, with the right training path, you should be able to write like Shakespeare, paint like Picasso, compose like Bach, act like Streep, or think like Einstein.

In practice, however, it is *impossible*. It will never happen because it can *never* happen.

From the moment your brain made contact with the world, it began its journey down a path that is uniquely your own. A path no brain had been on before or ever will again. A path that wrote your brain's custom software.

Your brain's present configuration is the sum total of all the experiences it's had up to this very moment. It is those experiences that determine what it's currently capable of. And that set of experiences is uniquely yours. No two brains are the same because no two training paths are the same.

Your Unique Signature

Consider the case of handwriting. We're all solving the basic problem when we write, which is to turn our thoughts into squiggly lines other humans can decode.

But no two solutions look identical. No two solutions are the same. Your handwriting networks are the product of every unique handwriting training run you've performed since you first picked up a pencil. Your handwriting algorithms are uniquely yours, which is why you can't write like someone else, and they can't write like you. Because no two paths will ever be identical.

Each brain has solved the problem effectively, in its own way, the product of a path that only that brain has taken. Your handwriting is uniquely yours because your training path was unique. And this applies to everything else you've ever learned.

You're No Einstein! (And He's No You!)

So yes, no matter how hard you try, and no matter how perfect your learning techniques, you will never write like Shakespeare, paint like Picasso, compose like Bach, act like Streep, or think like Einstein. You can't have the same experiences they had, because they already had them. That's the bad news.

But the far better, and liberating, news is that neither they nor anyone else could ever write, paint, compose, act, or think like you. Their brain has its own unique solution space, and so does yours. You can't think like Einstein, and he can't think like you.

The solution space in Einstein's brain encompassed many problems in theoretical physics, but relatively few in the realm of fashion or hairstyling. Einstein followed his natural curiosity, and so his brain developed expertise in the problems it had cared about. He obsessed about the same set of problems day after day, year after year. That curiosity-driven obsession is what created a solution space that was very different from anyone else's. Had he paid more attention to the sorts of things the Impostor cares about, he probably would've had a larger solution space for fashion and hairstyling. But we'd have traded in improved color coordination and a proper side part for the theory of relativity.

Uniquely Yours

A brain is a brain. Every one is magnificent, and every one becomes magnificently different. Each one of us was gifted with one of these magnificent objects at birth, and we get to spend our entire lives writing our own software to customize it to our specifications. Each day we also get to see all the cool and wonderful ways other humans have customized theirs, in many instances pushing the boundaries of what we thought these brains of ours were capable of.

Just don't let those cool and wonderful customizations that other brains have make you think less of yours. And don't make the mistake of chasing the impossible, of setting a goal that can never be reached. You can't replicate someone else's cool and wonderful customizations, but you can create equally cool and wonderful customizations of your own.

Don't stop admiring what other brains have accomplished. Those achievements are genuinely amazing and worth celebrating. But don't use them as evidence that your brain is defective. It's just running different software, created by their unique training data. You'll never be like them, and they'll never be like you. Your potential is boundless, but it is uniquely yours.

The fact that no two brains are the same makes our world endlessly fascinating, and better at collective problem solving. Each one is not better or worse; rather, each one has its own unique set of strengths and weaknesses. Not better or worse, but different.

So, embrace your uniqueness. Lean into it. Ignore the Impostor's ignorant attempts to judge your gifts in comparison to those of others. Your brain is not magnificent in spite of its uniqueness, but because of it. It's the only brain in the history of the universe that can see the world exactly the way you see it and solve problems exactly the way you solve them. It is what you and only you bring to this world. The world doesn't need another

Einstein because it already had one. Rather than trying to become a watered-down version of someone else, work toward becoming the best version of only you.

As e.e. cummings wrote:

> *To be nobody but yourself in a world which is doing its best, night and day, to make you everybody else means to fight the hardest battle which any human being can fight; and never stop fighting.*

Payback Time

Now you know the Impostor's playbook. His five genius-killing tricks. The methods he uses to dominate the cognitive conversation and keep the Genius silent.

But what to do about it? Understanding intellectually that the Impostor is lying to you doesn't magically make his voice suddenly disappear. He's been controlling the cognitive conversation for some time now and isn't going to suddenly stop chattering away. Remember, he thinks he has a very important job to do and will continue trying to do it.

The Impostor has hijacked the cognitive conversation, which is what gives his stories their power. We may not be able to shut him up, but we also don't have to listen. And taking back control of the conversation is how we neutralize his influence and unlock what the Impostor has spent a lifetime convincing you was impossible.

chapter summary

- **The Impostor shapes the future by shaping the story:** He can't control your actions directly, but by crafting the narrative of who you are, he steers your future behavior.
- **Trick #1—The hostile takeover:** In high-stakes moments, the Impostor seizes the cognitive conversation at precisely the moment you need your automated skills to run freely.
- **Trick #2—The gold star trap:** Achievement-driven learning exploits the Impostor's hunger for status but drives the Genius into hibernation.
- **Trick #3—The productivity myth:** The Impostor insists that rest is wasted time, but history's greatest breakthroughs came to minds that were toggling, not grinding.
- **Trick #4—The self-illusion:** The Impostor needs you to believe you are fixed and stable, because growth requires change and change threatens his story.
- **Trick #5—The thief of joy:** The Impostor uses others' achievements as evidence your brain is defective, when differences in ability reflect training history, not biology.

12

turning the tables

I am always doing what I can't do yet
in order to learn how to do it.

—Vincent van Gogh (artist)

So, all this time, you've had two personalities living inside your brain. Technically, more than two. But for this discussion, we're keeping it simple.

One of those personalities, the Genius, dominated your early life. The other, the Impostor, showed up a bit later and is now the mad king of his neural empire. One is a selfless, egoless master of learning and the repository of all your knowledge and skills. The other is a self-centered (literally!) bullshit artist.

If you're like most, you've spent much of your life inadvertently feeding the Impostor and starving the Genius. As a result, the Impostor has grown very strong and the Genius, weak. Now we must shift the balance of power.

Perhaps it is self-evident, but let's first clarify what's at stake. What do you stand to gain by shifting the cognitive conversation? What would it mean to be living a life where the Genius is greasing the synaptic gears?

Releasing the Genius doesn't necessarily mean achieving feats that others would label genius. That's the kind of goal the Impostor would chase, so that sort of goal might sabotage our efforts from the get-go. Besides, we've spent far too long making a fuss over feats of uncommon genius, and far too little making a fuss over the feats of genius every brain performs routinely. Were that not true, you'd already have a much better appreciation of what you were capable of, and I wouldn't have had to spend all this time writing a book to help you see it.

So, while it is true that unlocking your genius does offer you the best odds of achieving feats that others would marvel at and possibly even merit a major award, in the end what we're after is something much deeper and lasting than that.

In short, what we're after is for you to get the most out of that amazing brain you have. Not so you can show everyone how clever you are (nice try, Impostor!), but so you give yourself the best chance of reaching your most meaningful goals. To help ensure that you spend time and energy pursuing what really matters and enjoy every step on that journey. And to experience what it's like when the Genius is at the wheel, and your entire cognitive arsenal is back in the conversation. You had that once in your life, and you can have it again.

Honestly, if I've done my job up to this point, then much of what's in this chapter should be self-evident, as it flows from the model of cognition that we've worked through. You may already have your own ideas of how to transform that model into practical actions.

That said, I've had the advantage of thinking about these ideas for quite some time. Frankly, I've been a bit obsessed with the topic for as long as I can remember. As such, you may find some value in how I answer that question.

I do know that getting the most from your brain has far more in common with tending a garden than it does with building a bookshelf. We can't control or engineer the process, but we can try to create the conditions where it's more likely to emerge. We don't make the flowers bloom, but we can greatly enhance the odds that they will. And our job isn't to understand how to make the flowers, but rather how to care for the soil.

So, what I'm sharing here are my own personal guidelines. I'll provide the general contours and then let you take it from there as to how to apply these principles in your own life. Taking the time to figure out how to apply this framework to your own life and then using it as a lens for filtering your daily experiences is how you transform this from the abstract to the concrete.

Lastly, the following thoughts about unlocking your genius potential are predicated on the assumption that you believe that such a thing is *possible*. Otherwise, we're just spinning our wheels. I have spent several chapters trying to convince you of that, so I'm assuming you're still here because I was successful. If not, thanks for hanging in there until now. It's been real.

And now, without further delay and qualification, let's talk about how we can take back control of the cognitive conversation.

Quiet the Impostor

First things first, we have to deal with the monkey on our backs. Correction: the 2,000-pound gorilla with a loose relationship with the truth who's been weighing down the Genius for much too long.

Given the crushing impact of a back-riding gorilla, it doesn't make much sense to do anything else until we've shed those excess pounds, and all our efforts will be multiplied many times over after we do.

Translation: We must quiet the voice of the Impostor. Notice I didn't say *destroy* the Impostor? That's not possible. Not without brain surgery, at least. The chatter will never go away. But we can turn that chatter, and its influence, way, way down.

Understanding the Task

People have long recognized that there's a maniac chattering away inside our heads who doesn't always serve us well, and a great many people have spent a great many hours troubleshooting that problem. That means there are loads of resources out there for you centered around this topic, from stoicism to cognitive behavioral therapy to mindfulness to Buddhism. All of it revolves around how to free your mind from the tyranny of the self-module. What I present here has been filtered through my neuroscience lens and tailored for our specific aims.

Remember, all mental phenomena are implemented in the connections and communications between our neurons. And so the impact of these mental techniques is 100 percent physical. The Impostor's suppressive influence is ultimately implemented at the level of our synapses, and each of these techniques is designed to weaken it.

Technique #1: Notice and Name

Breaking the illusion begins with noticing it. Our goal is to create psychological distance. We are not the Impostor. The Impostor is just one of a great many task-specific modules running in our brain, his task being to maintain the self-illusion to ourselves and others.

We must learn, then, to recognize his voice. You might recognize some of his favorite phrases: "You're not good at that." "You're not smart enough." "You can't learn to do that." "You're too old to dance like that." "I wonder what they think of me." "Do I look dumb in this fedora?"

And last but not least, "Who do you think you are?"

To which you reply, "It takes one to know one."

You know he's talking when the topic is *you*, and especially your set of attributes and features that must be preserved. Our identity must be protected at all costs, and so any threatening thoughts of growth or change must be shut down. He is preoccupied with how others see us, and with ensuring that their perception aligns with the story he's been telling.

When you do identify his voice, call him out. Either in your head or out loud if you want. "Hello, Impostor. I hear you. Thanks for trying to help, but I've got this." You can be snarky and patronizing with that last sentence if you want.

Speaking of patronizing, in general, the more pathetic and small you make him seem, the less you'll care about what he has to say. Giving him a name is one step in that direction—one that helps create psychological distance between you and the Impostor. I've already given him an unflattering name. But feel free to change it from the Impostor to one of your own, like goober, dillweed, or Chad. No offense, Chad. "Evil Chad" is fine, too.

Don't feel bad about it. He's probably called you a few names over the course of your life. You can mentally roll your eyes at him when he speaks, too. Any way to let him know you see through the bullshit.

The key practice here is simple: any way to create distance between "you" and "him" weakens his power. Each time you recognize his voice, each time you name him as separate from yourself, you chip away at the illusion. Over time, those chips add up. Quieting the Impostor isn't about silencing doubt; it's about preventing doubt from making your decisions.

Sarah is sitting at her kitchen table, laptop open. Her company is offering free courses in data analytics. The email says space is limited. She hovers over the "Register" button.

Data analytics? You? You're not so hot with numbers, remember? You'll just embarrass yourself. Everyone will see you struggle with something that comes easily to them. Stay in your lane, Sarah.

Two months ago, Sarah would have closed the email. That voice was her voice, and that story was her story. She would have told herself she was "being realistic" about her limitations and protecting herself from inevitable disappointment.

She smiles and clicks the button. "Nice try, Chad," she says to an empty room. With a mix of nervousness and exhilaration, the outlines of a story she would've never before thought she could inhabit are starting to take shape.

Technique #2: Starve the Impostor

Once you start noticing and naming the Impostor, pay attention to the places where his voice is loudest. The places where you most feel his presence. What are the environments and activities where he prevails?

For example, you may find his voice is deafening when you're engaged with social media. Some platforms more than others. Social media is the digital playground built by and for the Impostor. It is purified status signaling, and he can't get enough of it.

In a survey I recently conducted of nearly a thousand adults, when asked to rate on a scale of 1 to 10 how worthwhile their time spent on social media platforms that included Facebook, Instagram, Twitter/X, and TikTok was, the average rating was 1.8. Spending time with friends, listening to music, and reading books? A 9.2.

When the Impostor is the only voice in the room, we feel miserable. When he vanishes, we feel at our best.

You'd think this would mean we'd be spending almost none of our time on the former and almost all of it on the latter. Yet we know the reality. The Impostor isn't just controlling the conversation inside our minds; he's controlling the one outside of it, too.

That's not to say you must abandon all activities where his voice is louder. But do recognize that any time spent there is strengthening his influence and weakening the Genius. Be *intentional.*

Other Impostor-amplifying environments share common features. Anywhere that's focused on competition for status, external validation, performance for judgment, or comparison with others. These aren't inherently bad, but they do feed the Impostor. Be mindful of the trade-off and be prepared to counter the tales he will tell.

On the flip side, pay close attention to circumstances where the Impostor's voice softens or disappears entirely. The times when you, quite literally, "lose yourself." When you lose the sense of you as a distinct being separate from your surroundings. When you're fully absorbed in something, be it a book, an idea, a project, a song, a conversation, a card game, a tennis match, and so on.

These are the moments when the Genius can come out and play. Oftentimes, they're the moments when he is already playing. Moments when time disappears and self-consciousness vanishes. What activities produce this for you? What environments? What people?

When we intentionally spend more time doing what quiets the voice of the Impostor and less time doing what amplifies it, we use plasticity to our advantage. The pathways we use grow stronger. The pathways we neglect weaken.

As an easy exercise, list three activities where you lose yourself. List three environments where the Impostor is loudest. Commit to more of the former, less of the latter. Start small and be specific. "Thirty minutes of reading before bed" is better than "Read more." "Thirty minutes of social media per day" is better than "Spend less time on social media."

Feed the Genius

Just by quieting the Impostor's voice, you will have gone a long way toward releasing and realizing what's already there. Removing his tyranny over the cognitive conversation alone will greatly expand your accessible solution space.

Now, we'll take it to the next level. With the Genius released from confinement, it's time to feed him. Because after years of achievement-driven learning and productivity myths, he's quite famished!

Feeding the Genius means building the scaffolding that expands our solution space—the sum total of problems or tasks our brain has the capacity to solve or complete. When we solve an algebra problem, throw a slider, make biscuits, or do the hokey-pokey, our brain is solving a problem. These things are within its solution space. That space is the product of all that you've fed the Genius up until that moment.

There are four core techniques for ensuring the Genius is adequately nourished:

Technique #1: Lead with Curiosity

Much of the software you've written is a result of what you've paid attention to. Externally and internally, we direct our attention to what we care about. And as you know, what the Impostor cares about and what the Genius cares about are two very different things.

The genius exists so that you can learn, grow, and understand. The Genius is the source of our natural curiosity about the world. Our curiosity *reveals* what the Genius cares about, and as such is a valuable signal for what truly matters to us. Following that signal is how to ensure we don't regret where we've placed our attention. Paying attention to what the Genius cares about also helps to ensure you'll grow as a result, since Genius-led learning is the most effective kind.

The Impostor loves to ride the bandwagon. He wants you to pay attention to what's popular because he thinks being different is dangerous. He wants you to follow the herd. From his perspective, nothing good comes from following your curiosity.

That's all fine and good if you want to think like everyone else. The closer your mental diet is to the herd's, the more similar your solution space. You'll succeed in blending in but have a hard time contributing anything original.

YOUR FUEL IS YOUR FATE

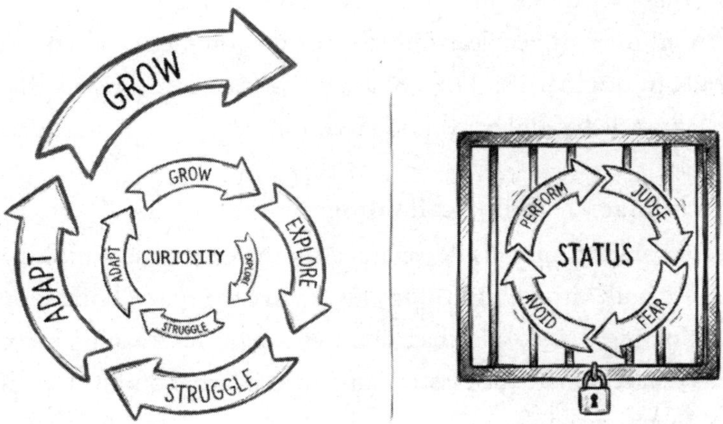

THE GENIUS CYCLE
(FUELED BY CURIOSITY)

THE IMPOSTOR TRAP
(FUELED BY STATUS)

YOUR PROGRESS IS DETERMINED BY YOUR FUEL SOURCE.

THE GENIUS CYCLE RUNS ON CURIOSITY. IN THIS CYCLE, STRUGGLE IS A NECESSARY SIGNAL FOR ADJUSTMENT, LEADING TO THE CONSTRUCTION OF NEW SCAFFOLDING AND CONTINUOUS GROWTH.

THE IMPOSTOR TRAP RUNS ON STATUS. STRUGGLE IS PERCEIVED AS A THREAT TO IDENTITY, TRIGGERING FEAR AND AVOIDANCE. STAGNATION PREVAILS.

Notice what genuinely engages you. Not what you think should interest you, not what would impress others, but what truly captures your attention. What questions do you naturally ask? What are the sorts of things you're doing when time melts away? When your sense of self melts away? Follow those signals.

Don't worry if your curiosities seem odd or impractical. Trust the Genius.

Here's an exercise: List three topics you're drawn to but have avoided because they seemed "impractical." Commit to exploring one. No need to justify it. Just follow the curiosity.

Curiosity-driven learning creates deep understanding and leads to original thinking. Status-driven learning creates shallow knowledge and conventional thinking.

Technique #2: Build Scaffolding

Your solution space is determined by the cognitive scaffolding you've built through learning. To expand the space, build more scaffolding. Easier said than done, as it requires learning methods that stimulate the plastic reorganization that builds the scaffolding we need.

Our existing scaffolding, whether it's in the realm of thinking, perception, or motor skills, determines what we are capable of now, and what is within reach. It represents what we've mastered, and what we're mastering.

To continue progressing in learning anything, all we ever really need to know is the next best step to expand our scaffolding. As long as learning is in the Goldilocks Zone of optimal challenge, progress is a biological certainty. But this requires knowing what we know (our existing scaffolding), knowing what we don't know, and knowing what's within reach.

There are three core requirements for building scaffolding effectively:

Requirement #1: Provide Optimal Challenge

How do we stimulate growth in our muscles? By sending a signal that our current capabilities are insufficient. Why doesn't lifting a 1-pound weight off the floor ten times stimulate muscle growth? Because you can already do it! It's already well within your capabilities, and your body isn't going to waste resources building and supporting extra muscle tissue to give you capabilities you don't need.

Why doesn't trying and failing to lift a 1,000-pound weight off the floor stimulate muscle growth? Because it's too heavy for you to generate any productive muscle activity. It's too far beyond your capabilities.

However, if you lift a 100-pound weight off the floor five times, and then struggle to lift it a sixth and a seventh time, what does that signal? That there's a capability you need that is just beyond where you are right now, and so resources spent to build that extra capability are going to be well spent. This is what exercising in the Goldilocks Zone looks like. That 100-pound weight is providing the optimal challenge.

Our goals with learning are precisely the same, except that we're trying to stimulate brain tissue growth, or rewiring. But brains don't lift heavy things; they solve problems.

So we stimulate growth by operating at the edge of our problem skills. If our brain can solve all the problems we throw at it—if they are all within our solution space—then it has no reason to grow and change. Our efforts won't send a stimulation signal. In this case, our capabilities are perfectly tailored to our needs.

If our brain can solve none of the problems we throw at it—if they are all outside our solution space—then it has nothing to base its growth on. Even if we send a stimulation signal, it has no idea how to rewire itself to support progress. It has no scaffolding upon which to build.

However, if our brain can solve some but not all the problems we throw at it—if they are just at the edge and outside of our solution space—then we have everything we need. We've (1) sent the signal that our present capabilities are insufficient and (2) provided feedback on the rewiring that would result in progress. This is the Goldilocks Zone of learning, where we're providing our brain with an optimal challenge.

But how do you know you're in the zone?

The simple answer is that things are not too easy and not too hard. When the level of difficulty is "just right." When what you're trying to learn is challenging but attainable.

More specifically, research on optimal learning conditions across domains consistently points to a success rate of 60–85 percent. That means we're succeeding a little over half the time.

That rate provides enough errors to signal the brain that a change is needed, but enough wins to show what patterns should become permanent. That sweet spot should also feel good. It's not so easy that you're bored, but not so hard that you're frustrated. It should feel like you're stretching but not breaking.

When you notice you're out of the sweet spot, when your attention is drifting from boredom or your mouth starts emitting colorful language, it's time to adjust. Bring it back into the zone. Make it harder if it's too easy. Break it into smaller steps, or shrink the gap, if it's too hard.

Remember that if you're learning successfully, then your Goldilocks Zone is a moving target. What's optimal today likely won't be optimal next week. That's what happens when you build scaffolding. Problems that were once too hard become too easy. Tasks automate and your skills scale.

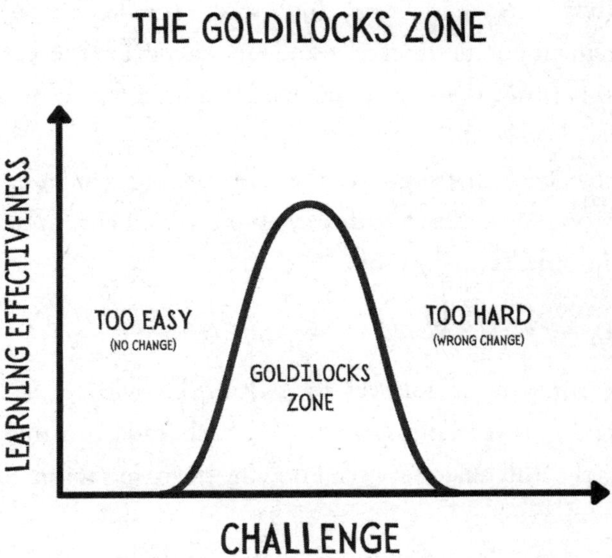

THE GOLDILOCKS ZONE OF LEARNING IS WHERE THE TASK IS OPTIMALLY CHALLENGING AND PROGRESS IS A BIOLOGICAL CERTAINTY.

IF IT'S TOO EASY, OUR EFFORTS WON'T STIMULATE CHANGE.

IF IT'S TOO HARD, OUR EFFORTS MAY STIMULATE THE WRONG KIND OF CHANGE (BAD HABITS).

Requirement #2: Seek Ongoing Feedback

Effective learning happens when we're operating at the edge of our capabilities. We need mistakes to signal that change is needed, and we need wins to know what that change should look like. But distinguishing between the two requires *feedback*. We have to know how we're doing.

It may sound obvious, but "learning" in a feedback vacuum is extraordinarily common, including in the place where most of us went to do our learning. Traditional school feedback is infrequent (tests every few weeks), high stakes (grades matter), for measurement not modification, and separated from the learning process. It is not the sort of feedback required for stimulating and steering growth.

The feedback that supports effective learning is ongoing, low stakes, for modification rather than measurement, and integrated into the learning process.

Requirement #3: Attach to Existing Scaffolding

New learning must connect to existing knowledge. Isolated facts are cognitive islands. As physicist Richard Feynman put it, "There's the difference between knowing the name of something and knowing something."

Words are cognitive shortcuts that compress knowledge into single sounds. If all you know is the sound, it's not knowledge, it's trivia. Much of school learning involves memorizing isolated facts such as state capitals, dates, and formulas. Good for acing tests or winning trivia contests, but not for building scaffolding.

Because it is enabled by change and growth in neural tissue, building scaffolding takes time. It's why both the duration and sequence in learning any complex skill, from learning to walk to doing a backflip to calculating the second derivative, requires a minimum amount of time and follows a stereotyped progression.

Why have there been virtually no major scientific or creative breakthroughs from child prodigies? Why no transformative works of genius? Because while their atypical interests generate atypical scaffolding for their age, it's not atypical compared to adult experts. A prodigy's brain is constrained by the same limits of biology as every brain, and there's just simply not enough time in childhood to create the necessary scaffolding. Feats of genius require uncommon scaffolding, built through many years of consistent and effortful learning.

A focus on building scaffolding helps us avoid the illusion of knowledge. If you're leading with curiosity, this will usually take care of itself. And if you're learning facts, make sure they're attached to something, and it's not just memorization for its own sake.

For much of our lives, the goal when we "learned" was not to understand, but to produce the right answer. This is still what learning means and what counts as intelligence to the Impostor.

Here's an exercise: Pick one skill you're working on or you want to develop. Assess your current level. Identify what's just beyond that. What feels challenging but within your reach? How will you get feedback to know when you've made mistakes and when you've succeeded?

Progressive composition through optimal challenge, ongoing feedback, and connection to existing knowledge builds real scaffolding. Once it's built, it's yours for good. If you've truly learned something, you still know it. If you've only memorized it, you've forgotten it soon after the test.

Technique #4: Always Be Creating

We live in an age of infinite consumption. We can watch lectures, read articles, and scroll through tutorials until the end of time. The Impostor loves this mode. Passive consumption feels productive—"I'm researching!"—but it is safe. As long as you are consuming, you can't fail. You can't look foolish.

But you also cannot grow.

The Genius is not a consumer; the Genius is a builder. We are the species that makes things. We chip arrowheads, weave baskets, compose symphonies, and write code. Evolution didn't design your brain to be a hard drive for storing facts, but a tool for manipulating the world. The deep learning that writes software into your neural tissue only happens when you move from consumption to creation.

This is what I meant earlier by "active knowledge construction." You must take the raw information you've consumed and forge it into something new. You have to get your hands dirty.

So, don't just read about history. Write an argument about it.

Don't just watch a coding tutorial. Build a broken app that does nothing but display a picture of a cat.

Don't just listen to a podcast about woodworking. Go sand a board.

Creation acts as the ultimate stress test for your scaffolding. When you consume, you can trick yourself into thinking you understand. The moment you try to create, however, your gaps in understanding are instantly exposed.

That exposure makes the Impostor squirm, because to him it looks like failure. He will scream, "You don't know what you're doing! Stop before someone sees!"

But the Genius loves it. To the Genius, that gap between what you know and what you're trying to make is the virtuous cycle of growth in action. It is the friction that builds scaffolding.

And here is the most important rule for this technique: Create for the sake of it. You built the most advanced cognitive abilities we humans possess during your childhood. Back when you created for the sake of it. Children are driven to create, day after day. Why? Because the Genius is still running the show. And the Genius only cares about growth and understanding.

The Impostor will want you to create for status. He will want to know if the painting is "good," if the app will "make money," or if the essay will "get likes." If you focus on the outcome, you will freeze. You will judge your work before it even exists.

The Genius loves the process. The Impostor loves the outcome. So build things that are ugly. Write songs that don't rhyme. Write code that is inefficient. It's not the product, but the neurological activity required to produce it, that matters.

The Irony of Impact

The irony here is that creating for the sake of it is the only path to achieving the recognition that the Impostor so desperately craves. The only way he'll ever get it is by no longer wanting it.

The Impostor wants the applause, but he wants to skip the struggle. He wants the breakthrough without the breakdown. But you cannot fake scaffolding. Shallow, status-driven work produces shallow, derivative results. It might get a few likes today, but it vanishes tomorrow.

Deep, robust, and original scaffolding can only be built

through the honest, messy work of creation for its own sake. It is built in the hours when nobody is watching, when you are wrestling with a problem purely because it fascinates you.

The creators of history's most celebrated works didn't produce them because they were hungry for recognition. The work wasn't a means to an end. The work was the end. The accolades, which the Genius couldn't care less about, were a side effect of their curiosity-driven obsessions.

When you create to learn, you build a unique solution space that produces work that the world actually values. By ignoring the Impostor's demand for instant validation, you inadvertently build the very thing that eventually earns it.

Technique #5: Cross-Train Your Brain

Our cognitive machinery evolved to support three primary domains of cognitive skills: motor, perceptual, and symbolic (thinking). The latter was the last to appear on our evolutionary timeline.

Somewhere along the way, a nasty rumor spread that intelligence only pertained to thinking skills. As I mentioned in a prior chapter, this likely had something to do with wanting our brains to be at the tippy top of the intelligence hierarchy, since thinking skills were our brain's signature move.

But you are now cured of such intellectual snobbery. You now realize that thinking skills have no privileged position in the pantheon of intelligence. Problem solving is problem solving. All domains of intelligence require cognitive scaffolding, and there's a strong argument to be made for building all three.

Outwardly, speaking Spanish, riding a skateboard, performing in a musical, or playing the tuba may look very different. But inwardly, it's still all about patterns. It's all enabled by cognitive scaffolding. The more unique your scaffolding, the more unique your solution space, the more likely novel solutions and insights are to emerge.

A study of more than one thousand scientists found that Nobel laureates were fifteen to twenty-five times more likely than their peers to engage in writing or performing arts. All in all, the evidence shows that developing a diverse set of expertise greatly enhances the odds of making a scientific breakthrough. A unique solution space enabled by unique scaffolding.

Novel solutions and insights often come from identifying shared factors in seemingly disparate domains. From noticing similarities in patterns nobody has noticed before. So, the larger and more diverse your pattern library, the more likely that is to happen. Building intelligence in one domain enhances all others. The mechanisms are the same, and the patterns inform each other.

Technique #6: Learn How to Learn

Learning how to learn is the ultimate metaskill. The one skill that rules them all. Ironically, and tragically, it isn't taught in school. Even worse, most of us must *unlearn* the habits school instilled in order to learn effectively.

In school we learned to wait for instructions, seek a single right answer, avoid mistakes, limit learning to formal settings, ask few questions, quit when challenged, and follow the rules even when they're clearly wrong.

Effective learning involves curiosity-driven exploration, multiple solution paths, productive failure, persistence through difficulty, asking questions, and adaptation when an approach isn't working.

I think learning how to learn is such an important topic, I decided to write an entire book on it called *Anyone Can Play Music*. It's specifically focused on learning a musical instrument but uses that as a vehicle for discussing why and how we can learn anything, at any age.

Technique #7: Leverage AI as a Learning Partner

This is the most wonderful time to be a curious human. By far. This was already true when the internet gave us access to the entire catalog of human knowledge at our fingertips. But with the advent of Large Language Models (LLMs), we now have access to the most powerful learning tool in human history, one that helps us turn that knowledge into capability.

AI tutors are available 24/7, never tire of answering questions, can adapt to any learning level, and possess expert knowledge across virtually every domain. But whether those interactions end up feeding or starving the Genius depends entirely on how you use them.

To appreciate why AI represents such a massive opportunity for learning for us all, we need to look at what decades of research has revealed about the most effective way to educate.

The Two-Sigma Problem

In 1984, educational psychologist Benjamin S. Bloom published findings from a study comparing three different instructional settings.

The first was conventional classroom instruction. You know

that scene: rows of desks, a single teacher, and twenty to thirty students.

The second setting was "Mastery Learning," where students progressed at their own pace with materials tailored to their current abilities. Assessments were performed at the end of every unit of instruction to determine if the student was ready to move on.

The third was one-on-one tutoring. The format mirrored Mastery Learning, except that if gaps were found after an assessment, the tutor would provide specific instruction to fill them.

The results were both extraordinary and alarming: 84 percent of students in Mastery Learning outperformed their classroom peers.

But one-on-one tutoring was in a league of its own, with a staggering 98 percent of tutored students outperforming their classroom peers! That's two standard deviations from the norm, or two "sigma" in statistical jargon. This means that the *average* student given one-on-one instruction would outperform 98 percent of students in a conventional classroom.

Many in the field were shocked by these results. It was a finding entirely at odds with the Special Brain Story. It showed that if you provide any brain with an optimal path to success, then success is virtually guaranteed. It showed that *how* we learn matters far more than the brain we're born with.

Bloom was unsettled by the findings. They plainly demonstrated how much potential was being left unrealized by a one-size-fits-nobody approach to education. But providing one-on-one tutoring for every student was a fantasy. Bloom challenged educators to find approaches that could replicate these effects at scale, but the "two-sigma problem" remained unsolved for forty years.

That may soon change. Because AI can already deliver what Bloom dreamed of. It can deliver personalized instruction that's always in the Goldilocks Zone. And it can do so anytime, anywhere. We may soon move from a "two-sigma problem" to a "twenty-sigma solution" at the societal level. But we already have what we need to realize those benefits at the personal level.

Forklift or Dead Lift?

There's a healthy dose of hand-wringing and brow-furrowing happening right now around what AI is going to do to our brains. It bears a striking resemblance to the fears that accompanied technologies like the printing press, the calculator, and the personal computer. The fear is that if we let the machines do all our thinking, our thinking skills will wither.

This is an understandable concern. But most of those concerns revolve around its broad use in education. On a personal level, ensuring your AI interactions are feeding and not starving the Genius is pretty straightforward. It's a matter of being intentional. Along those lines, one simple question to ask yourself with each interaction is, Am I using AI like a forklift or a dead lift?

This handy metaphor comes from Kevin Roose, a technology columnist for the *New York Times*. A forklift is a machine that does work for us. It literally does our heavy lifting so we don't have to. Using AI as a forklift means we're letting it do the work for us. It is removing any challenge.

In a dead lift, however, we do the heavy lifting. We bend over and pick a barbell up off the floor. What for? Not because we need to move it anywhere, but because the effort stimulates muscle growth. That is the objective of any learning we do. If you're using AI to maintain your learning in the Goldilocks Zone of optimal challenge, it will promote growth.

More generally, our goal is to ensure that our AI usage is human-centered, not machine-centered. In my own efforts to ensure my usage meets that objective, I find it helpful to think of it in three broad categories.

The first is "Drudge AI." This is AI that we use to relieve us from intellectual drudgery. Just as machines like the dishwasher and the washing machine relieved us from physical work that drained our energy and sucked our souls, Drudge AI does this for cognitive work. These are the cognitive tasks with no redeeming neurological value, where outsourcing them brings nothing but upside. Think audio transcription, proofreading for typos, scheduling appointments, formatting citations, sorting emails, and so on. Here, we're intentionally using AI like a forklift. Offloading those tasks to AI won't feed the Genius directly, but it frees up cognitive resources that you can direct toward more worthwhile pursuits.

The second category is "Boost AI." These are the tasks where we use AI to become better together. Here, AI acts like a cognitive orthotic, enhancing our capabilities. It's not relieving us of cognitive work; it's just making the work we do more effective. Boost AI makes us more capable *today*.

The third category, and my favorite use case of all, is "Mentor AI." This is the use case that can solve Bloom's two-sigma problem. Here, AI is facilitating Genius-led learning, nurturing our curiosities and tailoring instruction to our present needs and ability. Our interactions build cognitive scaffolding and expand our solution space. Mentor AI makes us more capable *tomorrow*. This is using AI to *expand* human intelligence, not replace it.

The Struggle Is the Point

Remember, you're using AI like a forklift if you're copying its answers without understanding how it arrived at them, using it to complete assignments rather than understand concepts, feeling no cognitive strain during the interaction, or asking "What's the answer?" instead of "How do I figure this out?"

In the end, if you're leading with curiosity, you're virtually assured to have productive, growth-promoting interactions with AI. Because when you're leading with curiosity, learning is the point. The goal is to build scaffolding that creates capability and cultivates understanding. That's the reward. Outsourcing that to AI is like having it eat your ice cream for you.

Using AI just to get the answers is an Impostor goal. Because to the Impostor, the appearance of competence is just as good as actual competence. When incentives are designed to appeal to the Impostor, cheating is to be expected. In that case, the problem isn't the tool; the problem is the system. Using AI to "cheat," or shortcut the learning process, is only a concern in Impostor-led cultures of achievement, not in Genius-led cultures of curiosity.

In an age of AI, this distinction forces us to redefine the value of human cognition. For centuries, we measured intelligence by the result—who could calculate the fastest, who knew the most facts, who could produce the cleanest copy. The Impostor loves results because results confer status.

But if machines can provide the result instantly, then the value of a human being is no longer the output, but the struggle itself. The "Genius" isn't the part of you that knows the answer; the Genius is the part of you that enjoys the confusion of finding it. In a world of infinite forklifts, the only thing that separates us from the machines is our willingness to deadlift. The Impostor wants the answer; the Genius wants the struggle. The struggle is the point.

Support the Hardware

I would be remiss if I didn't mention the importance of tending the hardware that cognition runs on. Effective learning depends on the growth and reorganization of living tissue. Responding to that stimulation requires materials (nutrients) and time. Just as your muscles can't grow in response to the stimulation of a workout without protein, your brain can't grow in response to the stimulation of learning without brain tissue–building materials.

Our lifestyle determines the return we get on our efforts to stimulate growth and change. And our main lifestyle levers are diet, physical activity, and sleep.

Diet provides the nutrients we need to build tissue and to perform all the life-sustaining chemical reactions. Physical activity drives blood flow to the brain and triggers the release of growth factors essential for building new connections. Sleep is when almost all our brain growth occurs. We don't build scaffolding while we're learning; we build it while we're *sleeping*, based on the signals we sent during our waking hours. Sleep is also when the brain recovers and restores from the activity of the day, replenishing our tank of cognitive resources.

I also think the evidence is clear that learning is the single best thing we can do to boost and maintain the health of our brain, provided that our lifestyle supports those efforts. The full details of how to do so are beyond the scope of this book, but my good friend, colleague, and podcast cohost, Dr. Tommy Wood, has published the definitive guide on it: *The Stimulated Mind*, which I strongly encourage you to give a read.

Sarah's daughter Emma comes home on a regular Tuesday afternoon in October. She's nine years old. She drops her backpack by the door and heads straight to the kitchen, shoulders slumped.

"How was school?" Sarah asks, looking up from her laptop, where she's been working through a particularly tricky data visualization problem for the analytics course.

"Fine," says Emma.

Sarah is not convinced. Her maternal intuition suggests she probe further. She closes her laptop. "Tell me what happened."

Emma hesitates, then pulls a paper from her backpack. A math quiz. And a red 62 percent at the top.

In that instant, Sarah is transported thirty years to the back seat of her mom's car. Her mother's voice echoes in her mind, suggesting a response: *It's okay, sweetie. Not everyone is good at math. You're more creative, like me.*

And a few months ago, she would have said those exact words. She would've believed them completely and meant them as kindness.

But three months ago, she also would have said she could never do data analytics. Would have closed that course registration email without a second thought. Would have been certain that quantitative work "just wasn't for her."

And yet, right now, open on her laptop, is a regression analysis she's halfway through. Getting to this point hasn't been easy. There have been fits and starts. She's had to revisit basic math concepts from her high school days. She's had to rewatch lectures. She's had to be patient with herself and consistently remind herself that growth takes time. That you aren't born good at things but become good at them. That building the neural scaffolding that can solve these data analytics takes time, and occurs on an individual's own schedule, not anyone else's.

She looks at Emma's quiz more carefully. "Can I see what you got wrong?"

Emma points to a word problem about fractions. "I didn't understand what it was asking."

"Okay," Sarah says. "Let me see if I understand it." She reads through the problem slowly. "So they're asking how many pizzas you'd need if each person eats three-quarters of a pizza and there are eight people . . ."

She works through it out loud, making a mistake, catching it, correcting it. The same way she works through her analytics problems—trying, failing, adjusting, trying again.

"Wait," Emma says. "So it's six pizzas?"

"I think so. Let's check." They work through it together.

When they're done, Emma looks up. "You're good at math."

Sarah almost laughs. She has to stop herself from correcting Emma. The old story is as automatic as breathing.

Instead, she says, "I'm learning. Same as you. I've just been at it longer. I'm taking a class right now that's pretty hard, but I'm figuring it out."

Emma's eyes widen slightly. "Really?"

"Really. I got a problem wrong yesterday. I had to try it three different ways before I got it!"

"But you figured it out?"

"Eventually, yeah."

Emma nods, already pulling out her homework. "Can you help me with the rest?"

"Absolutely. We'll figure it out together."

Later that night, after Emma's asleep, Sarah sits at the kitchen table with her analytics homework. She thinks about her mom, who meant well. Who was just passing down what she'd been told. Who was trying to comfort her daughter the only way she knew how.

She thinks about the presentation that went south, the decades of avoiding anything with numbers, the opportunities she'd turned down because they "weren't for someone like her."

She thinks about Emma working through that homework, not ashamed of getting it wrong, just trying to figure it out.

Sarah had believed the story her mother told her. Believed it so completely she almost told Emma the same one.

Looking back, she can now see it all so clearly. The thing that was keeping her back all this time was that *story*. A story based on a myth, perpetuated until it had become an accepted truth. Seeing through that story has opened up an ocean of possibility. Recognizing the depth of her own potential has changed everything.

Your North Star

Many volumes could be spent on this topic. Replacing the Special Brain Story with the Every Brain Story is the single most important step you can take. That is the Impostor's greatest lie.

Beyond that, what's most important are the three steps: quiet the Impostor, feed the Genius, and support the hardware. All else is details.

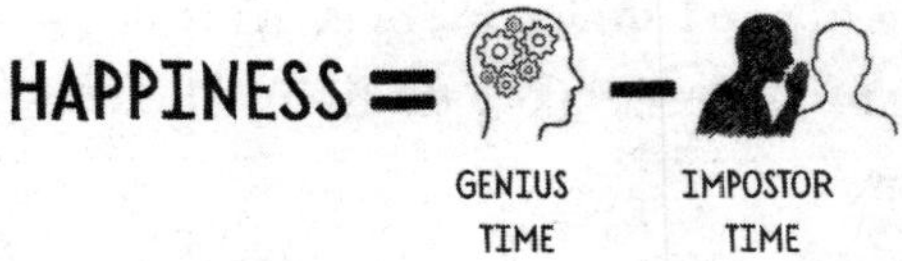

And if you were to force me to boil it down into just one single guideline for a genius-led life, it would be this: curiosity-driven lifelong learning. That's my North Star.

We began with the mystery of Einstein's ordinary brain. How could a brain so extraordinary look just like mine and yours? Now we have the answer: intelligence isn't born; it's built through curiosity-driven learning. Just as Einstein suspected.

It's easy to follow the Impostor's priorities of wealth, status, and power, as he will always be trying to convince you of their importance. But pursuing those goals won't get you anywhere close to finding out what your brain is capable of, nor would they lead to lasting fulfillment.

chapter summary

- **Quiet the Impostor:** Recognize his voice and create psychological distance. Name him, limit time in environments where he's loudest, and spend more time in activities where he disappears.
- **Feed the Genius:** Expand your solution space through curiosity-driven learning. Stay in the Goldilocks Zone of optimal challenge, seek ongoing feedback, and connect new knowledge to existing scaffolding.

- **Leverage AI as a learning partner:** AI is a powerful learning tool, if used like a dead lift. The struggle is the point.
- **Support the hardware:** Diet provides the materials, physical activity drives growth factors, and sleep is when the brain actually builds scaffolding. Lifestyle determines the return on your learning efforts.
- **Lead with curiosity:** The key to a Genius-led life is following your curiosity.

13

the genius of doing nothing

At the moment when I put my foot on the step the idea came to me, without anything in my former thoughts seeming to have paved the way for it.

—Henri Poincaré (mathematician and physicist)

You've spent time dutifully building your cognitive scaffolding. You've followed your curiosity, pursued challenges in your Goldilocks Zone, and developed skills across perception, movement, and thought. Your potential solution space, representing the sum total of "problems" your brain could theoretically solve, has expanded by leaps and bounds.

Yet, at any given moment, you can only access a fraction of it.

This chapter is about the final piece of the puzzle: deliberately shifting the routing architecture to access different parts of your solution space. We've seen how Mendeleev's breakthrough came during sleep, how Einstein's insights emerged during walks, how study participants solved problems during rest that focused effort couldn't crack. How breakthrough solutions appeared, time and again, when least expected.

Which is why regular, intentional mode shifting is key to releasing your potential. The Impostor wants you in task-positive mode all the time, grinding away, proving to everyone how "productive" you are. But some of your best work, quite possibly the most impactful work you could create, can only happen when you toggle away from that mode entirely.

Imagine a smartphone loaded up with apps of all kinds. Apps for navigation, photo editing, word processing, language translation, calculating, music streaming, and so on. Each app has its own specific capabilities, determined by its underlying code.

But, at any given time, only some of the apps are accessible. And only a subset of those are able to exchange information back and forth. As a result, what your smartphone can do at any given moment depends on the apps you can access, and how they communicate with each other. A Spanish translation app can't help you find a bathroom in Acapulco if you can't open it.

That's essentially how your brain operates. Except you wrote the code for your cognitive apps through learning.

All that scaffolding you've constructed through learning, along with the solution space it creates, exists as patterns of connections in your neural tissue. But which patterns you can currently access depends on your brain's present routing architecture. That routing architecture determines which modules can participate in the cognitive conversation at this moment.

And that routing architecture is always in flux as your brain toggles between modes large and small.

The same brain that during a dinner conversation can't remember the word for that thing you use to strain noodles will effortlessly recall the word "colander" while daydreaming in the shower. The marketing strategy that eluded you all day at the office arrives out of the blue during a run that evening. The answer you couldn't conjure while sitting at your desk taking a test pops into your mind a few moments later as you're walking across campus.

We are all familiar with these moments. It's reasonable to see them as evidence of a brain that's fickle or unreliable. Or insufficiently caffeinated. That sometimes it's firing on all cylinders, and other times it can't find a spark. But it's not. These moments reveal a brain working exactly as designed.

Different modes of brain operation—from sleep to wakefulness and everything in between—create different routing architectures. Those routing architectures determine which cognitive modules can communicate, which determines what you can think, perceive, remember, and do in that moment.

You don't have one static solution space that's always there. You have multiple, each one specific to a particular brain mode. If our capabilities depend on our current mode, then expanding what we can do isn't only about building more scaffolding. It's also about learning to shift between modes, or learning to *toggle*. In the last chapter, we discussed how to train our brain to build scaffolding and solution space. Now it's time to talk about how to toggle to get the most out of those efforts.

The Practice of Toggling

Most people spend too much time in focused, task-positive mode. Or at least trying to spend time there. We've absorbed the cultural message that productivity means focused work. That time not spent executing specific tasks is time wasted. That if we're not actively working, we're not contributing.

This is the Impostor's voice, and it's killing our potential.

We've seen the evidence throughout this book. Breakthrough after breakthrough emerging not in spite of rest, but because of it.

Yet we're still convinced that intelligence comes from effort alone. From pushing harder. From maximizing every minute of "productivity." We've built entire cultures around this belief, and in doing so, we've locked ourselves out of much of what our brains can do. Leonardo da Vinci understood this tension centuries ago when he observed that "men of lofty genius when they are doing the least work are most active." The solution isn't to spend less time working; it's to redefine what "working" means. To fully comprehend what we lose out on when we undervalue rest, and what we stand to gain when we prioritize it. That we understand that rest isn't the absence of work but work of a different kind. It's when your brain does its heaviest reorganization. It's when learning transfers to unconscious networks. It's when the routing architecture shifts to unlock solution spaces that focused effort couldn't reach.

So what does this look like in practice? The general goal is to regularly engage in a diversity of mental states beyond focused, or "task positive," mode. While much of this exists along a spectrum, at a minimum we want to regularly engage in the three primary forms of rest.

The first form is full cognitive rest. In this state, attention is free floating and not directed toward anything specific. Lying in the grass watching the clouds drift by. Sitting on a bench in a park to people watch. Lying in a bathtub looking at the bubbles. The sorts of stuff we all used to do before screens made boredom optional.

The second is active rest. Any activity where your body is in motion but your attentional demands are low. Just enough to move safely and smoothly, but not enough to create cognitive strain. This can include light forms of cardio like walking, hiking, running, sailing, cycling, rowing, and so on. But it can also include things like washing dishes, gardening, and showering. In all likelihood, these each produce nonoverlapping routing architectures and solution spaces. So the more, the merrier.

Whenever possible, get yourself into natural environments. Nature is particularly effective for triggering our default mode, while built environments require constant cognitive processing that adds cognitive load. Nature provides genuine rest. Who knows how much of our modern world we owe to long walks through the woods?

And last but not least of our crucial forms of rest is sleep. It's the time when our brain constructs scaffolding. And it's the time for mode shifts that allow for cognitive conversations that could never happen during wakefulness, enabling the kind of creative problem solving that waking hours cannot touch.

None of this happens automatically. The current of modern life will sweep away your opportunities for rest if you allow it. Build them into your day like you build in work time. It's especially crucial if creativity and originality are important to you. Your best ideas and breakthroughs will almost always occur when you're not expecting them. They come from the Genius, and he lives deep underground.

Beware, the Impostor will try to undermine your efforts here. He'll accuse you of being lazy. He'll tell you that producing more always comes from grinding harder. So, there's one more Impostor-neutralizing trick I want to share with you. It involves wielding his own desperate need for self-preservation against him.

The Impostor's Paradox

The Impostor's influence is peculiar. On the one hand, he is clueless and powerless. He has no access to the gears that control our actions, nor does he have any idea why we do the things we do. If he can't influence our current actions, how does he influence us at all?

By shaping our future actions.

By crafting the story of who we are, the Impostor shapes who we become. He can't control our current behavior directly, but he doesn't have to. All he needs is for us to buy into the story. The story becomes the compass our unconscious networks steer our actions by.

All too often, conforming to the story results in lives of increasing stagnation. We spend countless time and energy maintaining a version of us that deep down doesn't feel true. We become who the Impostor says we are. We become the story we tell. We become the identity the Impostor creates.

Research supports the powerful influence of identity over behavior. Much of our current cultural and political polarization is the result of digital technology that's been expertly weaponized to manipulate our need to preserve it.

But we can flip the script. We can use our identity—and the Impostor's need to preserve it—in our favor. How? By identifying first and foremost as a lifelong learner.

The problem with identifying as someone who is smart, slow,

fast, strong, weak, liberal, conservative, musical, mathematical, funny, artistic, and so on, is that it creates strong incentives to make that appear so to others as well as to ourselves. At least from the Impostor's perspective. And so we will avoid anything that threatens, or undermines, that identity.

Challenges are to be avoided. Mistakes are the enemy. The incentives align around comfort, safety, and stagnation.

But precisely the opposite is true if I identify as a lifelong learner. Challenges are opportunities. Mistakes are essential for growth. If others see me screw up, or if I see it, it's proof that I am who I say I am. Someone who is always learning.

I've met and worked with many people in my life. I've spent considerable time in the halls of elite institutions. Without question, the "smartest" people I've known, the most original and innovative thinkers, the ones who blew my mind with their ideas, creativity, and insights, have never been those with the highest IQ scores, GPAs, or academic pedigrees.

They have always been the ones who are the most curious. The ones who are always questioning, always reading, always learning, unafraid to put themselves out there and risk looking ignorant or stupid. Curiosity, and the desire to learn, always mattered most. If you identify as a lifelong learner, in order for the Impostor to save himself, he must become the Genius.

Sarah stares at her laptop screen. Her analysis of the customer retention data is solid, clearly showing that churn rates spike at the three-month mark across all segments. But she can't figure out how to best visualize it for the nontechnical executive team.

She's been wrestling with the problem all week, and her presentation is tomorrow morning.

Stop trying so hard. Trust yourself.

She closes the laptop and laces up her running shoes.

The trail through the park is quiet in the evening light. Oak trees overhead casting long shadows. Ten minutes in, with music blaring and her feet locked in rhythm, an image pops into her mind. It's a heat map, color-coded by cohort, with time on the x-axis. The perfect visualization for presenting her analysis.

She stops, pulls out her phone, records a quick voice note. Then keeps running.

Her mind wanders as her pace quickens again. She can hardly believe how much has changed over the last six months. In some ways, she barely recognizes herself. But in other ways, she's more like herself than she's ever felt. Like she's reconnected with something essential that had been lost. Or hidden.

She's moving through life with an easy confidence. Living on her own terms. The voice of doubt is down to a whisper, replaced by a belief and a trust in herself that she hasn't experienced in ages. It fills her with a sense of possibility she finds exhilarating.

The hardest part now is deciding what she'll tackle next.

chapter summary

- **Your solution space depends on your current mode:** Scaffolding determines potential, but your brain's current routing architecture determines what you can access.

- **Rest is not the absence of work:** During rest, the brain reorganizes, consolidates learning, and accesses cognitive conversations that focused effort cannot reach.
- **Practice the three forms of rest:** Full cognitive rest, active rest, and sleep each produce distinct routing architectures. Accessing more modes unlocks more potential.
- **The Impostor's paradox:** Identifying as a lifelong learner flips the Impostor's self-preservation in your favor, making challenges, opportunities, and growth the path of least resistance.

the genius operating system

A Field Manual for Human Potential

WARNING: *This manual assumes an ordinary human brain.*

OBJECTIVE: *To override default social programming (The Impostor) and reengage the native learning engine (The Genius).*

1. System Architecture: Know Your Components

Your brain runs two conflicting operating systems. Use this comparison table to identify which one is currently active.

THE GENIUS (Optimal)	THE IMPOSTOR (Malware)
Drive: Curiosity and Mastery	**Drive:** Status and Validation
Goal: Understanding the unknown	**Goal:** Looking smart and safe
Method: Trial, Error, and Feedback	**Method:** Comparison and Avoidance
Reaction to Failure: "Interesting data."	**Reaction to Failure:** "I am a fraud."
Time Orientation: Deep Present (Flow)	**Time Orientation:** Future/Past (Anxiety)

2. System Diagnostic: Who Is Driving?

Instructions: For each check, mark the statement that matches your current state of mind. Tally your score at the bottom.

1. Voice Check: What Is Your Inner Dialogue Saying?

- ☐ A. "I wonder how this works." / "Let's try and see."
- ☐ B. "What if I mess this up?" / "They are judging me."

2. Motivation Check: Why Are You Doing This?

- ☐ A. To understand, explore, or solve a problem.
- ☐ B. To look smart, avoid embarrassment, or gain status.

3. Challenge Check: How Does the Task Feel?

- ☐ A. Engaging struggle. Hard but possible.
- ☐ B. Overwhelming (Panic) *or* Boring (Autopilot).

4. Curiosity Check: What Are You Wondering?

- ☐ A. "I have a specific question about the content."
- ☐ B. "I hope I'm doing this right." / Nothing specific.

Mostly A's: GENIUS ACTIVE.

Protocol: *Maintain momentum. Ensure you get sleep tonight to join this scaffolding.*

Mostly B's: IMPOSTOR HIJACK.

Protocol: *STOP immediately. Do not push harder and risk further psychic injury.*

Use the Troubleshooting Matrix in Section 4, following.

3. The Learning Engine: Calibration Guide

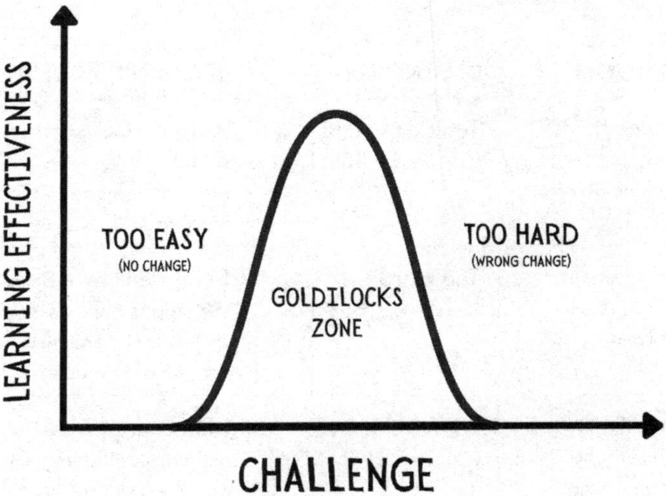

Figure 1: *The Learning Curve. Learning effectiveness peaks when the challenge is just manageable (60–85 percent success rate). Below this zone is boredom (no growth); above it is anxiety (shutdown).*

Effective learning only happens in the **Goldilocks Zone** (60–85 percent success rate). Use this symptom checker to adjust your difficulty level.

SYMPTOM	DIAGNOSIS	REQUIRED ACTION
Boredom, mind wandering, checking phone.	**Too Easy** (Success > 85%)	**Increase Constraints:** Add speed, remove tools, or combine with another skill.
Rage, despair, feeling "stupid," paralysis.	**Too Hard** (Success < 60%)	**Scaffold Down:** Break the step in half. Ask, "What is the smallest version of this I can do?"
Time dilation, engagement, frequent small mistakes followed by correction.	**OPTIMAL** (Success 60%–85%)	**Maintain:** You are building scaffolding. Do not stop until fatigue sets in.

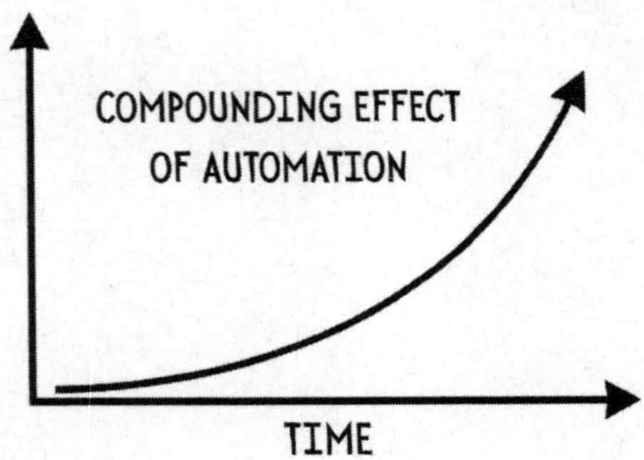

Figure 2: The Genius Advantage. Conscious effort (linear) is limited by attention. Once a skill is automated (moved to unconscious competence), it compounds exponentially, freeing up resources for the next layer of scaffolding.

4. Troubleshooting Matrix (Threat Detection)

When you feel stuck, identify the "Error Message" (Feeling) to find the Fix.

ERROR MESSAGE	ROOT CAUSE	THE FIX
"I'm a fraud" / "I can't do this."	Impostor Hijack	**Notice and Name:** Say, "I see you, [NAME]." Shift focus from "Me" to the specific "Task."
"I'll do it later."	Fear / Pressure	**Lower Stakes:** Reframe the life-or-death task as a "silly experiment" or "rough draft."
Brain Fog / Stuck	Routing Error	**Toggle Mode:** Stop thinking. Go for a walk, shower, or nap to access a different solution space.
Envy / Jealousy	Comparison Virus	**Reframe:** Their brain has a unique solution space you cannot replicate. Focus on your unique path.

5. Advanced Protocol: AI Use Without Brain Rot

Be intentional. AI makes a terrible master but an excellent sparring partner. Before interacting, identify your use case.

- **DRUDGE AI:** Outsource the task. You are saving cognitive energy that you can spend elsewhere.
- **BOOST AI:** Use AI to scale your output or iterate faster.
- **MENTOR AI:** Use AI to adjust the weight, not lift it.

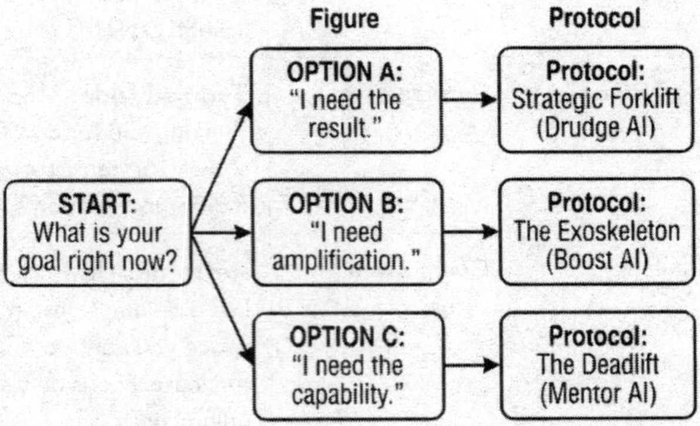

***Figure 3:** The AI Decision Tree. Determine if you are using AI to Outsource (Forklift), Amplify (Exoskeleton), or Learn (Deadlift).*

6. Daily Log: The 3-Minute Review

Use it at the end of the day to track your system performance.

1. **The Genius Check**
    - Did I focus on building capability (scaffolding) today, or just on getting results?

2. **The Impostor Check**
    - Did the Impostor try to hijack me today?
    - If yes, what triggered it? (e.g., comparison, difficult task, fatigue)

3. **The Mode Check**
    - Did I engage in **Active Rest** (motion without focus: walking, gardening)?
    - Did I give my brain **Full Rest** (nap, mind-wandering)?

a word of thanks

Any attempt to fully acknowledge everyone who has contributed to this work is bound to be hopelessly inadequate. So here is my hopelessly inadequate attempt to do so.

My formal obsession with the brain began at thirteen. Tasked with devising an experiment for the school science fair, my mom suggested I explore the hemispheric lateralization of the brain. While intriguing in its own right, the topic's appeal was further boosted by the fact that our home was already filled with a small library of books on the subject, a major convenience in the days before Google search.

That science project was the catalyst for a journey that, several decades later, I am still traveling. It is a path that led through a college major in neuroscience, medical school, a neurology residency, years of work as a clinical neurologist and researcher, and eventually the founding of a neuroscience-based music education company.

It is the culmination of a life lived across many domains, spanning the focused intensity of the clinic, the collaborative flow of a music jam, the strategic competition of the tennis court, and the chaotic joy of family life. Every one of these experiences, and the people who have been part of them, has been integrated into this book. As such, it can be fairly described as my life's work.

The Intellectual Foundation

The neuroscience portion of my brain has been shaped by many. There are those I have never met—or have only encountered briefly—but whose work provided the scaffolding for my own thinking: Oliver Sacks, Douglas Hofstadter, Richard Dawkins, Carl Sagan, Michael Merzenich, Terrence Deacon, Barbara Oakley, Anders Ericsson, Sam Harris, Robert Sapolsky, Michael Gazzaniga, and Norman Geschwind.

Then there are the mentors, colleagues, and sanity checkers I've had the privilege of working with directly: Kenneth Heilman, Edward Valenstein, Steven Nadeau, Linton Hopkins, Michael Okun, Allan Berlind, John Jacobson, Timothy Lo, Corey Schuman, Tommy Wood, and Daniel Pardi. Most importantly, I want to thank the thousands of patients I've served; they have been my greatest teachers, providing the lessons that no textbook ever could.

The complete list is much longer and far beyond the limits of my memory or awareness to recall in full. And while the words here may be my own, I consider this work to be as much theirs as it is mine. The good parts, at least.

The Community

Because this book is a product of my whole life, it owes a debt to those who keep that life balanced and vibrant. I am grateful to my tennis partners and my many jam and bandmates for the lessons in rhythm, resilience, and connection that inevitably found their way into these pages.

To the team who brought this vision to the finish line: my agent, Jill Marsal; my editor, Jacob Surpin; and Lota Erinne, whose advice and patience were indispensable.

Family

Finally, I must thank my family.

My parents, Bob and Lyn, for being my most enthusiastic and generous supporters from the beginning. My mom also deserves special credit for suggesting that science project all those years ago, setting off the chain reaction that led to this very moment.

My older brother, Rob, for instilling a necessary balance of humility and confidence via the precisely calibrated ratio of private beatdowns and public praise.

My children, Jules and Tucker, for being my most important work and for helping to keep everything else in perspective.

And finally, my wife, Jenny, without whom none of this would be even remotely possible.

notes

Chapter 1: The Special Brain ~~Story~~ Lie

5 **I am, somehow, less:** Stephen Jay Gould, "Wide Hats and Narrow Minds," in *The Panda's Thumb: More Reflections in Natural History* (W. W. Norton, 1980).

11 **A measly 1,230 grams:** Sandra F. Witelson, Debra L. Kigar, and Thomas Harvey, "The Exceptional Brain of Albert Einstein," *The Lancet* 353 (1999): 2149–53.

11 **And the race was on:** Virginia Hughes, "The Tragic Story of How Einstein's Brain Was Stolen and Wasn't Even Special," *National Geographic*, April 21, 2014, https://www.nationalgeographic.com/premium/article/the-tragic-story-of-how-einsteins-brain-was-stolen-and-wasnt-even-special.

13 **It is an irony of fate that I myself:** Albert Einstein, *The World as I See It* (Philosophical Library, 1949), 10.

Chapter 2: The Survival Machine

21 **We have a brain for one reason:** Daniel Wolpert, "The Real Reason for Brains," TED Global, 2011.

24 **You'd see roughly eighty billion neurons:** F. A. C. Azevedo, L. R. B. Carvalho, L. T. Grinberg, J. M. Farfel, et al., "Equal Numbers of Neuronal and Nonneuronal Cells Make the Human Brain an Isometrically Scaled-Up Primate Brain," *Journal of Comparative Neurology* 513, no. 5 (2009): 532–41.

29 **This processing is "cognition":** Marcus Kaiser, "A Tutorial in

Connectome Analysis: Topological and Spatial Features of Brain Networks," *NeuroImage* 80 (2013): 174–88.

32 **To answer the question posed:** Peter Sterling and Simon Laughlin, *Principles of Neural Design* (MIT Press, 2015).

34 **Having the longest period:** Barry Bogin, "The Evolution of Human Childhood and Development," *Annual Review of Anthropology* 28 (1999): 109–53.

44 **Recursion is what makes:** Marc D. Hauser, Noam Chomsky, and W. T. Fitch, "The Faculty of Language," *Science* 298 (2002): 1569–79.

45 **As biologist François Jacob:** François Jacob, "Evolution and Tinkering," *Science* 196 (1977): 1161–66.

Chapter 3: Genius in Training

49 **We are faced with a paradox:** Stanislas Dehaene, *How We Learn: Why Brains Learn Better Than Any Machine . . . for Now* (Viking, 2020).

53 **That's followed by plosives:** Patricia Stoel-Gammon, "Normal and Disordered Phonology in Children," *Journal of Speech and Hearing Disorders* 52 (1987): 283–318.

55 **Children learn nouns first:** Sharynne McLeod and Kathryn Crowe, "Typical Speech Sound Development," in *The SLP's Guide to Speech Sound Disorders* (SLP Now, 2019); Kristen Syrett, Sudha Arunachalam, and Sandra Waxman, "Slowly but Surely: Adverbs Support Verb Learning in 2-Year-Olds," *Language Learning and Development* 10, no. 3 (2014): 263–78.

58 **Children who aren't exposed:** Rachelle Pufahl, "Feral Children," in *Psychology of Language* (Pressbooks, 2017).

59 **If they aren't free:** April R. Levin et al., "Motor Outcomes in Children Exposed to Early Psychosocial Deprivation," *Journal of Pediatrics* 164, no. 1 (2014): 123–29.

Chapter 4: The Problem Solver

65 **All life is problem solving:** Karl Popper, *All Life Is Problem Solving* (Routledge, 1999).

77 **It is comparatively easy:** Hans Moravec, *Mind Children* (Harvard University Press, 1988).

Chapter 5: The Engine of Intelligence

82 **Civilization advances by extending:** Alfred North Whitehead, *An Introduction to Mathematics* (Henry Holt, 1911).

86 **In a 2005 study:** Russell A. Poldrack, Fred W. Sabb, Karin Foerde, Sabrina M. Tom, et al., "The Neural Correlates of Motor Skill Automaticity," *Journal of Neuroscience* 25, no. 22 (2005): 5356–64.

88 **Importantly, this consolidation:** Susanne Diekelmann and Jan Born, "The Memory Function of Sleep," *Nature Reviews Neuroscience* 11, no. 2 (2010): 114–26.

95 **By age five:** L. Fenson, P. S. Dale, J. S. Reznick, E. Bates, et al., *Variability in Early Communicative Development*, Monographs of the Society for Research in Child Development 59, no. 5 (1994).

98 **IQ scores are a poor:** Ed Diener and Shigehiro Oishi, "IQ and Subjective Well-Being," in *The Science of Well-Being*, ed. Felicia A. Huppert, Nick Baylis, and Barry Keverne (Oxford University Press, 2005), 165–83.

98 **They're also not good:** Dean Keith Simonton, *Scientific Genius: A Psychology of Science* (Cambridge University Press, 1988).

100 **Flynn found that IQ:** James R. Flynn, "Massive IQ Gains in 14 Nations: What IQ Tests Really Measure," *Psychological Bulletin* 101, no. 2 (1987): 171–91.

102 **Research shows that cognitive:** Andrew R. A. Conway, Michael J. Kane, and Randall W. Engle, "Working Memory Capacity and Its Relation to General Intelligence," *Trends in Cognitive Sciences* 7, no. 12 (2003): 547–52.

107 **And his delayed:** Donna Beeston, "The Early Years of Albert Einstein: When Viewed Through the Lens of Current Theory and Research Were There Signs of Giftedness?," *Apex* 15, no. 1 (2009): 65–77.

107 **At age five:** Walter Isaacson, *Einstein: His Life and Universe* (Simon & Schuster, 2007).

Chapter 6: Genius Never Stops

113 **Every man can:** Santiago Ramón y Cajal, *Recollections of My Life* (Original Spanish: *Recuerdos de mi vida*), 1901.

113 **Everything may die:** Santiago Ramón y Cajal, *Degeneration and Regeneration of the Nervous System*, trans. R. C. Fraser (Clarendon Press, 1928), 741.

114 **Using microelectrodes, Merzenich:** Michael M. Merzenich et al., "Cortical Representational Plasticity," in *Neurobiology of Neocortex*, ed. W. J. Miller (Springer, 1988), 41–48.

115 **In the first part:** A. Pascual-Leone, D. Nguyet, L. G. Cohen, J. P. Brasil-Neto, et al., "Modulation of Muscle Responses Evoked by Transcranial Magnetic Stimulation During the Acquisition of New Fine Motor Skills," *Journal of Neurophysiology* 74, no. 3 (1995): 1037–45.

118 **We have the longest:** David F. Bjorklund, "The Role of Immaturity in Human Development," *Psychological Bulletin* 122, no. 2 (1997): 153–69.

122 **Research also shows that:** David F. Bjorklund and Kayla B. Causey, *Children's Thinking: Cognitive Development and Individual Differences*, 6th ed. (Sage, 2017).

122 **Research shows that there:** Susan A. Ambrose, Michael W. Bridges, Michele DiPietro, Marsha C. Lovett, et al., *How Learning Works: Seven Research-Based Principles for Smart Teaching* (Jossey-Bass, 2010).

124 **The workplace of the 1920s:** Raymond E. Callahan, *Education and the Cult of Efficiency: A Study of the Social Forces That Have Shaped the Administration of the Public Schools* (University of Chicago Press, 1962).

Chapter 7: The Disconnected Mind

129 **What we call the self:** Marvin Minsky, *The Society of Mind* (Simon & Schuster, 1985).

129 **At autopsy, it was:** Paul Eling and Harry Whitaker, "Chapter 36: History of Aphasia: From Brain to Language," in *Handbook of Clinical Neurology*, ed. Michael J. Aminoff, François Boller, and Dick F. Swaab (Elsevier, 2009), 95: 571–82.

131 **Gall not only believed:** O. Parker Jones, F. Alfaro-Almagro, and S. Jbabdi, "An Empirical, 21st Century Evaluation of Phrenology," *Cortex: A Journal Devoted to the Study of the Nervous System and Behavior* 106 (September 2018): 26–35.

132 **This term, coined by:** H. L. Teuber, "Physiological Psychology," *Annual Review of Psychology* 6, no. 1 (1995): 267–96.

134 **Half the subjects had:** K. M. Heilman, R. Scholes, and R. T. Watson, "Auditory Affective Agnosia. Disturbed Comprehension of Affective Speech," *Journal of Neurology, Neurosurgery, and Psychiatry* 38, no. 1 (1975): 69–72.

134 **In addition to conveying:** E. D. Ross, "The Aprosodias: Functional-Anatomic Organization of the Affective Components of Language in the Right Hemisphere," *Archives of Neurology* 38, no. 9 (1981): 561–69.

139 **This is also referred:** Kenneth M. Heilman and Edward Valenstein, *Clinical Neuropsychology* (Oxford University Press, 2011).

142 **I knew this because:** Jules Dejerine, "Sur un cas de cécité verbale avec agraphie suivie d'autopsie," *Mémoires de la Société de Biologie* 4 (1892): 61–90.

146 **In 1965, Boston University:** Norman Geschwind, "Disconnexion Syndromes in Animals and Man. I," *Brain: A Journal of Neurology* 88, no. 2 (1965): 237–94.

Chapter 8: A Brain in Flux

151 **Do I contradict myself:** Walt Whitman, "Song of Myself," *Leaves of Grass*, 1855.

158 **Loads of evidence:** J. Eric Ahlskog, Yonas E. Geda, Neill R. Graff-Radford, and Ronald C. Petersen, "Physical Exercise as a Preventive or Disease-Modifying Treatment of Dementia and Brain Aging," *Mayo Clinic Proceedings* 86, no. 9 (2011): 876–84.

161 **If blocking adenosine's effects:** Theresa E. Bjorness and Robert W. Greene, "Adenosine and Sleep," *Current Neuropharmacology* 7, no. 3 (2009): 238–45.

161 **The second cluster:** Elda Arrigoni and Patrick M. Fuller, "The Sleep-Promoting Ventrolateral Preoptic Nucleus: What Have We

Learned over the Past 25 Years?," *International Journal of Molecular Sciences* 23, no. 6 (2002): 2905.

166 **The authors described:** M. E. Raichle, A. M. MacLeod, A. Z. Snyder, W. J. Powers, et al., "A Default Mode of Brain Function," *Proceedings of the National Academy of Sciences* 98, no. 2 (2001): 676–82.

169 **According to neurologist:** Oliver Sacks, *Uncle Tungsten: Memories of a Chemical Boyhood* (Alfred A. Knopf, 2001).

170 **In a landmark 2004:** Ullrich Wagner, Steffen Gais, Hilde Haider, Rolf Verleger, et al., "Sleep Inspires Insight," *Nature* 427, no. 6972 (2004): 352–55.

172 **In one study:** Benjamin Baird, Jonathan Smallwood, Michael D. Mrazek, and Julia W. Y. Kam, "Inspired by Distraction: Mind Wandering Facilitates Creative Incubation," *Psychological Science* 23, no. 10 (2012): 1117–22.

173 **For many, only a relatively:** Alex Soojung-Kim Pang, *Rest: Why You Get More Done When You Work Less* (Basic Books, 2016).

174 **Virginia Woolf, who authored:** Mason Currey, *Daily Rituals: How Artists Work* (Knopf, 2013).

175 **As philosopher Friedrich Nietzsche:** Friedrich Nietzsche, *Twilight of the Idols* (1889), in *Twilight of the Idols and The Anti-Christ*, trans. R. J. Hollingdale (Penguin Classics, 1990), 33.

Chapter 9: Hidden Genius

183 **To see is to forget:** Paul Valéry, *Introduction to the Method of Leonardo da Vinci*, 1894.

191 **By around age three:** Claire Golomb, *The Child's Creation of a Pictorial World*, 2nd ed. (Lawrence Erlbaum Associates, 2004).

194 **That's exactly what:** Allan Snyder, Homayoun Bahramali, Tobias Hawker, and D. John Mitchell, "Savant-like Numerosity Skills Revealed in Normal People by Magnetic Pulses," *Perception* 35, no. 6 (2006): 837–45.

Chapter 10: An Unreliable Narrator

199 The first principle: Richard P. Feynman, "Cargo Cult Science," Caltech Commencement Address, 1974.

202 The official name: Emad Singer, Kinal Bhatt, Adesh Prashad, Larri Rudman, et al., "Diagnosis and Management of Marchiafava-Bignami Disease, a Rare Neurological Complication of Long-Term Alcohol Abuse," *Discoveries (Craiova)* 11, no. 2 (2023): e168.

202 Back in the early: W. P. Van Wagenen and A. Herren, "Surgical Division of Commissural Pathways in the Corpus Callosum," *Archives of Neurology and Psychiatry* 44, no. 4 (1940): 740–59.

203 In the mid-twentieth: Roger W. Sperry, "Cerebral Organization and Behavior," *Science* 133, no. 3466 (1961): 1749–57.

203 Since the visual cortices: Michael S. Gazzaniga, Joseph E. Bogen, and Roger W. Sperry, "Some Functional Effects of Sectioning the Cerebral Commissures in Man," *Proceedings of the National Academy of Sciences* 48, no. 10 (1962): 1765–69.

206 Dr. Michael Gazzaniga: Michael S. Gazzaniga, *The Social Brain: Discovering the Networks of the Mind* (Basic Books, 1985).

207 In a social species: R. Trivers, "The Elements of a Scientific Theory of Self-Deception," *Annals of the New York Academy of Sciences* 907, no. 1 (2000): 114–31.

208 Except that's exactly: Shai Danziger, Jonathan Levav, and Liora Avnaim-Pesso, "Extraneous Factors in Judicial Decisions," *Proceedings of the National Academy of Sciences* 108, no. 17 (2011): 6889–92.

209 But the truth was: Richard E. Nisbett and Timothy DeCamp Wilson, "Telling More Than We Can Know: Verbal Reports on Mental Processes," *Psychological Review* 84, no. 3 (1977): 231–59.

209 In a study published: Piotr Winkielman, Kent C. Berridge, and Julie T. Wilbarger, "Unconscious Affective Reactions to Masked Happy Versus Angry Faces Influence Consumption Behavior," *Psychological Science* 16, no. 6 (2005): 452–57.

211 Absurd as it sounds: Dan Ariely, George Loewenstein, and Drazen Prelec, "'Coherent Arbitrariness': Stable Demand Curves Without Stable Preferences," in *The Construction of Preference*, ed. Sarah Lichtenstein and Paul Slovic (Cambridge University Press, 2006), 246–70.

211 In a famous study: Donald G. Dutton and Arthur P. Aron, "Some Evidence for Heightened Sexual Attraction Under Conditions of High Anxiety," *Journal of Personality and Social Psychology* 30, no. 4 (1974): 510–17.

212 In a study published in 2005: Petter Johansson, Lars Hall, Sverker Sikström, and Andreas Olsson, "Failure to Detect Mismatches Between Intention and Outcome in a Simple Decision Task," *Science* 310, no. 5745 (2005): 116–19.

213 In a study published in 1999: Daniel M. Wegner and Thalia Wheatley, "Apparent Mental Causation: Sources of the Experience of Will," *American Psychologist* 54, no. 7 (1999): 480–92.

214 Subjects were hooked up: Benjamin Libet, Curtis A. Gleason, Elwood W. Wright, and Dennis K. Pearl, "Time of Conscious Intention to Act in Relation to Onset of Cerebral Activity (Readiness-Potential)," *Brain* 106, no. 3 (1983): 623–42.

224 It's no coincidence: David G. Blanchflower and Andrew J. Oswald, "Is Well-Being U-Shaped over the Life Cycle?," *Social Science & Medicine* 66, no. 8 (2008): 1733–49.

Chapter 11: The Impostor's Playbook

227 We are what: Kurt Vonnegut, *Mother Night* (Harper & Row, 1961).

236 Worse yet, research shows: Edward L. Deci, Richard Koestner, and Richard M. Ryan, "A Meta-Analytic Review of Experiments Examining the Effects of Extrinsic Rewards on Intrinsic Motivation," *Psychological Bulletin* 125, no. 6 (1999): 627–68.

237 Research shows that effective: National Academies of Sciences, Engineering, and Medicine, *How People Learn II: Learners, Contexts, and Cultures* (National Academies Press, 2018).

239 Studies show that, compared: Eliza G. Liquin and Alison Gopnik, "Children Are More Exploratory Than Adults: A Meta-Analysis," *Developmental Review* 65 (2022): 101014.

250 **On the other hand:** Eric Turkheimer, "Three Laws of Behavior Genetics and What They Mean," *Current Directions in Psychological Science* 9, no. 5 (2000): 160–64.

Chapter 12: Turning the Tables

256 **I am always doing:** Vincent van Gogh, Letter to Anthon van Rappard, 1885.

271 **Why have there been:** Dean Keith Simonton, "Age and Outstanding Achievement: What Do We Know After a Century of Research?," *Psychological Bulletin* 104, no. 2 (1988): 251–67.

275 **A study of more than one thousand:** R. Root-Bernstein, L. Allen, L. Beach, R. Bhadula, et al., "Arts Foster Scientific Success: Avocations of Nobel, National Academy, Royal Society, and Sigma Xi Members," *Journal of Psychology of Science and Technology* 1, no. 2 (2008): 51–63.

276 **In 1984, educational psychologist:** Benjamin S. Bloom, "The 2 Sigma Problem: The Search for Methods of Group Instruction as Effective as One-to-One Tutoring," *Educational Researcher* 13, no. 6 (1984): 4–16.

281 **We don't build scaffolding:** Björn Rasch and Jan Born, "About Sleep's Role in Memory," *Physiological Reviews* 93, no. 2 (2013): 681–766.

Chapter 13: The Genius of Doing Nothing

287 **At the moment when:** Henri Poincaré, *Science and Method* (Original French: *Science et Méthode*), 1908.

292 **Research supports the powerful:** Daphna Oyserman, "Identity-Based Motivation: Implications for Action-Readiness, Procedural-Readiness, and Consumer Behavior," *Journal of Consumer Psychology* 19, no. 3 (2009): 250–60.

index